2nd Edition

Make Your Own Living Will

by enodare publishing

D0905649

Bibliographic data
- International Standard Book Number (ISBN): 978-1-906144-44-9
- Edition: Second Edition (2012)
- Printed in the United States of America
- First Printing: December 2010

Published by: Enodare Limited
                                   Athlone
                                   Co. Westmeath
                                   Ireland

Printed and distributed by: International Publishers Marketing
                                   22841 Quicksilver Drive
                                   Dulles, VA 20166
                                   United States of America

For more information, e-mail books@enodare.com.

IMPORTANT NOTE

This book is meant as a general guide to preparing your own living will. While considerable effort has been made to make this book as complete and accurate as possible, laws and their interpretation are constantly changing. As such, you are advised to update this information with your own research and/or counsel and to consult with your personal legal, financial and medical advisors before acting on any information contained in this book.

The purpose of this book is to educate and entertain. It is not meant to provide legal, financial or medical advice or to create any attorney-client or advisory relationship. The authors and publisher shall have neither liability (whether in negligence or otherwise) nor responsibility to any person or entity with respect to any loss or damage caused or alleged to be caused directly or indirectly by the information or documents contained in this book or the use of that information or those documents.

ABOUT ENODARE

Enodare, the international self-help legal publisher, was founded in 2000 by lawyers from one of the most prestigious international law firms in the World.

Our aim was simple - to provide access to quality legal information and products at an affordable price.

Our Will Writer software was first published in that year and, following its adaptation to cater for the legal systems of over 30 countries worldwide, quickly drew in excess of 40,000 visitors per month to our website. From this humble start, Enodare has quickly grown to become a leading international estate planning and asset protection self-help publisher with legal titles in the United States, Canada, the United Kingdom, Australia and Ireland.

Our publications provide customers with the confidence and knowledge to help them deal with everyday estate planning issues such as the preparation of a last will and testament, a living trust, a power of attorney, administering an estate and much more.

By providing customers with much needed information and forms, we enable them to place themselves in a position where they can protect both themselves and their families through the use of easy to read legal documents and forward planning techniques.

The Future….

We are always seeking to expand and improve the products and services we offer. However, in order to do this, we need to hear from interested authors and to receive feedback from our customers.

If something isn't clear to you in our publications, please let us know and we'll try to make it clearer in the next edition. If you can't find the answer you want and have a suggestion for an addition to our range, we'll happily look at that too.

USING SELF-HELP BOOKS

Before using a self-help book, you need to carefully consider the advantages and disadvantages of doing so – particularly where the subject matter is of a legal or tax related nature.

In writing our self-help books, we try to provide readers with an overview of the laws in a specific area. While this overview is often general in nature, it provides a good starting point for those wishing to carry out a more detailed review of a topic.

However, unlike an attorney advising a client, we cannot cover every conceivable eventuality that might affect our readers. Within the intended scope of this book, we can only cover the principal areas in a given topic, and even where we cover these areas, we can still only do so to a moderate extent. To do otherwise would result in the writing of a text book which would be capable of use by legal professionals. This is not what we do.

We try to present useful information and documents that can be used by an average reader with little or no legal knowledge. While our sample documents can be used in the vast majority of cases, everybody's personal circumstances are different. As such, they may not be suitable for everyone. You may have personal circumstances which might impact the effectiveness of these documents or even your desire to use them. The reality is that without engaging an attorney to review your personal circumstances, this risk will always exist. It's for this very reason that you need to consider whether the cost of using a do-it-yourself legal document outweighs the risk that there may be something special about your particular circumstances which might not be taken into account by the sample documents attached to this book (or indeed any other sample documents).

It goes without saying (we hope) that if you are in any doubt as to whether the documents in this book are suitable for use in your particular circumstances, you should contact a suitably qualified attorney for advice before using them. Remember the decision to use these documents is yours! We are not advising you in any respect.

In using this book, you should also take into account the fact that this book has been written with the purpose of providing a general overview of the laws in the United States. As such, it does not attempt to cover all of the various procedural nuances and specific requirements that may apply from state to state – although we do point some of these out along the way. Rather, in our book, we try to provide forms which give a fair example of the type of forms which are commonly used in most states. Nevertheless, it remains possible that your state may have specific requirements which have not been taken into account in our forms.

Another thing that you should remember is that the law changes – thousands of new laws are brought into force every day and, by the same token, thousands are repealed or amended every day! As such, it is possible that while you are reading this book, the law might well have been changed. Let's hope it hasn't but the chance does exist! Needless to say, we take regular steps (including e-mail alerts) to update our customers about any changes to the law. We also ensure that our books are reviewed and revised regularly to take account of these changes.

Anyway, assuming that all of the above is acceptable to you, let's move on to exploring the topic at hand......Living Wills.

 CD-ROM & Downloadable Forms

Blank copies of all of the forms contained in this book are available on the CD-ROM which accompanies this book. Alternatively all forms can be downloaded from the enodare website.

Web: http://www.enodare.com/downloadarea/

Unlock Code: XYZ10412

enodare

TABLE OF CONTENTS

AN INTRODUCTION TO LIVING WILLS

Not many of us actually relish the thought of making a will or an estate plan. Even fewer look forward eagerly to nominating what sort of medical treatment we would want if we were too ill or too badly injured to speak for ourselves at the time. It's hardly the kind of scenario we like to dwell on.

However, we do need to face the facts - a great many people really do drop off the proverbial twig with little or no warning, with their affairs in a muddle, and totally unprepared as far as arrangements regarding their estate are concerned.

At the same time, road accidents alone leave thousands of victims in a state of limbo each year, not to mention workplace accidents, hunting, boating and skiing accidents, accidents around that highly dangerous place we can't avoid, the home, and unforeseen illnesses of every kind.

What's more, it's been said that western medicine is the next biggest killer after heart disease, cancer and stroke. So just spending an extended period in a hospital puts large numbers of people in mortal peril.

Sounds crazy, but it's true. A study was done a few years ago, and it was found that more patients die each year in U.S. hospitals from incorrect dosages alone, than died over the entire period of the Vietnam War. Yet because most people put doctors and modern medicine into a category almost beyond questioning, we hear these things... but nobody marches on Washington. Nobody burns their Medicare card. Instead, we blithely tune out such figures, dismiss any suggestion that doctors and nurses frequently get it wrong, and pretend that it's all good down at County General.

But however delusional we may be about hi-tech medical marvels, or even about living to a healthy 95 and dying peacefully in our sleep; whatever natural or completely unexpected cause sets up your checkout time and mine — our door knock from the celestial bell-hop, as it were — when you get right down to it, one thing's for certain: nobody gets out of this world alive.

And the only question is: 'When my turn comes, what will it be like for me?'

Sometimes of course, the lights just go out. There's nothing more for us to think about, and no more to do. Whatever needs to be done is perforce a matter for others.

But with higher and higher-tech medicines adding weeks, months and sometimes years to our lives (though not necessarily life to our years), there are serious questions to ponder.

Questions like:

- When I get to the final countdown, and my quality of life is virtually non-existent, do I really want to stretch it out on life support... or would I rather let nature take its course?

- What if I'm to all intents and purposes out of it? Not able to speak, not really registering a thing, and no real hope of any improvement on that?

- Or what if I'm in a fully-fledged coma? And the only thing keeping me going is some kind of respirator, and a feeding tube?

- Or worse, what if I'm in a lot of pain? Hey, what if I'm racked with pain, but I can't *tell* anyone, and nobody even realizes it?

- How far would I want to take that kind of a deal? Where would I draw the line?

Unfortunately, a lot of people actually find themselves in those or similar situations. Without warning, in many cases.

Have you ever thought about what you would like to have happen if an illness or an accident leaves you in a coma or in a 'persistent vegetative state'? One from which you may well never emerge?

Probably not. As we said, no one looks forward to this kind of event, and we tend to put off thinking about it. Which is a natural enough reaction.

But just picture this scenario for a moment:

- By illness, age or misadventure, you're in the ICU. Your eyes are closed, you're attached to various tubes and scopes, and you're not looking all that chipper.

- For all anyone can tell, you're oblivious to what's going on, and nobody knows for sure whether you'll wake up or not. They only know that it's not looking good. Machines monitor your vital signs; others provide a constantly adjusted cocktail of medications. Time ticks by.

- You may not even be aware of the passing of time, or of having your bodily functions taken care of by attendants and nurses; nor of being washed while you lie there supine; knowing nothing, experiencing nothing.

Based on this picture, let's consider your present thoughts on the matter:

- In a case like this, would you want to have your life prolonged by any means available? Or would you prefer to have certain high-tech treatments either withheld or discontinued, and just to be kept as comfortable as possible, allowing a natural death to come as your irreparably damaged (or worn out) systems wind down?

- Suppose you opt for a natural death. Not being able to speak for yourself, wouldn't it be extremely valuable to have a legal document and/or a spokesperson to make your decision known, and to ensure that it gets carried out?

Important Note

But even better than this might be to:

1. have your legal document,

2. appoint your authorized spokesperson, and also

3. have your intentions understood and accepted by your family, by openly discussing your thoughts and reasons with them beforehand.

Hopefully, this open discussion will avoid well-meaning objections to your spokesperson's announcement of your wishes, if and when the day to implement them arrives.

- Here's another thought: whatever of the quality of your existence, how would you feel about the emotional and financial burdens your enduring vegetative condition would place on your loved ones, for an indefinite period of time?

- Despite these burdens, are your family going to switch off your life support? Or are they more likely to say 'we have to mortgage the home (or even sell the place) if it keeps mum or dad alive?'

- Finally, would your answers be different if you were under 40, or over 70?

We're certainly not here to tell you what you should or shouldn't think, or do; just to prompt you to think. We're here to ask 'What's your position on these sorts of issues?' and then raise the question, 'Does anyone else know how you feel?'

And even if your sister (or some other family member) knows, maybe she thinks you don't really mean it, or else that you need protecting from yourself. Ask yourself... 'If the time ever came, am I confident she'd support me? And even if she did, how sure am I that she'd carry the day with the rest of your family?'

And while we're on the subject, here's another interesting question: 'Would you want to have someone else who knows where you stand to not just make your wishes known, but actually step in and make these sorts of decisions for you, in the light of all the facts as they stand at the time, when you no longer can?'

Well, now you can let your wishes on all these matters be known in advance! What's more, you can do it in a way which has the prior approval of the courts.

Making these choices for yourself is what living wills are all about.

Remember, we're not talking right or wrong here, nor are we suggesting this way is good, that way is bad. We are talking purely about one thing, namely....your personal preferences!

Furthermore, your own wishes on these matters supported by your personal beliefs and values, whichever way they lean, may become important for your family and your care providers to know about should something like this ever happen to you.

A living will is about deciding these things now, while you can. It's about doing it calmly and without any pressure, and then making your wishes known in a legal document that will go on your medical record.

A document that will be there to guide your medicos and your friends and family members alike, if and when you come into the emergency room or the ICU in no fit state to hold a conversation.

Important Note

Suppose you were inclined to this point of view: 'If there's any area where I'm entitled to have my wishes respected, it would have to be my choice of whether to lie there insensate on life support for an indefinite period, or to die with dignity when nature says 'it's time'.'

If you strongly felt that situation was definitely your call, and nobody else's, we do believe that most people would agree with you.

Our sincere hope for this book is that it will help you to better understand your rights, and avoid some of the unnecessary traumas that too many others have been through.

However, before diving into living wills and how they operate, we'll take a quick look in Chapter 1 at how they came to be.

CHAPTER 1:
THE DEVELOPMENT OF ADVANCE MEDICAL DIRECTIVES AND LIVING WILLS

Chapter Overview

In this chapter, we will explain what living wills are and how they came to be. We will also introduce you to some real life examples of instances where living wills could have alleviated vast amounts of suffering for individual patients and their families.

Chapter 1

CHAPTER 1

THE DEVELOPMENT OF ADVANCE MEDICAL DIRECTIVES AND LIVING WILLS

What Is an Advance Medical Directive?

An advance medical directive (or an "AMD" as it is also called) is a written statement in which you set out the medical care that you wish to receive during any period in which you are unable to make decisions on your own behalf. It also allows you to direct how medical decisions are to be made on your behalf during any such period of incapacity and even to appoint someone to make these decisions for you.

Why Do I Need an Advance Medical Directive?

In the absence of having an AMD, state laws will generally allow your close family members to make medical decisions for you during any period in which you are incapacitated and unable to make these decisions on your own behalf. While this can of course be beneficial for you, there is always a risk that your family members will make decisions based on what they believe is best for you rather than what you would have actually wanted in the circumstances. More importantly, there is the added risk that the person making these decisions for your might not be someone that you would have entrusted this responsibility to had you the choice. It was in anticipation of these very issues that AMDs were developed. Thankfully, all states now have provisions that allow for the use of AMDs so that people can exercise some control over the medical treatment they receive during periods of incapacity. The two most common types of AMD currently in use are living wills and healthcare powers of attorney. While we will primarily focus on living wills in this book, we will also review healthcare powers of attorney briefly in Chapter 6

What Is a Living Will?

A living will is a legal document that allows you to instruct healthcare providers regarding the use or non-use of certain life-prolonging medical procedures in the event that you become terminally ill or permanently unconscious and unable to communicate your own wishes.

Important Note

Please note each of the <u>emphasized points in the preceding paragraph.</u> They all come into play with a living will, so it's immediately evident that there are a number of limits on when a living will can operate.

Nonetheless, it remains a very powerful document for those who want control over their medical treatment during their final days.

The life-prolonging medical procedures in question are sometimes referred to as 'heroic measures' and are generally aimed at keeping the patient alive rather than fixing the underlying problem (which is often virtually untreatable, like multiple organ failures or severe brain damage). As a general rule, living wills only come into effect if you're no longer able to make your own healthcare decisions. For example, if you suffer serious brain damage in an accident or suffer an incapacitating stroke, you may be permanently unconscious and unable to communicate your wishes to your doctor. In this case, a living will lets your doctor know your wishes concerning the receipt or non-receipt of certain medical procedures. It also allows you to designate a person who can either enforce or revoke the decisions made in your living will.

Development of Living Wills

The development of living wills can be viewed as a legal response to advancements made in the medical field over the last 100 years. During that period, both medicine and medical techniques advanced to a point where physicians can sustain life even in the most dire of situations including situations that were once fatal. Physicians can treat diabetes, cancer and even organ failures. In many cases, patients can lead a relatively normal life following the treatment. However, in other cases, the quality of life of the patient is severely affected. In some instances, physicians can keep the body alive but are unable to restore movement or brain activity and the patient is left in a permanent vegetative state. The ability to keep a person alive in such a condition has invariably led to conflicts between the families of the patients and the physicians providing medical care to the patient. Notwithstanding that families may wish to have their loved ones pass away where there is no reasonable prospect of the patient surviving, medical practitioners will wish to exercise a moral and professional obligation to keep the patient alive. Given this clear conflict of interest, it may surprise you to learn that living wills have only been legal for a relatively short period of time.

In fact, the concept of facilitating dying people's rights to control decisions about their own medical care was first raised by attorney Luis Kutner in 1967. It was taken up the following year by Florida legislator Dr Walter Sackett, who unsuccessfully introduced a bill to allow patients make binding decisions about the use or non-use of life-sustaining methods.

Dr Sackett's bill was defeated again when he reintroduced it five years later.

Then in 1974 state senator Barry Keene presented similar bills in California, initially with the same result. Keene's mother-in-law had been unable to control her medical care in relation to a terminal illness in 1972, which she attempted to do via a power of attorney.

The bill finally passed in 1976, when Sen. Keene reintroduced it. Thus in September 1976, California became the first state to legally sanction a form of living will. By 1977, living will legislation had been introduced in 43 states and adopted in seven. Over the next 15 years, all 50 states plus the District of Columbia passed some form of advance directive or living wills legislation.

In 1976 the New Jersey Supreme Court handed down a landmark decision on machine-sustained 'life' versus the right to die, in the case of Karen Ann Quinlan. The facts in this case were as follows. In April, 1976, shortly after she turned 21, Karen attended a birthday party. Friends said she had been on a radical diet, and hadn't eaten a meal in 48 hours. She had a few drinks and swallowed a tranquillizer, began to feel faint, and was taken home to bed. Fifteen minutes later, she was found to be not breathing.

Her friends attempted mouth-to-mouth resuscitation, and called an ambulance. She remained unconscious, but some color returned to her cheeks. Karen was admitted to hospital in a coma and was kept alive for several months on a mechanical ventilator and feeding tube, but without improvement. In fact she became prone to violent and unpredictable limb movements. It appears that she may have choked on her own vomit after returning from the party, causing respiratory failure for a period of 15-20 minutes. In that period, she seems to have suffered irreversible brain damage.

Her parents requested that she be removed from active life support and be allowed to die. The hospital refused their request. In the subsequent court case, Chief Justice Hughes of the New Jersey Supreme Court ruled that:

- If patients are mentally incapable of making treatment decisions, someone else (e.g. a parent) can do it for them.

- Decisions that could lead to the death of such patients are better made by families with advice from their doctors, than by courts.

- End-of-life care decisions should consider both the invasiveness of the treatment and the patient's chances of recovery.

- Patients have the right to refuse treatment, even if doing so might cause their death.

As a result of the Court's judgment, the right of Karen's parents to make healthcare decisions on her behalf was upheld, and she was gradually weaned off the ventilator at their request. Unfortunately, Karen remained in a coma until her death from pneumonia in 1985.

Supreme Court Intervention

In 1990 the United States Supreme Court agreed to hear its first case on the right to refuse or terminate life-sustaining treatment.

The facts in this case, Cruzan vs. Director, Missouri Department of Health, were that on the night of January 11, 1983 Nancy Cruzan rolled her car and was found face down in bushes neither breathing nor with any detectable heartbeat. Paramedics restored both functions but she remained unconscious.

At the hospital, surgeons implanted a feeding and hydration tube but all efforts at rehabilitation proved unavailing as Nancy, though able to breathe, fell deeper into a persistent vegetative state. That is, she exhibited motor reflexes but gave no indications of cognitive function. For six years her physical and mental state grew steadily worse. It became clear that Nancy had no chance of regaining her faculties and her parents asked the hospital to turn off her artificial nutrition and hydration processes. All agreed that this would cause her death and, as a result, the hospital declined to do so without court approval.

Chief Justice Rehnquist, expressing the 5-4 majority view, described the case as 'the first case in which we have been squarely presented with the issue of whether the United States Constitution grants what is in common parlance referred to as a "right to die.'

Important Note

The Supreme Court affirmed that a competent person has the constitutionally protected right to refuse medical treatment, even life-sustaining treatment. The same did not apply to an incompetent person, and the question came down to whether a surrogate could make such a decision on their behalf.

Missouri had legislated to permit this in a limited way, subject to the procedural safeguard that there was 'clear and convincing evidence' that the patient while competent had expressed the desire not to be kept alive in a permanently vegetative state.

The court found that Missouri's high standard of proof here was both permissible and constitutional. In the majority's opinion, the State Supreme Court was entitled to decide that this standard of proof had not been satisfied. In reaching this conclusion, the court affirmed the state court's decision against the petitioning parents.

The minority judges upheld Nancy's right to die, based on evidence of her preferences in serious conversations with close friends not long before her accident, and testimony of friends and family as to her beliefs and values. They gave weight also to her extreme physiological dissolution, ending the remotest chance of rehabilitation, and her apparent experience of pain indicated by grimaces at various painful stimuli.

There is a 'happy ending' to the Nancy Cruzan saga. Her family was able to continue assembling further proof of her wishes not to be kept on life support, which in the end was sufficient to satisfy Missouri's 'clear and convincing evidence' test.

They eventually won a court order to discontinue her life support (though we wonder at what cost), and she finally died 11 days later on December 26, 1990.

Important Note

It is important to note that at all material times, the State of Missouri had living wills legislation which would have permitted Nancy to express her wishes in writing, and allowed her to appoint a surrogate to ensure their full recognition. By this simple procedure, the entire painful, exhausting, emotionally draining and no doubt ruinously costly saga could have been avoided entirely.

Note the similarities and differences between the Karen Ann Quinlan and Nancy Cruzan cases. Both dealt with young, physically strong women who had the misfortune to fall into a persistent vegetative state. Quinlan's case established the right of an individual to appoint a healthcare proxy, while the Cruzan case confirmed that a healthy adult had the constitutional right to create a binding living will.

Federal Intervention

Congress has now mandated a regime to publicize and support the state laws. It goes under the name 'Advance Medical Directives' (AMDs) of which the living will and the healthcare power of attorney are two elements. (For information on the latter please see Chapter 6, and also see our book on Powers of Attorney.)

The AMD law emanates from the federal Patient Self-Determination Act 1991 (the 'PSDA'), passed a short while after the Cruzan decision. The PSDA requires that adult patients admitted to medical care facilities in receipt of federal funding be apprised of their rights to prepare advance healthcare directives, which are then entered on their medical records. This law does not of course create any new forms of directives. It simply validates state laws which create AMDs.

The information given to patients under the PSDA explains their rights under what's sometimes referred to as 'natural death' legislation, and the different state requirements for living wills and healthcare powers of attorney. Remember, exactly what can be included in a living will and what cannot depends on state law, and therefore varies somewhat from one jurisdiction to the next.

Also bear in mind that a living will normally comes into effect ONLY when you are:-

- suffering a terminal illness, irreversible coma or permanent unconsciousness, and

- physically unable to make and communicate your own healthcare decisions.

Up until that moment, you can continue to give personal instructions to your healthcare providers, even though you've made an advance directive. In other words, the directive is there to widen your ability to express your wishes, not to narrow or obstruct it in any way.

The same philosophy applies to a medical (or healthcare) power of attorney.

The Story of Terri Schiavo

In recent years, much has been recorded and stated about the plight of Terri Schiavo. While this case was by no means the first of its kind, it certainly garnished a huge degree of public attention. For that reason alone, we will mention it here in passing.

In 2005, Terri Schiavo, who had been in a coma since 1990, became the center of a national debate about when it was appropriate to turn of life support on someone, and who has authority to make that decision.

The principal parties in the conflict were Terri Schiavo's husband, Michael, and her parents, Bob and Mary Schindler. Michael Schiavo, who was also Terri's court appointed guardian, had been informed by doctors that his wife was in a "persistent vegetative state" and that there was no hope that she would recover from that position. On that basis, he requested the withdrawal of nutritional support which was then been administered via a feeding tube. However, her parents refused to give up hope and sought to continue the administration of tube feeding.

A legal battle ensued for many years as a result of the divergence of views. The courts however sided with Michael Schiavo despite numerous protests from high-ranking members of Congress. Interestingly, the United States Supreme Court refused on numerous occasions to hear the case, instead upholding the decisions of the U.S. District Court and the Florida State Court.

On March 18, 2005, Terri Schiavo's feeding tube was removed, and she died 13 days later.

It's worth noting that Terri Schiavo did not have a living will and this was most certainly a contributing factor in the resulting court cases. Had such a document been available, matters may well have been less heavily disputed.

CHAPTER 2:
HOW LIVING WILLS WORK

Chapter Overview

In this chapter we look at how living wills work, when they take legal effect and review the various life sustaining measures that can be encompassed in a living will.

Chapter 2

CHAPTER 2

HOW LIVING WILLS WORK

How Living Wills Work

As mentioned above, a living will allows you to state whether you want your life prolonged in the event that you are suffering from a terminal illness, or are in a permanent state of unconsciousness. Your living will indicates whether you want certain treatments withheld or withdrawn if their function is only to prolong the dying process or to keep you 'alive' where there is no realistic hope of recovery.

For example, if you suffer serious brain damage in an accident, or suffer an incapacitating stroke, you may be permanently unconscious and unable to communicate your wishes to your doctor. In this case, a living will lets your doctor know the kinds of medical procedures and treatments you are (a) willing to accept and (b) not willing to accept.

In understanding how living wills work in practice, it's important that you realize that living wills only come into effect when:

(i)   you are suffering from a terminal condition, a persistent comatose condition or in a permanent vegetative state;

(ii)   there is no real prospect of recovery; and

(iii)   you are unable to make and communicate your own healthcare decisions.

It is only at this point will the person nominated under your living will have any ability to enforce or revoke any of the instructions that you have set out in your living will. However, before this person can lawfully act, the law in the majority of states and indeed the terms of most living wills require that one or in some cases two doctors must first personally examine you and agree that you satisfy the conditions referred to above and that the application of medical procedures would only prolong the dying process. If the doctor or doctors agree that this is the case, then the medical procedures may be withdrawn or applied, depending on the choices expressed in your living will.

What Is a Terminal Condition?

A terminal condition is an incurable condition caused by disease, illness or injury with the consequence that there is no reasonable prospect that the patient's condition will improve and the expected result is death. Such diagnoses are often common with progressive diseases such as cancer or advanced heart disease.

Important Note

A terminal condition is referred to in some states as a terminal illness, a terminal injury or an incurable or irreversible illness.

Often, a patient is considered to be terminally ill when the life expectancy is estimated to be six months or less, under the assumption that the disease will run its normal course. In many cases, where people are correctly diagnosed as being terminally ill, they will cease to be able to properly communicate towards the final stages of their illness. It is in these very situations that living wills can be most beneficial. By creating a living will, a patient can choose whether or not they want to receive life-sustaining treatments that would serve only to prolong their life.

Important Note

You will notice that some of the state forms at the back of this book provide that the terms of the living will shall only be implemented where the patient will die irrespective of "whether or not life sustaining procedures are implemented or not". The suggestion that death must be inevitable before life sustaining procedures can be withdrawn runs somewhat contrary to the intention behind living wills. Remember, living wills are designed to allow a person to die a natural death in circumstances where they could be artificially kept alive for years - in other words, where death was not necessarily inevitable. This language seems to be good example of poor draftsmanship on the legislator's behalf. It remains to be seen whether a literal interpretation of the provision will be upheld or whether states will simply abide by the general spirit and intent of the legislation and allow living wills to be used in the manner that they were intended. In using forms with this language, you may wish to add an addendum to your living will to clarify the position. See Appendix F at the back of this book.

What Is a Persistent Comatose Condition?

A persistent comatose condition can generally be described as a profound or deep state of unconsciousness where there is no reasonable prospect of regaining consciousness. In other words, while we are in fact alive, we are effectively asleep and unable to respond to life around us. This condition, which is often caused by accidents or traumas, is similar to a coma save that with a coma there is often an expectation that the patient will regain consciousness at some time in the future.

Where a patient is diagnosed as being in a comatose condition, a living will can direct doctors as to whether the patient wishes to receive life sustaining procedure or not. Of course, two physicians will need to certify that the patient has met the required conditions for a living will to take effect in that state.

What Is a Persistent Vegetative Condition?

A persistent vegetative state, which sometimes follows a coma, is a condition which results in a person losing all cognitive neurological function and awareness of the environment around them. However, despite this neurological illness, the individual retains non-cognitive functions and a disrupted sleep-wake cycle.

A living will can allow you direct whether you wish to receive life sustaining procedures if you are in a permanent vegetative condition.

What Life Support Choices Do I Have Within My Living Will?

There are, generally speaking, three different choices you can make in regards to life-sustaining measures:

- *Option 1* – You can require doctors do everything in their power to keep you alive.

- *Option 2* – You can provide that the only life-sustaining measures you desire to have are artificial tube feeding for nutrition (food) and hydration (water).

- *Option 3* – You can have all artificial life-sustaining treatment withheld, including nutrition and hydration.

Of course, you can to a degree mix some of the above options. However, no matter which of these three options you choose, you will generally always be provided with all necessary pain medication and comfort medication. In addition to the provision of treatment for pain and comfort there are a number of different treatments available to help keep you alive. We'll discuss some of the principal procedures below.

Life Sustaining Procedures

Life sustaining procedures can be described as any medical procedures or interventions which serve only to prolong the dying process. They do not prevent death, just delay it.

Remember, there's a big difference between 'life saving' (rescuing someone from deadly peril, so they can return to a normal life) and 'life sustaining' (keeping someone's basic systems, circulation, respiration, nutrition, hydration, elimination, etc, ticking over, with no guarantee that the patient will be able to lead more than a bedridden and perhaps even comatose life). If your values include things like independence, self-sufficiency and active participation in life, these differences could be crucial. To you, a comatose life might be no life at all.

Many modern medical treatments, which at times can be lifesaving, are often merely life-sustaining. In order to assist you determining which procedures you would life to receive and which you would not, we have provided a brief explanation of each procedure below. If, however, you are in any doubt regarding the nature of the procedure or the consequences of accepting or rejecting it, you should speak to your doctor or physician.

Surgery

Surgery is a medical specialty that uses operative manual and instrumental techniques on a patient to investigate and/or treat (by means of cutting, removing or changing the body) a disease or injury. Surgery is generally performed by a physician with specialist training in operative procedures; more commonly called a surgeon.

There are many surgical specialties providing treatment in all areas of the human body including the brain, lungs, heart and bones. Surgeries can be minor or they can be life saving such as in the case of a heart or kidney transplant. The specific advantages and disadvantages associated with surgery can vary from case to case. As such, it's important that you address these issues with your doctor particularly if you are intending to specify in your living will that you do or do not wish to receive a particular treatment.

Respiratory Support

In addition to the heart, the lungs play a crucial role in keeping us alive. Our lungs are responsible for the exchange of gases in our body; taking fresh oxygen-rich air from the atmosphere into our blood stream and releasing carbon dioxide from the bloodstream into the atmosphere.

The working of the lungs is controlled by the diaphragm, a large thoracic muscle which contracts to expand thoracic volume and thereby reduce chest cavity pressure. This lowered pressure creates suction, which draws outside, oxygenated air into the airways and lungs, whence it travels through the bronchial tubes to ever-smaller passages and finally to the alveoli. These extremely thin-walled, cauliflower-like endings of the respiratory tree (300,000,000 in each lung) are tiny air sacs containing minute capillaries, tiny blood vessels which interface with the pulmonary capillaries.

Meanwhile, the heart pumps oxygen-poor, carbon dioxide-rich blood returned to it via the veins out through the pulmonary arteries and capillaries, where it meets the alveoli of the lungs. There, oxygen passes into the pulmonary capillaries, while in exchange carbon dioxide passes into the alveoli, the crucial gas exchange takes place.

To complete the cycle the heart pumps the freshly-oxygenated blood flowing back to it from the lungs via the pulmonary veins, to all parts of the body, initially via the large arteries beginning with the aorta and eventually through tiny capillaries. At the same time, the diaphragm relaxes, the chest cavity shrinks, pressure in the lungs is increased, and 'bad air' is expelled, exhaled into the atmosphere.

Any interference with this process creates problems for the body. Interferences can be caused by conditions such as asthma, chronic obstructive pulmonary disease (COPD), emphysema, pneumonia, pleurisy, pulmonary embolism, cystic fibrosis, hypertension and viral infections.

Equally, there may be a wide range of heart disease problems in the equation which affect the respiratory process.

Finally, things like obstructive sleep apnea (OSA), excessive alcohol use, too little or too much iron in the body, obesity, thyroid disease, coronary artery disease and of course chest trauma through accident can also contribute to breathing difficulties.

Important Note

Many treatments are available for inadequate spontaneous ventilation, depending on the cause of the breathing problem, its severity and urgency. The area that concerns us most here is of course being kept alive artificially to no good purpose, and where that's most likely to occur is in the hospital ER/ICU environment.

So what we're really looking at is the long-term use of a mechanical ventilator to ensure enough airflow, where our own system has either stopped working or is working inadequately.

A mechanical ventilator is a sophisticated pump for moving air and oxygen into and out of the lungs. It regulates the air-oxygen mix, plus the rate and amount of air delivered with each breath. As well as hospitals and similar institutions (e.g. nursing and convalescent homes), ventilators are also made for private home use. Here the patient is usually under the care of a home nurse.

As long as a patient is conscious, can communicate and is in other ways able to enjoy at least a minimal quality of life, a ventilator or respirator has its rightful place in their treatment regime. It is also a valuable temporary support mechanism, while other treatments and therapies are helping to bring about a recovery.

However, the value and use of a ventilator is often called into question where its sole purpose is to assist a person to breath while permanently unconscious or comatose and in receipt of nutrition and hydration through tubes. It is in these very situations that living wills can express a person's desire as to whether the respirator should be allowed to remain on with what some might regard as a meaningless existence.

Dialysis

Dialysis is a treatment that replaces the function of the kidneys, which normally act as a natural filter for the body. The treatment involves the use of a blood filter and a chemical solution known as dialysate in order to remove waste products and excess fluids from the bloodstream. Dialysate is a chemical that is used to extract waste products out of the blood. For patients whose kidneys are no longer capable of removing these waste products and fluids from their bloodstream, dialysis represents the only treatment available to them apart from kidney transplantation.

The principal types of dialysis treatment include hemodialysis and peritoneal dialysis, the former being the treatment most frequently prescribed in the United States.

Hemodialysis dialysis involves the circulation of a patient's blood outside of their body through a dialysis circuit consisting of plastic blood tubing, a filter known as a dialyzer (artificial kidney) and a dialysis machine that administers dialysate while at the same time monitoring and maintaining blood flow. Patients undergoing this type of treatment typically require three treatments per week, each such treatment taking approximately three to four hours.

Peritoneal dialysis, on the other hand, involves the use of the patient's abdominal lining as a blood filter. A tube, which is surgically inserted into the patient's abdomen, is used to fill the abdominal cavity with dialysate. Once the dialysate has mixed with the waste products and fluids in the patient's bloodstream, usually after 24 hours or so, waste filled dialysate solution is drained from the abdomen, and replaced with clean dialysate.

Where an injury or disease cause your kidneys to fail in the manner outlined above, dialysis is the only means by which you can prevent internal poisoning short of a kidney transplant. Failing to avail of either treatment will eventually result in death. As such, the decision whether to undergo transplant surgery or receive dialysis can ultimately be classified as an end-of-life decision.

Antibiotics

Antibiotics can be described simply as drugs that can be administered either topically, orally, intravenously, or intramuscularly and are used to cure or treat numerous bacterial, viral, and fungal infections.

However, notwithstanding the success of antibiotics in reversing life-threatening infections, infectious diseases still constitute a real threat to elderly people. Even though medical technology has advanced to a position where it can support body functions virtually indefinitely, infection still accounts for approximately 30 percent of all deaths amongst elderly people. While antibiotics are of course useful in treating many of these infections, they often cannot cure the underlying disease or condition. In many cases, life-threatening infections are superimposed on terminal or incurable illnesses. Where this happens, it can be said that the administration of antibiotics used to treat these infections (such as in the case of dialysis, for example) actually acts as a means of prolonging the dying process and, in some cases, the patient's suffering unnecessarily. It is for this reason that thought should be afforded to the administration of antibiotics in your living will.

Important Note

All antibiotics are potentially life-sustaining. They enable other technologies to sustain lives.

Cardiac Resuscitation

In classical belief the heart is the very seat of our being, and our emotional center. But in reality the heart is just a fancy pump, a pump made of meat, at that. It operates in close conjunction with the lungs to send freshly-oxygenated blood throughout the body via inch-thick to hair's breadth tubing known as the vascular system. In doing so, it helps provide oxygen, nutrients and hormones to cells, and carry away waste and oxygen-poor blood for recycling.

While the heart is very robust, it can cease beating (pumping) from a variety of causes. Without fresh blood, our brain is quick to suffer irreparable damage, and unless the heart is restarted within minutes all our other systems will quickly shut down. Some can be restarted, but others are beyond repair.

Restarting a stopped heart and having it continue beating of its own accord is called cardiopulmonary resuscitation (CPR). Hearts can be restarted by using chest compressions, drugs, electric shocks, and artificial breathing aimed at reviving a person who is on the point of dying.

The heart's job can be taken over temporarily in an operating room setting by a heart-lung machine, while the heart itself is worked on, or even replaced. The heart can often be jump-started by delivering an electric shock via a 'defibrillator.' But one way or another, without a working heart and a reasonable vascular system, the human body will die.

If such a resuscitation is likely to be truly lifesaving, then obviously you'd want to have CPR if you ever needed it; you'd want it to be 100 percent successful, and you'd want to go on from there. On the other hand, if by reason of advanced age, multiple organ failures, severe trauma, brain anoxia, or for some other reason, your doctors conclude that you're not likely to survive very long anyway, that all you can look forward to is being kept 'alive' by machines, you may prefer not to be resuscitated. Would you want to prolong dying if that's all it's going to do?

And what if they predict that as a result of your illness or injury, your life will be one long round of seizures, amnesia, hallucinations, and sundry psychological and neurological abnormalities? Again, what's to look forward to in a life of dementia, confusion and other mental disorders?

This is exactly the situation where, if you so choose a 'Do Not Resuscitate' ("DNR") order or an advance directive can help by letting medical personnel know that you do not want to be resuscitated and instead want a natural death to follow. The precise form of a DNR Order varies from state to state. As such, you should contact your local medical care provider or lawyer to obtain a copy of a form suitable in your state. For more information on DNR Orders, see Chapter 6.

However, the decision to refuse CPR is of course not one that should be made lightly. A lot will depend on your age, your current state of health and indeed your personal preferences. Before making a DNR order or providing for non-resuscitation in your living will, we recommend that you speak with a doctor as, unlike other life sustaining procedures, you do not need to be terminally ill before the order is implemented.

Important Note

If you have any queries regarding the above treatments or would like further information in respect of same, we recommend that you contact your doctor.

Blood Transfusions

Blood transfusion is the process of transferring blood or blood-based products from one person into the circulatory system of another. They can be life-saving in situations such as where an individual has suffered massive blood loss due to trauma or surgery. In addition, they can be vital for those requiring chronic transfusions associated with the treatment of conditions such as chronic amnesia, chemotherapy, or bone marrow transplant. In each case, the receipt of blood transfusions can be life saving.

The decision to receive blood can be directly impacted by a person's religious beliefs. Indeed, many people prepare living wills solely for the purpose of ensuring that their religious beliefs regarding the non-receipt of blood and organs form third party donors are respected in times when they themselves are unable to communicate their wishes to medical personnel.

Tissue and Organ Donation

Tissue can most easily be described as a group of specialized cells which perform a specific function. An organ, in turn, is a group of tissues that work together to perform a specific set of functions such as the lungs, heart or kidneys.

Organ transplantation refers to the transplantation of organs or tissue from one person to another following the death of the former. Such transplantations are carried out to save the life or improve the quality of life of the recipient. As transplantation has now become a regular medical procedure, more and more patients have a chance of benefiting from transplants.

The range of organs and tissue currently used for transplantation include the kidneys, heart, lungs, liver, pancreas, corneas, heart valves, bones and tendons, small bowel and skin.

Similar to the position outlined above in respect of the receipt of blood, the receipt of an organ may be something you feel strongly about due to your religious beliefs. If so, you may want to make specific provisions within your living will to deal with the receipt of such organs.

Nutrition and Hydration

Either intravenously through a tube (known as an 'IV tube') placed into a vein in a patient's arm or leg or through a tube into the stomach or nose, it's not uncommon these days for patients who can't swallow, or who are unconscious, in a coma, or in a persistent vegetative state to receive nutritional support and hydration (water).

Where a patient's prognosis is positive, that is where his or her underlying illness or trauma is treatable, and the patient is responding to treatment (for example, where their double pneumonia is responding to antibiotics), there is no doubt that support of this kind is both warranted and welcome. However, where the patient is suffering from catastrophic or untreatable damage or disease, is comatose, unable to communicate, and barely alive, the case for keeping them in suspended animation while knowing that they may not make a recovery or may not be able to live anything remotely like a normal life again is by no means open and shut.

With artificial nutrition and hydration, patients can live for a number of years despite the fact that they are in a permanent state of unconsciousness. The removal of such support would of course lead to death. Of course, any such removal of this support is usually done in such a manner as not to cause discomfort to the patient.

In making your living will, you will need to decide whether or not you wish to have this support applied or withheld. Of course, you can attach conditions to your living will such that your decision to remove this support will only take effect if you were in a permanent state of unconsciousness for a particular period of time. The decision is yours to make.

Important Note

State forms differ when it comes to nutrition and hydration. Some are silent as to the provision of same, some require it to be provided and some allow you to have them withheld or withdrawn. If you are not happy with the choices given under the form required for your state living will, then you should consider creating an addendum to your living will which correctly sets out your choice. See Appendix F. Remember your new choice will only be valid if permitted under state law.

Pain Relief and Palliative Care

While you may state that you do not wish to have your life prolonged through medical means, this does not mean that you must forgo treatment to alleviate pain and discomfort. Palliative care or comfort care focuses on improving the quality of life for a patient rather than prolonging the life of the patient. This allows the patient to receive treatments which alleviate pain and discomfort while still respecting any wishes that they may have outlined in their advance directive. This type of treatment can be appreciated widely by both patients and family members as it allows the patient to retain dignity until their death occurs.

Palliative care seeks to:

- provide relief from pain;

- enhance the quality of the patient's life;

- integrate the psychological and spiritual aspects of patient care with medical care;

- offer patients support to help them live as actively as possible until their death occurs; and

- offer support to the families of terminally ill patients in preparing for the patient's eventual death and, following the patient's death, in their own bereavement.

Care in the Home

In many cases, given the option, people would prefer to die at home surrounded by their loved ones rather than in a hospital or care facility. If you would prefer this, then you can make provision for same in your living will. However, before you do so you should discuss your wishes with both your family and your doctor. These discussions should ensure that you are made fully aware of the pros and cons of making such a decision – both from your point of view and that of your family's.

One of the most important considerations when deciding whether or not to receive palliative care at home is the availability of additional medical treatments in the home. In many cases, these treatments are only available in hospital. As such, before you make a final decision to receive palliative care at home, you should discuss the availability of additional medical treatments at home and also any other available options in terms of the receipt of such treatments. This is particularly important where you wish to receive life sustaining procedures while at the same time avail of palliative care at home. Remember, it may not be possible to have it both ways!

In order to alleviate the possibility of providing conflicting instructions under your living will, it's often useful to include a stipulation in your living to the effect that you only want to receive palliative care at home if it means that you will not have to forego any or all particular types of life sustaining procedure.

If you ultimately decide in favour of home care, you should then have a discussion with both your family and medical team as to how you can best receive the required support and resources in the home. Particular attention will be required should you be in need of 24 hour care. In such circumstances, one or more family members will usually need to agree to be available to tend to your needs. This would most likely require a big commitment from them. As such, it would be useful to discuss this with them in advance. You may also wish to make arrangements for your medical team or a home carer, such as a hospice nurse, to visit you at regular intervals while at home.

Pain and Distress

While most people faced with terminal illness fear pain other symptoms can be much more distressing. In fact, there is a variety of different problems associated with terminal illnesses and unfortunately most patients will suffer from some of them. The most common conditions and their frequency are as follows:- insomnia (59%), anorexia (48%), constipation (33%), sweating (28%), nausea (27%), dyspnoea (24%), dysphagia (20%), neuropsychiatric symptoms (20%), vomiting (20%), urinary symptoms (14%), dyspepsia (11%), paresis (10%), diarrhoea (6%), pruritus (6%) and dermatological symptoms (3%)[1].

Over the years, the hospice movement has done a great deal to develop knowledge about the management of pain and distress in the treatment of terminally ill patients. As such, where home care is being considered, it's often very beneficial to have a hospice nurse or similar home carer attend you at home.

In selecting an appropriate carer regard should be had for the carer's experience and expertises as well as the cost of the carer. As the role can be quite demanding, and often requires 24 hour availability in the case of emergency, it's important that the carer is both willing and able to cope with the physical and emotional demands involved in caring for the terminally ill.

Emotional Needs

Often, when death becomes imminent, the emotions of both a patient and family run high. Fear, anxiety, uncertainty and helplessness are quite common. In such times, people often turn to God whether for the very first time or for the first time in a long time. As such, you may wish to consider having a minister of religion available just in case. Religious ministers can often provide valued guidance and comfort to all concerned during the end stages of an illness.

---

1 Figures from Grond S, Zech D, Diefenbach C, et al; Prevalence and pattern of symptoms in patients with cancer pain: a prospective evaluation of 1635 cancer patients referred to a pain clinic; J Pain Symptom Manage. 1994 Aug; 9(6):372-82

Important Note

If estate planning provisions have not been made before an illness becomes terminal, then this should be tended to as soon as possible so as to avoid dying intestate. Dying intestate (without a will) will almost certainly cause complications.

CHAPTER 3:
STATE REQUIREMENTS FOR LIVING WILLS

Chapter Overview

Each state has different laws regarding the content, operation and execution of living wills. We'll examine each of these issues in general in this chapter before covering state specific requirements in relation to the format of living wills later on in this book.

CHAPTER 3

STATE REQUIREMENTS FOR LIVING WILLS

State Requirements for Life Sustaining Medical Treatment

Although you may have a living will, certain states have legal restrictions and requirements concerning medical treatment that must be adhered to notwithstanding the terms of your living will. For example, some states require that patients receive medical treatment for a certain period of time before the provisions set out in their living will can be implemented. Some states even prevent the provisions of a woman's living will from being implemented if she is pregnant. As such, in order to understand the effectiveness and legality of your living will, you will need to determine what legal provisions apply in your state. We will examine some of the more common requirements and restrictions below. However, we recommend that you supplement the information we provide you by carrying out some independent research of your own.

Who Can Create a Living Will?

In general there are few specific requirements which a person must satisfy before becoming entitled to make a living will. However, as a basic legal requirement, a person wishing to make a living will should be able to understand the meaning and purpose of the document. It is for this very reason that all states require a person to have attained a specific age before being lawfully able to make a living will. In the majority of states, the general requirement is that a person must have reached the age of 18 years before making a living will or other healthcare directive. There are, however, two notable exceptions to this general requirement. In the states of Alabama and Nebraska a person must be at least 19 year old before they can make a living will, while the later state also permits a person under the age of 19 years to make a living will if they are married.

Receipt of Minimum Medical Treatment

As mentioned above, in some states, if you are diagnosed to be in a state of permanent unconsciousness, laws may require that you receive medical treatment for 60 or 90 days before the doctors can make a decision to implement your wishes as stated in your living will. Alternatively, if your condition shows zero brain activity, laws may require that you receive medical treatment for a certain number of hours before the terms of your living will can be implemented.

What Happens During Pregnancy?

In many states, the provisions set out in your living will cease to apply if you are pregnant. Instead, doctors will usually do all in their power to keep you alive until the unborn child is born. Of course, not all states have this requirement – see the chart further on in this chapter for further information on the states which have this requirement. If you are a female resident of one of these states and intend on making a living will then you should expressly state in your living will whether you want life sustaining procedures to be applied if you are pregnant. Even where you decide to withhold life sustaining procedures during your pregnancy, your medical attendants may refuse to honor your request if your pregnancy is well advanced or if such an action runs contrary to their hospital policy in such matters.

When Does My Living Will Become Effective?

Your living will become's a legal document once it is validly signed and witnessed in accordance with the laws of your state of residence. However, notwithstanding that it is legal, it will only become effective once one or more doctors (depending on the requirements set out in the living will itself) determines that you lack the capacity to make your own healthcare decisions and that you are suffering from a terminal illness or permanent vegetative condition.

Formalities

In order for a living will to be valid, it must comply with the relevant state laws in terms of format, signature, witnesses and notarization. We'll discuss each of these requirements in further detail below.

State Living Will Forms

All states with the exceptions of Massachusetts and Michigan have adopted specific forms of living wills. Depending on the state in question, you will be either required to use the specific form set out in legislation (or a form in substantially the same form) or you will be able to use your own form provided that it deals with certain minimum requirements.

We have included state specific forms at Appendix A in the back of this book. These forms have been taken directly from the relevant state codes and, in many cases contain instructions on how they should be completed. Be sure to read these instructions carefully. Some of these forms are relatively straightforward requiring only that you date and sign same as required under state law. Others however allow you to specify the particular life sustaining procedures that you want applied or withheld; while others actually incorporate provisions of a healthcare power of attorney.

If the form provided for your state does not include a provision that you would like to include in your living will, then you should either write the provision in on the state form or attach a separate page to the form setting out your desired provision. Remember to be very clear and precise when writing your provision. Alternatively, you could use the forms set out in this book to help you prepare your own custom living will form (such as the in Appendix B). Of course, it will need to be signed in the same way as any other living will made in your state.

Where the living will provisions are contained within a power of attorney and you do not wish to create a power of attorney, then just complete the living will provisions leaving the remainder of the form blank and execute the form in the required way.

If you live in Massachusetts or Michigan, you could use the sample form set out in Appendix B. However, before doing so, you should check your state laws to ensure that it has not yet prescribed a particular form for use in your particular state.

To see a sample of how a living will can be completed, see the sample completed forms for Alaska contained at Appendix C.

Important Note

Living will forms vary in content from state to state. They can include provisions for appointing someone to revoke or enforce your living will, donating organs and tissue, specifying which procedures to withhold and which to apply, designating guardians and primary physicians. Be sure to read your living will form carefully before signing it!

Witnesses

In order to ensure that a living will is the voluntary act of the person making it, and that this person has not been unduly influenced by their medical condition or by other persons, certain states have limitations on when a living will can be made and who can serve as witnesses.

In several states, you cannot make a living will while you are in the hospital or in a nursing home. It must be made before you go to the hospital (or at least, after you have been discharged, and before you're readmitted with your 'final illness'). In other instances specific conditions will apply before you can make a living will in hospitals. For example, under Georgia law, if you wish to make a living will while you are a patient in a hospital or resident in a nursing home, you will need to have an additional person to witness you signing your living will form. In the case of a hospital, this third witness must be the chief of the hospital staff or a physician not participating in your care. In the case of a nursing home, it must be the nursing home's medical director or a staff physician not participating in your care.

In most cases, you will need two witnesses to witness the signing of your living will. However, you should be aware that a number of states prohibit certain people from acting as a witness to the signing of a living will. In fact, some of the state forms expressly specify who cannot act as a witness. You should be sure to check the laws of your state to determine who can and cannot act as a witness to your living will. In general, however, the following people are precluded from acting as witnesses in most states: your spouse, children, grandchildren, parents, grandparents, siblings, or any lineal ancestors or descendants. Also included are spouses of any of these people. Other persons who should not be witnesses of course would include a person who is named in your last will or who would benefit from your estate (if you died intestate), someone who is a beneficiary of a life insurance policy on your life and finally a person who is directly responsible for your medical care (including employees, agents and patients of any hospital or nursing home that you might be in). The rationale here is that each of those people may potentially gain upon your death and may make decisions based on self-motivation.

You should also avoid using minors or anyone named as an agent in your healthcare power of attorney.

Notarized Signatures

The laws of certain states require that living wills be signed and witnessed in front of a notary. Details of states with such requirements are set out in the table on the next few pages.

While some states do not require that your living will be notarized, it often makes sense to have it notarized as it makes it more unlikely that a legal challenge will be mounted against the validity of the signatures appearing on the document (including your own) and this in turn increases the likelihood that your healthcare providers will accept it as valid.

We have attached affidavit forms at Appendix D which you can attach to your living will (if it doesn't already contain one) in order for it to be notarized.

Important Note

Certain states have specific wording which needs to be used for notarizing a document. Be sure to check with your notary that the wording contained in your living will is suitable in your state.

State	Overview of state requirements for AMDs
Alabama	Two witnesses required for AMD. An AMD will not be valid if the patient is pregnant.
Alaska	No witnesses required for a living will. Two witnesses are required for a healthcare power of attorney.
Arizona	A witness and a notary are required for both a living will and a healthcare power of attorney.
Arkansas	Two witnesses required for both a living will and a healthcare power of attorney. Neither will be valid if the patient is pregnant.
California	Two witnesses required for both an AMD and a healthcare power of attorney. A healthcare power of attorney can also be witnessed by a notary.
Colorado	Two witnesses required for an AMD. A healthcare power of attorney does not require any witnesses.

State	Overview of state requirements for AMDs
Connecticut	Two witnesses required for both an AMD and a healthcare power of attorney. The signatures must be notarized. Neither will be valid if the patient is pregnant.
Delaware	Two witnesses required for both a living will and a healthcare power of attorney.
District of Columbia	Two witnesses required for both a living will and a healthcare power of attorney.
Florida	Two witnesses required for both a living will and a healthcare power of attorney.
Georgia	Two witnesses required for both a living will and a healthcare power of attorney. A living will is not valid if the patient is pregnant.
Hawaii	Two witnesses required for both a living will and a healthcare power of attorney. The healthcare power of attorney must be notarized. A living will is not valid if the patient is pregnant.
Idaho	Two witnesses required for both a living will and a healthcare power of attorney. A notary can also witness a healthcare power of attorney. A living will is not valid if the patient is pregnant.
Illinois	Two witnesses required for a living will. A living will is not valid if the patient is pregnant. One witness required for a healthcare power of attorney.
Indiana	Two witnesses required for a living will. A living will is not valid if the patient is pregnant. A notary is required for a healthcare power of attorney.
Iowa	Two witnesses and a notary required for both a living will and a healthcare power of attorney. A living will is not valid if the patient is pregnant.
Kansas	Two witnesses or a notary are required for a living will.
Kentucky	Two witnesses or a notary required for a living will. A living will is not valid if the patient is pregnant.

State	Overview of state requirements for AMDs
Louisiana	Two witnesses required for both a living will and a healthcare power of attorney.
Maine	Two witnesses required for both a living will and a healthcare power of attorney.
Maryland	Two witnesses required for both a living will and a healthcare power of attorney.
Massachusetts	No provision for a format of living will. Two witnesses required for both a living will and a healthcare power of attorney.
Michigan	No provision for a format of living will. Two witnesses required for both a living will and a healthcare power of attorney.
Minnesota	Two witnesses and a notary required for both a living will and a healthcare power of attorney. A living will is not valid if the patient is pregnant.
Mississippi	Two witnesses required for an advanced healthcare directive (includes both a living will and a healthcare power of attorney in the one document).
Missouri	Two witnesses required for both a living will and a healthcare power of attorney. A notary can also witness a healthcare power of attorney. A living will is not valid if the patient is pregnant.
Montana	Two witnesses required for a living will.
Nebraska	Two witnesses and a notary required to witness a living will.
Nevada	Two witnesses required for both a living will and a healthcare power of attorney. A notary can also witness a healthcare power of attorney.
New Hampshire	Two witnesses or a notary required to witness both a living will and a healthcare power of attorney.
New Jersey	Two witnesses or a notary or a lawyer is required to witness both living wills and healthcare powers of attorney.

State	Overview of state requirements for AMDs
New Mexico	No witnesses required for either a living will or a healthcare power of attorney.
New York	Two witnesses required for both a living will and a healthcare power of attorney.
North Carolina	Two witnesses required for both a living will and a healthcare power of attorney. A living will is not valid if the patient is pregnant.
North Dakota	Two witnesses required for both a living will and a healthcare power of attorney. A living will is not valid if the patient is pregnant.
Ohio	Two witnesses or a notary required for both a living will and a healthcare power of attorney. A living will is generally not valid if the patient is pregnant.
Oklahoma	Two witnesses required for both a living will and a healthcare power of attorney. A living will is not valid if the patient is pregnant.
Oregon	Two witnesses required for both a living will and a healthcare power of attorney.
Pennsylvania	Two witnesses required for a living will (includes a healthcare power of attorney in the same document). A living will is not valid if the patient is pregnant.
Rhode Island	Two witnesses or a notary required for both a living will and a healthcare power of attorney. A living will is generally not valid if the patient is pregnant.
South Carolina	Two witnesses or a notary required for both a living will and a healthcare power of attorney. A living will also requires a notary to act as a witness.
South Dakota	Two witnesses required for both a living will and a healthcare power of attorney. A healthcare power of attorney can also be witnessed by a notary. A living will is generally not valid if the patient is pregnant.
Tennessee	Two witnesses required for both a living will and a healthcare power of attorney. A healthcare power of attorney can also be witnessed by a notary.

State	Overview of state requirements for AMDs
Texas	Two witnesses required for both a living will and a healthcare power of attorney. A living will is generally not valid if the patient is pregnant.
Utah	Two witnesses required for a living will. A living will is generally not valid if the patient is pregnant. A notary is required for a healthcare power of attorney.
Vermont	Two witnesses required for both a living will and a healthcare power of attorney.
Virginia	An advance medical directive requires two witnesses.
Washington	Two witnesses required for a living will. A living will is generally not valid if the patient is pregnant. No witnesses are required for a healthcare power of attorney.
West Virginia	Two witnesses and a notary required for both a living will and a healthcare power of attorney.
Wisconsin	Two witnesses and a notary required for both a living will and a healthcare power of attorney. A living will is not valid if the patient is pregnant.
Wyoming	Two witnesses are required for both a living will and a healthcare power of attorney. A notary is also required for a healthcare power of attorney. A living will is not valid if the patient is pregnant.

Out-of-State Directives

People often wonder whether advance directives made in one state will be honored in other states. This is primarily because it is by no means inconceivable that you could end up in hospital in another state. The good news is that the laws of many states provide for the recognition of living wills made in other states provided that the living will complies with the laws of your state of residence. However, there are some states where the law is simply not clear on the issue. While there is a degree of ambiguity in these states, the practical reality is that most healthcare providers will try to abide by your wishes irrespective of whether you use an out-of-state form or not.

Important Note

Subject to some exceptions, a person is generally deemed to be resident in the state in which he or she is registered to vote, holds their driving license and bank and investment accounts.

In situations where you spend much of your time between a few different states, it might be useful to make a living will in each state just to cover off the possibility that a healthcare provider refuses to recognize an out-of-state living will. It might even be practical to have different healthcare agents in each such state but this is something that you will have to consider carefully.

Life and Health Insurance

Unlike suicide, life and health insurance companies generally don't refuse to pay out under their policies where you die as a result of the withdrawal of life sustaining procedures.

What if My Doctor or Hospital Refuses to Follow My Advance Directive?

Doctors are generally free to refuse to follow the provisions set out in your living will. They may choose to do so because it doesn't fit in with their personal beliefs or because it's the policy operated by the hospital or nursing home where they are employed. They may also do so where they believe your instructions run contrary to what is considered acceptable medical practice. Where a doctor or healthcare facility refuses to honor your wishes, they should assist you in locating a facility that will honor your requests and, if appropriate, transfer you to that facility. Of course, if the reason for refusing to follow your wishes in the first instance is based on the fact that your wishes fall below what is considered to be acceptable medical practice, it's unlikely that another institution will honor your requests.

Healthcare providers are required under federal law to advise you of your right to make an advance medical directive and of their policies in that respect. They should also be able to advise you of their policies in advance of admission if you so request. Where you are terminally ill and likely to be admitted to a particular hospital or care facility, you should consider requesting details of their policies in relation to advance directives before admission.

As outlined above, the one exception to the foregoing arises in the case of pregnancy. In such cases, living wills can cease to apply.

Immunity for Healthcare Providers

As with all medical professionals, your healthcare providers will be immune from prosecution if they follow the provisions set out in your living will or the instructions provided by your agent. Of course, they will need to check the terms of your living will closely and verify the authority of your agent to act on your behalf.

Do I Need a Lawyer to Help Me Make a Living Will?

No. There is generally no need to have a lawyer assist you with the preparation of your living will. In most cases, you can complete the state forms yourself or use a self-help book such as this one to assist you. However, if you are in any doubt as to what you are doing or believe that you might need a specially drafted form to cover your specific requirements, you should contact a lawyer for assistance. Alternatively, you could contact the Division of Aging Services.

Should I Involve My Doctor in Making My Living Will?

While there is no need to involve your doctor in the process, it is often useful to discuss your choices and options with your doctor before making your living will. In this way, you will be sure to fully understand the import of the decisions that you are making within your living will.

CHAPTER 4:
HEALTHCARE AGENTS

Chapter 4

Chapter Overview

Choosing a healthcare agent could be one of the most important decisions you ever make. To guide you through the selection process, we will identify in this chapter the main traits that you should look for in an agent. We will also examine both the responsibilities and authority of healthcare agents.

CHAPTER 4

HEALTHCARE AGENTS

What Is a Healthcare Agent?

A healthcare agent is a person you choose under a living will or a healthcare power of attorney to make certain decisions for you in the event that you are unconscious or otherwise unable to make these decisions for yourself.

An agent appointed under a living may have authority to make end-of-life decisions on your behalf based on the provisions you have set out in your living will. The degree of authority which you can give to your healthcare agent will vary depending on the laws of the state in which you are resident and, of course, the contents of your living will. In most cases, you can either grant authority to the agent to make end-of-life decisions on your behalf or appoint them for the sole purpose of enforcing or revoking the terms of your living will.

Important Note

In certain states, a healthcare agent can be referred to as a healthcare proxy or surrogate or an attorney-in-fact.

A healthcare agent appointed under a healthcare power of attorney has somewhat broader powers. They will generally be able to make decisions regarding your medical treatment as a whole rather than being confined to end-of-life decisions. Of course, similar to living wills, their authority to make these decisions will be restricted by state law and the terms of the healthcare power of attorney.

Appointing an Agent to Revoke or Enforce Your Living Will

As already mentioned, some states allow you to name an agent who may either revoke or enforce your living will. It is generally considered that when you name an agent, you are giving that person the power and authority to go to court on your behalf and ask a judge to either revoke or enforce the terms of your living will. However, in some cases, depending on the content of your living will, the agent does not need to go to court, but can merely instruct the medical care providers to either disregard or to enforce your wishes as set out in the living will. Alternatively, the agent may only be able to temporally suspend the operation of your living will so that it is not used at a specific time, but may be used later.

Important Note

Even if you don't appoint an agent under your living will, healthcare facilities and physicians are still obliged to follow the provisions set out in your living will.

Appointing a person to enforce or revoke your healthcare decisions can be useful because it allows for advocacy on your behalf which could help get over difficulties in interpreting your living will. It's also worth remembering that if physician refuses to respect the terms of your living will you have the right to be transferred to another physician or hospital that will honor the document. An agent can be very useful in ensuring that this happens.

Choosing an Agent

Given the authority granted to healthcare agents, it should go without saying that your choice of agent could be one of the most important decisions you ever make. It should not therefore be made lightly and should only be made after due consideration and forethought. Remember, unless you provide a stipulation to the contrary or expressly set out your desires regarding end-of-life treatment in your living will, your agent could have the same authority to make end-of-life decisions on your behalf as you would have if you were conscious and fit to make these decisions. Your choice of agent is therefore extremely important.

Important Note

Remember to choose an agent who is going to be on hand to make decisions when the time requires. If your illness is prolonged, they may have to spend a good degree of time overseeing that your wishes regarding end-of-life treatments are complied with. It may not therefore be advisable to appoint someone who lives a long distance from you or who will have limited availability when needed.

Your agent should be someone you know and trust and whose judgment you know you can depend on. The person should be someone with whom you've discussed your desires regarding end-of-life treatment and who understands, respects and accepts your views regarding such treatment. Often, people will choose their spouse or other close family members to act as their agents as they are often the people who satisfy these criteria.

If you believe that your choices may be met with adversity from either family members or medical personnel, be sure to appoint someone who is strong willed and assertive.

However, before appointing someone, it's important that you discuss your decisions with them and ensure that when the time comes that they will be willing to act on your behalf to uphold your decisions.

It's worth mentioning that, similar to the position regarding a witness, most states preclude you from appointing a person who is directly responsible for your medical care (including employees, agents and patients of any hospital or nursing home that you might be in) as your agent. Some states allow you to name family members as healthcare agents while others allow you to name colleagues if you work in a healthcare facility. However, before appointing any such persons, you should check the laws of your state. If you believe that a particular doctor is best placed to act as your agent under a living will then you can request that he or she ceases to act as your healthcare provider. If they agree and you no longer receive any medical care in the facility where they are employed, it should be possible for them to act as your healthcare agent.

If you are in any doubt that your agent will perform his or her tasks, you may wish to chose an alternative agent or appoint a second agent who independently has full authority to carry out your instructions. However, we would not ordinarily recommend the appointment of joint agents as it can lead to arguments and conflicts between them which could, in turn, result in delays in important medical decisions being made.

Appointing an Alternate Agent

When making your living will, it's always a good idea to appoint one or more alternate agents just in case the first appointed agent is unable or unwilling to act for any reason. An alternate agent is someone who will perform the duties of the first named agent should he or she be unable or unwilling to act (for whatever reason). If the alternate agent is required to act, he or she will be bound by the same duties and responsibilities as the original agent.

You should consider the appointment of an alternate agent in the same careful way that you considered the appointment of the primary agent.

Responsibility of an Agent

Your agent will have no authority to act under your living will until such time as you are diagnosed as suffering from a terminal illness, being in a persistent comatose condition or in a permanent vegetative state and unable to communicate your own wishes. Until that point, you are free to direct what terminal care you wish or do not wish to receive, as the case may be.

Once your agent becomes authorized to act on your behalf he or she must make decisions that are consistent with the instructions set out in your living will. If you have not made your wishes clear in your living will, your agent may, depending on the terms of your living will, have authority to decide what is in your best interests having regard to your personal values and any wishes which you have expressed directly to your agent or to your medical practitioners and family.

In many cases, however, your agent's responsibility will be limited to ensuring that your healthcare wishes as set out in your living will are honored by the medical personnel treating you and by your family. If there is resistance from either of these parties, your agent will be able to seek court intervention to order the medical personnel to comply with your wishes. If they refuse to do so, your agent can assist in making arrangements to have you transferred to a facility that will honor your wishes.

Living wills can also give your agent discretionary authority to revoke your living will if he or she deems fit. This can be important where circumstances make it undesirable to follow the provisions set out in your living will. In granting your agent this power, it's important to ensure that he or she is fully aware of your wishes, respects your wishes and is assertive enough to withstand pressure from medical personnel or your family members. It's therefore important to choose your agent carefully. Remember 'with great power comes great responsibility!'

Restricting Your Agent's Authority

Once you have decided on someone to appoint as your agent you will need to carefully consider whether any limitations should be placed on the scope of his authority. Of course, any such consideration will be influenced by the level of authority that your agent has actually been given.

Typically, people who place restrictions on their agent under their living will tend to restrict them from revoking the provisions set out in their living will or from making any other life sustaining decisions apart from those expressly included in the living will. In this way, the creator of a living will can be confident that the agent can only do what he or she is expressly authorized to do and, as such, cannot force a decision on the creator which he or she may not have approved of had he or she been conscious.

However, despite the clear advantages in limiting your agent's authority there is also a disadvantage. It's often quite difficult to predict how your medical situation will evolve over time. This being so, there is an argument for allowing your agent sufficient discretion to be able to respond to developments in your medical condition. Maybe a new medical treatment has become available to treat your terminal illness or maybe you are showing signs of a miraculous recovery? Were this to happen, would you want your agent to have authority to revoke the provisions of your living will? Maybe the right to revoke should only arise in certain circumstances? Maybe your agent should be given a right to suspend the application of your living will for a period of time rather than revoke it? In what circumstances should your agent be allowed affect this suspension? Maybe you would simply prefer to accept that your time has come and therefore give your agent no powers of revocation or suspension, just a power of enforcement?

It follows that, in determining whether or not to impose limitations on the scope of your agent's authority, you will need to carefully weigh up the pros and cons of restricting your agent's authority. These pros and cons will be determined by your own attitudes and feelings towards end-of-life treatment and death. Whatever your decision is be sure to document it clearly in your living will using simple and precise language.

Will My Healthcare Agent Be Responsible for My Medical Bills?

No! As with virtually all medical treatments, the patient will be responsible for the payment of his or her medical fees. Your agent will not therefore be held accountable for these fees.

There is however one exception to the above general rule. In certain states, an agent can be held liable for the costs of disposition of your body if proper provision has not been made for same. However, in most cases, either your family or your estate will pick up the cost.

CHAPTER 5:
SHOULD I MAKE A LIVING WILL?

Chapter 5

Chapter Overview

A living will should never be made without due thought and consideration. In this chapter, you will be asked to consider whether a living will is suitable for you or not. If a living will is for you, then we've got some useful and practical tips on preparing a living will.

CHAPTER 5

SHOULD I MAKE A LIVING WILL?

Should I Make a Living Will?

Whether or not you decide to make a living will is completely up to you. In making that decision, you will need to consider situations that might leave you in a persistent state of unconsciousness or indeed cause your death. Understandably, these are situations you might prefer not to think about. However, with high-tech medicine adding weeks, months and sometimes years to our lives we all run the risk of being incapacitated before we die. This leaves some serious questions for you, and indeed everyone, to ponder and to plan for.

Consider what you would want to happen if a serious accident or illness left you in a situation where:-

- you were unable to speak, move, feel or, worse still, you were in constant pain;

- only a respirator and feeding tube were keeping you alive; and

- your quality of life was virtually non-existent and there was no real hope of improvement.

Would you want to stretch your life out on life support or would you rather let nature take its course? Where would you want to draw the line? When should it end?

Unfortunately, far too many people actually find themselves, without warning and without the benefit of asking those questions, in those or similar situations. These people have no control over the medical care they are receiving. These people have no choice but to "live". You can avoid this lack of control if you are practical. Consider your alternatives and make a choice.

If this choice is hard for you to contemplate, think of how it will be for your loved ones if you do nothing. If anything should ever happen to you, they will be the ones who will have to bear the emotional trauma of dealing with your permanent incapacity. They will be the ones that will have to visit you in hospital and make the tough decisions for you. They will be the ones who have to consider how to foot the bill for years of hospital care notwithstanding that there might be no possible chance of recovery for you! They may even end up paying these bills themselves!

We don't mean in this chapter to scare you or to convince you that it's right or wrong to make a living will. We are here to prompt you to think —not to tell you what to think or what you should or should not do or think — just to prompt you into thinking about this very important matter for yourself.

Having the right to deicide what medical treatment you receive, if any, during a terminal illness is what living wills are all about. It allows you to decide these things now, while you can. It is about doing it calmly and without any pressure, and then articulating your wishes in a legal document that will be there to guide your doctors, friends and family if you ever come into the emergency room unable to tell them what you really want. The decision to make a living will is, of course, yours to make!

Why Should I Have a Living Will?

Well, the answer to this simple question is very straight forward. A living will gives you the opportunity to specify what life supporting treatments, if any, you wish to receive should you be terminally ill and unable to communicate your wishes. With it, you can provide a clear set of instructions for your medical team to follow. Also, by having your instructions detailed in a clear manner, it may save your family from making tough decisions which could have been quite difficult for them to make.

Living wills are also useful when it comes to ensuring that your religious and ethical beliefs are upheld by the medical personnel treating you. For example, you can stipulate that you don't want to receive blood transfusions or organ transplants.

In addition, it also allows you to appoint a trusted third party (your agent) who can either enforce or revoke the provisions set out in your living will.

Must I Have a Living Will?

No, there is absolutely no legal requirement whatsoever for you to have a living will or indeed any other type of advance directive. Healthcare facilities and hospitals cannot therefore refuse to provide you with medical care on the basis that you don't have a living will or other advance directive. Indeed, to the contrary, hospitals are generally required by the "Patient Self-Determination Act" to inquire as to whether you have a living will and, if not, whether you would like to make one. They cannot however insist that you do in fact make a living will before you receive medical care even if you are terminally ill and the provision of that medical care could leave you permanently unconscious.

What Happens if I Don't Make a Living Will?

If you fail to make a living will, state law will intervene to determine how decisions regarding your medical treatment are made. In most instances, the responsibility for making these decisions will fall to your family who will invariably be guided by medical personnel.

Of course, because you have not stated what life sustaining medical treatments you want or don't want, your family will have no real 'road map' to follow when making decisions for you. In these circumstances, family members could easily come to an impasse in terms of the treatment you should or should not receive, as the case may be. This impasse may well escalate to a court battle to resolve the issue. Indeed, this is exactly what happened in the Terri Schiavo case (see Chapter 1).

All of these possible problems and disagreements could be avoided by stating your wishes clearly in a living will.

What Should My Advance Directive Say?

While the terms of your living will can, to a large degree, be set out in a specific form in accordance with state law, the choices you make in terms of the receipt or non-receipt of life sustaining procedure is entirely up you. In most cases, these choices will represent your views on the receipt or non-receipt of life sustaining procedure.

Typically, you will use a living will to:-

- specify the life-sustaining treatments you want and don't want to receive. This may include matters such as organ transplantation, dialysis, blood transfusions and so on;

- specify whether you wish to receive artificial nutrition and hydration or not. In many states, in the absence of expressly setting out your wishes, it will be assumed that you wish to receive nutrition and hydration in all circumstances; and

- appoint an agent who can revoke or enforce the terms of your living will or, alternatively, make decisions regarding the receipt or non-receipt of life sustaining procedures on your behalf.

When Should I Refuse Medical Treatment?

Unfortunately, this is a question that we cannot answer for you. It really is a matter of personal choice for you. In many cases, however, there tends to be two main reasons why people refuse treatment. The first reason is because the risk attached to the treatment is too high. Of course, this is a matter of personal choice and dependent on each person's appetite for risk. Certain people will undergo risky medical procedures for an opportunity to extend life while others may be content with accepting a shorter life in order to avoid risky and invasive medical procedures.

The other reason why people refuse certain medical treatments is that they see them as merely prolonging life under conditions which may already be intolerable. For many, the idea of being terminally ill in a bed unable to communicate with the world is the last straw. It's when they finally decide to allow their life to come to an end naturally, without medical intervention.

Remember, if you don't want certain medical treatments, it's important that you clearly identify those in a living will.

Religious Views of Living Wills

Over the years, living wills have been accepted by many denominations and faiths including Baptists, Catholics, members of the Church of Christ, Methodists, Presbyterian and many more. Many believe in a person's right to allow nature take its course even where technology exists to delay that. However, this view is not shared by all. Some faiths have been quite vocal about their disapproval of living wills. If you are in any doubt as to what is acceptable having regard to your particular faith, we recommend that you speak to a minister of your faith.

Family Discussions

In practice, if you ever become incapacitated, your family will need to decide whether or not they wish to support the end-of-life decisions that you have made in your living will. The alternative would be to take court action to challenge the terms of your living will in order to either keep you alive or allow you to die naturally. The very fact that your living will, like your last will and testament and other legal documents, can be challenged by your family members (whether rightly or wrongly, successfully or unsuccessfully) makes it important to discuss your personal choices with close family members. At the very least, it will afford you an opportunity to try and bring them around to your way of thinking. Alternatively, it will open the door for a discussion that may provide you with useful feedback or may even present you with alternatives that you had not considered.

In discussing end-of-life decisions with your family, you should carefully explain the decisions you have made to them, what those decisions mean and why you have made them. This, ideally, should be done at the same time you make your living will. To help explain your decision, it may even be useful to refer to some of the high profile cases involving end-of-life care and decisions such as the Cruzan case or the more recent Terri Schiavo case. This will provide a useful real life scenario to help your family understand your wishes and the reasons for these wishes.

One of the most contentious areas of family discussions is often the choice of agent. Frequently, family members feel aggrieved that they were not considered for or indeed appointed to act as their loved one's agent. This same type of aggravation could have a direct impact on your family's willingness to abide by the wishes you have set out in your living will and indeed the decisions made by your agent. With this in mind, you should try to deal with this potential issue before it arises. In most cases, this can be achieved by discussing your choices with your family. In these discussions, it's important that you try and get them to accept the person that you have nominated as your agent under your living will. Otherwise, in addition to the emotional trauma, your family could find themselves amidst a grave conflict should you become incapacitated.

It follows that it is also very important that you discuss your wishes with your agent and ensure that he or she is fully aware of what you want to happen should you ever become permanently incapacitated. If you get both your family and agent in line with your thinking on the subject, matters should hopefully run smoothly as between them when the time requires.

Do I Need a Lawyer to Create a Living Will?

The simple answer to this question is no, you do not need a lawyer. By using this book and supplementing the information in it with your own research, you should have sufficient forms and resources to create your own living will. If however, you do not feel comfortable preparing the documents yourself, then we suggest that you contact your lawyer and/or doctor for assistance in completing your living will.

Finalizing Your Living Will

Once you have decided to make a living will, you should check the specific laws that may apply in your state. Many states have specific forms, and in a few states, required language that should be included in your living will. When you have determined the specific laws that apply in your state and what form you need to use, there are a few final steps you should take to ensure that your wishes will be respected when the time comes.

- specifically, you should discuss the terms of your advance directive with your doctor before you sign it. Make sure you are both comfortable with what it says. He or she may suggest something you hadn't thought of that you might decide to include;

- comply with your state's signature and witness requirements. As mentioned above, states have various requirements about who can be a witness, how many witnesses are needed, and if the directive must be notarized;

- keep the original in a safe place but also provide copies of the signed directive to (1) your doctor and hospital; (2) your agent if one is named; (3) family members; (4) your lawyer and (5) other significant people in your life.

What to Do With Your Living Will

After you have properly signed your living will, and had it witnessed and notarized, you need to take it to your doctor. (NB: this is not to get the doctor's advice. You've already done that before you finalized your living will.)

Ask your doctor to make a copy of the original living will and to put the copy in your medical records so that he/she will have it for future use. Keep the original living will in a safe place. If you go to the hospital, take the original living will with you.

Important Note

What do I do with my living will after completing it?

The original should be kept in a safe place with all your other important papers and legal documents. Copies should be given to your doctor, agent and other close family members to ensure that it's available when needed. It's also a very good idea to carry a small card in your wallet or purse that states that you have a living will and provides contact details for a person or organization that can provide it to medical personnel when required.

Legalvaults ™ Wallet Cards

When you have made your advance medical directive, it is a good idea to carry a card in your wallet or purse confirming that you have done so. This way, should you be admitted to a medical facility and unable to communicate, healthcare providers will be alerted to the fact that you have set out your requirements in relation to end-of-life treatments and will be legally bound to honor your wishes. By including on your card the contact names and numbers of key family members, details of your doctor and details of the location of your advance directives if you have any, your healthcare providers will be able to determine your healthcare wishes when most needed.

Important Note

For more information on obtaining wallet cards and storing your advance directives electronically so that physicians and medical personnel can easily access them in a time of emergency we recommend visiting the Legal Vaults™ website at www.legalvaults.com.

Terminating Advance Directives

As long as you remain mentally competent and able to manage your own affairs, you may terminate a living will that you have previously made at any time. Incidentally, the same applies to a healthcare power of attorney.

While your advance directive can be revoked orally, even as in some cases it can be made orally, we do not recommend doing so. It's simply too prone to challenge, and too difficult to prove. Rather we would recommend that you do one and, where possible, all of the following:

- physically destroy the living will by burning, tearing or shredding it and all copies of it;

- revoke the authority granted to an agent under a living will by serving a notice of revocation in writing on your agent, on all persons that hold a copy of your living will and all persons that might rely on it or your agent's authority;

- instruct your proxy or attorney-in-fact to revoke your directive where they have power to do so.

Ordinarily, revocation only takes effect when the revocation is communicated to the agent. The revocation is not effective with third parties who may deal with the agent until the third party receives notice of the revocation.

Not all states require that your written revocation be signed in front of witnesses, but a handful of states do. Even if your state does not require witnesses, it is a good idea to have them sign your notice of revocation. With witnesses, you minimize the chances that your revocation will be challenged or considered ineffective.

Important Note

We have included a notice of revocation of a living will as well as a notice of revocation of a power of attorney at Appendix E of this book.

The following persons should NOT act as witnesses:

- your spouse; your children, grandchildren, and other lineal descendants; your parents, grandparents, and other lineal ancestors; your siblings and their lineal descendants; or a spouse of any of these persons;

- a person who is directly responsible for your medical care;

- a person who is named in your will or, if you have no will, who would inherit your property by intestate succession; and

- a beneficiary of a life insurance policy on your life.

Ask the hospital personnel to make a copy and put the copy in your medical records. Put the original living will back in a safe place. This should not be somewhere which is hard to access, like a safe deposit box, just in case somebody you hadn't thought of does need to see it and you aren't able to communicate at the time.

CHAPTER 6:

HEALTHCARE POWERS OF ATTORNEY, DO NOT RESUSCITATE ORDERS AND ORGAN DONATION

Chapter Overview

In this chapter, we review other advance medical directives such as healthcare powers of attorney, DNR Orders and organ donations.

Chapter 6

CHAPTER 6

HEALTHCARE POWERS OF ATTORNEY, DO NOT RESUSCITATE ORDERS AND ORGAN DONATION

Healthcare Power of Attorney

As you will have no doubt gathered from the foregoing chapters, the principal limitation of living wills is that they only come into play when you are either terminally ill, or permanently unconscious, and cannot tell your doctors what you want done. It therefore does not apply where, for example, you are unconscious due to a minor accident, or illness, or where you are suffering from mental illness. This is where a healthcare power of attorney (HCPOA) comes into play.

Important Note

A healthcare power of attorney can also be referred to as a healthcare proxy, a durable power of attorney for healthcare, a medical power of attorney or a designation of healthcare surrogate.

A HCPOA is a document that appoints someone of your choice to be your authorized agent (also called an attorney-in-fact or proxy) for the purpose of making healthcare decisions on your behalf when you are unable to do so for yourself. You can give your agent as much or as little authority as you wish to make some or all healthcare decisions for you. And, in most states, you can include the same kind of instructions regarding life sustaining procedure that you would normally put in a living will.

The authority under a HCPOA becomes effective only when your attending physician or physicians (depending on state law and the terms of your HCPOA) determine(s) that you have lost the capacity to make informed healthcare decisions for yourself. However, as long as you still have this capacity, you retain the right to make all medical and other healthcare decisions.

In your HCPOA, you can limit the scope of your agent's authority to make healthcare decisions on your behalf. In the absence of limiting your agent's authority in this matter, your agent can have the same level of authority to make healthcare decisions for you as you would normally have. The authority of the agent to make healthcare decisions for you generally includes the authority to:

- give informed consent,

- refuse to give informed consent, or

- withdraw informed consent

to any care, treatment, service, or procedure designed to maintain, diagnose, or treat a physical or mental condition. Your agent will also be able to hire and fire doctors, decide which healthcare provider(s) to use, disclose your medical records to third parties and even limit your visitation rights. In addition, they can also make decisions following your death regarding the conduct of autopsies and the donation of your organs. It follows that you need to carefully consider the scope of the authority granted to your agent as well as the person who you wish to appoint as your agent.

Important Note

The rights of healthcare agents vary from state to state, so it's a good idea to ask your lawyer about the law in your state.

Choosing a Healthcare Agent

The person you choose to be your healthcare agent should be a trusted individual who is also knowledgeable and comfortable discussing healthcare issues. Because this person may need to argue your case with doctors or family members, or even go to court, an assertive yet diplomatic individual may be the best individual to represent your interests. You should discuss your healthcare choices with your agent before their appointment and ensure that they will support these choices.

For most, the person chosen to act as an agent is a spouse, partner or close family relative. However, while you invariably trust these people, you do need to consider whether they will have the resolve to make the tough decisions when the time comes. Remember, they may well be faced with dissenting family members and medical professionals. If you are in any doubt as to their resolve, you may wish to chose an alternative agent or appoint a second agent who independently has full authority to carry out your instructions. However, we would not ordinarily recommend the appointment of a second or joint agent as it can lead to arguments and conflicts between the two agents. This, in turn, often leads to delays in important medical decisions being made.

In choosing an agent, you should also consider the person's age, emotional ability, how well they know you, their views on your wishes, various medical treatments and the right to life generally, their religious beliefs, whether they have any financial or other interest in your survival or death and the availability and willingness of that person generally to act as your agent.

In certain states, a spouse can lose the right to act as an agent for his or her spouse if the couple are legally separated or divorced unless the incapacitated spouse's HCPOA provides otherwise.

Similar to the position with living wills above, your agent or healthcare proxy should not be someone attending to your healthcare as there is a danger of a conflict of interest arising in such circumstances as it is in the healthcare providers financial interest to keep treating you rather than curing you or allowing you to die!

Important Note

As a practical matter, it's useful to appoint the same person as your agent under both your living will and healthcare power of attorney – of course, the choice is up to you!

Alternate Healthcare Agent

Again, similar to the position with living wills, it's useful to appoint an alternate healthcare agent just in case the first named agent is unable or unwilling to act as your agent when the time comes. In selecting your alternate agent, it's important that you apply the same criteria as you did in choosing your primary agent. Also, remember to check that your alternate agent is willing to act as your agent.

Who Can Make a Healthcare Power of Attorney?

The requirements for making a HCPOA are quite similar to those that apply in relation to living wills. Generally, the person must have reached the age of majority in their state and must be able to understand what a HCPOA does and the content of their own HCPOA document.

Do I Need Both a Living Will and a Healthcare Power of Attorney?

Most estate planners agree that the best approach in dealing with healthcare issues is to have both a living will and a HCPOA. As already pointed out, using a living will in isolation is problematic as it only relates to end-of-life decisions. As such, in order to cover all other medical decisions, it's advisable to make a HCPOA to supplement it. It's even better when you can combine both into one document as it lessens the likelihood of any conflict arising where there are two separate documents. In fact, as already mentioned, many states allow you to combine the two documents.

Do Not Resuscitate Orders

Another form of medical directive goes by the name of a 'Do Not Resuscitate Order'. The name of the order varies from state to state and can also be referred to as a 'Do Not Attempt Resuscitation Order' or a 'DNR Order'. A DNR Order is often used in conjunction with a living will because it directs doctors, paramedics and emergency personnel not to give a person cardiopulmonary resuscitation (CPR) if they stop breathing.

Typically, if a person is in hospital and their heart stops beating and they stop breathing, the natural response of the emergency room team will be to immediately try and restore their heartbeat and breathing. This will happen as a matter of course unless the patient has elected in advance to refuse this particular form of treatment. A DNR order is used for this very purpose.

Important Note

Remember, depending on the terms of your HCPOA, your healthcare agent may have the right to make DNR decisions for you when you are no longer able to make them yourself.

CPR, like any other form of medical treatment, can be refused in advance either in a living will or in a separate DNR Order. This refusal can be conditional on the occurrence of certain events or it can be unconditional. Once made, the order should be placed with your medical records. In addition, you can also have details of the existence of your DNR order stamped on a bracelet which you wear. You can even keep a copy of the order at home in case paramedics, physicians or hospice nurses ever come to your home.

Important Note

You can also obtain a wallet card from Legal Vaults™ which will alert physicians and medical personnel to the fact that you have made a DNR Order. The Legal Vaults™ system can also be used to store your DNR Order electronically so that it can be retrieved quickly and easily in a time of emergency. For more information on Legal Vaults™, visit their website www.legalvaults.com.

Hospital and Non-Hospital DNR Orders

Generally speaking, there are two different types of DNR Orders - one for use in a hospital and one for non-hospital use.

DNR Orders made in hospitals are recognized in all states. If you are a patient in a public hospital, you may instruct your attending doctor to have a DNR Order placed on your medical records. If, during your stay in the hospital, you cease breathing then hospital personnel should honor your wishes and refrain from trying to resuscitate you. However, a DNR order made in a hospital is only valid in that hospital. It cannot be used outside the hospital.

A number of states do however have a special DNR Order for use outside of hospitals. This non-hospital DNR is intended for Emergency Medical Service (EMS) teams who answer 911 calls. EMS personnel are generally under orders to maintain and preserve life until the patient has been transported safely to a hospital.

Almost a half of all states have enacted legislation which gives validity to non-hospital DNR Orders. Under these laws, EMS personnel who are presented with a valid DNR order, signed by a physician, or who identify a standard DNR bracelet on a person, must comply with that order and refrain from administering CRP. However, if there is any ambiguity with the document or doubt as to its validity, the EMS team will most likely administer CPR.

The states that have enacted legislation authorizing the use of these non-hospital DNR Orders are Alabama, Alaska, Arizona, Arkansas, California, Colorado, Connecticut, Florida, Georgia, Idaho, Illinois, Kansas, Maryland, Michigan, Montana, Nevada, New York, Oklahoma, Rhode Island, South Carolina, Tennessee, Texas, Utah, Virginia, West Virginia, Wisconsin, and Wyoming. In states without laws providing for non-hospital DNR Orders, the EMS team will have no alternative but to administer CPR even if they are presented with a document or bracelet which indicates that the patient wishes to refuse CPR.

Validity of DNR Orders

For a DNR Order to be valid it must comply with the laws of the state in which it is to be made and used. These laws vary widely from state to state. In some states, you will be required to use a specific form of DNR Order while other states are a little more relaxed as to the precise form. For example, in Maryland, only DNR Orders in the prescribed state form are acceptable for use in the state. By contrast, in Virginia patients can use out-of-state DNR Orders with relative ease.

Important Note

Laws regarding DNR Orders vary from state to state. You should therefore check with your lawyer or physician to determine the precise requirements in your state.

In most states, you will need to have reached the age of majority in your state and be of sound mind before being able to validly execute a DNR Order. In addition, you will also need to have your DNR Order signed by your attending physician and two witnesses. Similar to the position with living wills above, there are a number of restrictions on who can act as your witnesses. Specifically, family members, physicians and employees of your healthcare facility are not permitted to act as witnesses to the execution of your order. If you are preparing a DNR Order, you will need to check the precise form of document required in your state as well as any requirements or limitations that may apply to the witnesses.

Who Can Make a DNR Order?

Any adult of sound mind may make a DNR Order. In addition, the parent or legal guardian of a minor child may also request a doctor to make a DNR order for that child.

Should I Make a DNR Order?

The decision as to whether you should or should not execute a DNR Order is entirely up to you. It will depend largely on your state of health and your underlying views and desires. In considering whether to make a DNR Order, there are a number of factors that you might wish to consider including:-

- How is your overall health?

- Do you have an existing illness or medical condition that is severely affecting your quality of life?

- Is your situation terminal?

- Are you intending to undergo a life-threatening procedure?

- Are you ready to stop fighting and let go?

- Does non-resuscitation coincide with your religious, cultural and philosophical beliefs?

Whatever you decide, remember that a DNR Order does not leave room for another person to act as your advocate or proxy in the same way as living wills or healthcare powers of attorney. They are absolute - if your heart or lungs fail, you will not be revived. You should therefore take your time and discuss your desires and thoughts with your family, friends and physicians before rushing off to make a DNR Order.

Can a DNR Order Be Revoked?

Either you or your healthcare agent (if permitted under the terms of your HCPOA) can revoke a DNR Order that you have made by either tearing it up or writing the word "Void" on the face of the document. Of course, the first method is the preferred choice. You should notify everyone who has received a copy of the DNR Order from you that the order is to be treated as void. You should request the immediate return of the order to you or confirmation that same has been destroyed and that no copies have been maintained. This process is very important because if an order remains on your medical file in a hospital then there will always be a risk that it may turn up and be used in deciding not to resuscitate you.

As an alternative, or even an addition, to the above, you could also complete a new DNR Order reflecting the fact that you do want CPR administered. Once completed, you should forward a copy to everyone who held a copy of your previous DNR Order.

Where to Keep Your Completed DNR Order

Once completed, you should keep your original DNR Order in a safe place with your other personal documents. You should also send copies to your physician and to the administration department of any care facility that you may be attending for inclusion on your medical records. You should also keep some spare copies so that you can bring them with you to any new healthcare facility that you might attend.

Finally, if you have a legal guardian or have named an agent under a healthcare power of attorney you should provide them with a copy or details of where they can locate a copy if and when required.

Do I Need a DNR Order, a Living Will and a Healthcare Power of Attorney?

The answer to this question may well be yes! In certain states, the forms of living will and HCPOA set out under law are such that they cannot adequately deal with issues such as CPR. This is because both documents allow for a third party to make decisions on your behalf when you are unable to make them yourself. In most cases, you will have had an opportunity to make these decisions with the benefit of time and after consultation with doctors. However, with a DNR Order, action must be taken immediately. There is time neither for consultation nor calling on a third party to make the decision for you. If CPR is to take place, it must be fairly immediate following the cessation of your breathing or of your heart beating. A DNR Order is ideal for this because your medical team, on foot of the instructions set out in your order, can act to save your life or allow your life to come to an end without the need for discussions with third parties.

Where to Obtain a DNR Order Form

If you are in hospital and wish to add a DNR Order to your records, just speak to your attending physician and they should be able to help you. Alternatively, for non-hospital DNR Orders, the best thing to do is to contact your local healthcare facility or general practitioner. They should be able to provide you with a form of DNR Order that is applicable in your state. Remember, however, that each healthcare facility is likely to have its own standard form of DNR Order. It is for this reason that it's often recommended that people should complete a new DNR Order every time they enter a new healthcare facility or change healthcare providers. This ensures that the facility or provider in question will abide by their DNR Order when the time comes.

Organ Donation

The Uniform Anatomical Gift Act, which has been adopted by almost all states, seeks to regulate the manner in which organ and tissue donations may be made. The act requires the donor to give a clear indication that she or he is willing to be an organ donor. This usually takes the form of an express statement in a will, advance directive or on an organ donor card. In addition, in order to make the process easier, many states also allow the donor to note their consent on the back of their driving license or state identity card. Surprisingly, however, notwithstanding that a person has given a clear indication of their desire to donate, the law still allows close family relatives to dissent to the procedure.

It also provides that, in the absence of any express statement by a deceased person indicating their desire to donate, the deceased's surviving spouse, or if there is no spouse, certain close relatives can give their consent to the making of the gift. However, to protect an individual against a spouse or family member deciding to donate the individual's organs against their wishes following death, the act also allows individuals to sign a refusal baring others from making any decisions in respect of the donation of their organs or tissues.

Uniform Anatomical Gift Act 2006

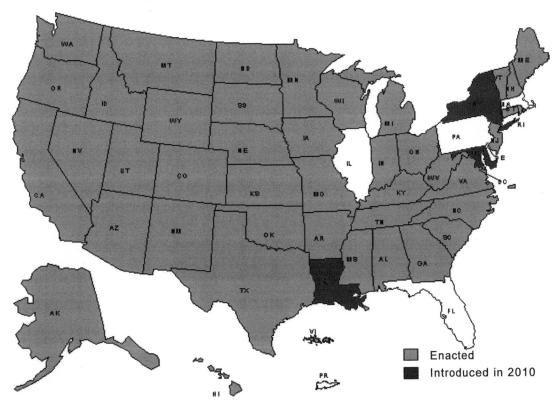

©Anatomical Gift Act

As mentioned above, a majority of states have signed up to the Uniform Anatomical Gift Act. Details of the states which have signed up to the act are set out in the table above.

Important Note

For more information on organ donation in your state visit www.anatomicalgiftact.org

SAMPLE DONOR CARD No.1

DONOR CARD

I wish to donate my organs, eyes, and tissue. I give:

- Any needed organs, eyes, and tissue; or

- ONLY the following organs, eyes, and tissue:

_____

Date: _____ Donor's Signature _____

SAMPLE DONOR CARD No.2

DONOR CARD

I wish to donate my organs, eyes, and tissue. I wish to give (complete either Section A, B, or C):

Subject of Gift:		Purpose of Gift:		
	Yes/No	Transplantation or therapy	Research or Education	Both
Section A				
ALL of my organs, eyes, and tissue				
Section B				

My Organs

My Eyes

My Tissue

Section C

Special Instructions (If none of the above apply), I wish to give ONLY:

_____

Date: _____ Donor's Signature: _____

SAMPLE DONOR CARD No.3

DONOR CARD

I give, upon my death, the following gifts for the purpose of (choose whichever applies): [ ] only transplantation and therapy, [ ] only research and education, [ ] transplantation, therapy, research, or education

For the purposes specified above, I give:

[ ] ALL needed organs, tissues, and eyes; or

(If you checked the box immediately above, you should not check specific boxes below).

[ ] Organs [ ] Tissues [ ] Eyes

If none of the above applies, I wish to give ONLY:

The following organs and tissues:_____

_____

Date: _____ Donor's Signature _____

CHAPTER 7:
LIVING WILL REVIEW

Chapter Overview

In this short chapter, we provide a final review of why it's important to have a living will, and give you instructions on how to make your own living will.

Chapter 7

CHAPTER 7

LIVING WILL REVIEW

Food for Thought....

If we've anywhere near hit our mark in this book, we've shown that there are ample reasons for having advance directives.

Life can be highly unpredictable, and unforgiving of momentary lapses. We know of a man whose mother, now 89, stepped off a train which had begun to move when she was aged 57. Now, six hip replacements later, she's had 32 years of pain and limited mobility, plus numerous hospitalizations, to rue that momentary error of judgment.

Seventeenth Century English philosopher Thomas Hobbes declared that the life of man is 'solitary, poor, nasty, brutish and short.' Some would say, 'Not much has changed.'

But even for the fortunate ones, those whose lives are sociable, rich, pleasant, cultured and long, all good things must come to an end. The world won't stop to let us off; eventually death, the great leveler, does for us all.

Shortly before the time of writing the first edition of this book, the second last living French veteran of World War I, and France's oldest man, M. Louis de Cazenave, died at the age of 110. His son reported a peaceful death at home, no doubt a perfect ending to long and full life. 'He had a peaceful death. He didn't suffer at all,' said Louis Jr.

Most of us would be more than happy to enjoy M. Cazenave senior's outcome, because as we know very well, 99.99 percent of humanity isn't so fortunate. In fact, living to over 100, and making our exit with peace and no suffering, is so rare that it makes the news.

That's why most of us would settle for 70 or 80 substantially healthy years, a comfortable place to live, a happy marriage, good kids, satisfying work with a fair income, a few years of retirement to do some of the things we didn't have time for earlier, and an exit that doesn't drag on too long.

But as we all know, things can sometimes go wrong in the best of families. That's why we insure our houses and cars (and very often ourselves). That's why we look both ways; that's why we go on diets.

That, in the simplest of terms, is why some of us create a 'Plan B' in relation to our date with destiny. Plan B, of course, is a strategy to cover the situation where things go amiss. Where your fond hopes and dreams are rudely derailed by an unexpected mischance.

As we said at the very beginning of this book, making a will is not the world's most popular activity. Nor is cleaning your teeth, but if you don't do it two or three times a day, you get to learn the meaning of the word 'edentulous' (which means toothless), and you get to pay the price of being that way.

In this book we've looked at two (sadly) famous examples where things went badly amiss, and life extracted a fearsome price for what was probably no more than a momentary lapse. The price was not the death of the unfortunate victims (Nancy Cruzan or Terri Schiavo); it was that they were compelled to remain in a living hell for years, a 'glass bubble' where they couldn't move or speak, when had they had a Plan B, they would have at least shared M. Cazenave's 'peaceful death' and suffered very little, if at all.

Are these situations rare, so rare in fact that we can safely disregard them? No, unfortunately they are not. Thousands more must occur than are ever reported in the press, or even the law reports, obscure as they are for most of us.

They just happen, because 'that's what the law says'. And because the unfortunate person thought they didn't need to take an action so trifling, so easy and quickly attended to that it makes cleaning your teeth every day look like the labors of Hercules.

Plan B. Spend the small time it takes to create whatever form of advance directives your state allows. If you wish, spend the small amount of money it requires to consult an attorney and/or go visit your doctor, to make absolutely sure that you've got it right. Then, rest assured in the knowledge that you've at least taken an important step in providing for your future medical care in the manner that you want. You family and friends may well be relieved of making some tough decisions!

How to Write Your Own Advance Directive

First things first! Read this book in its entirety. If you wish, supplement that reading with any research you feel necessary, particularly in relation to the laws applicable in your state. The idea is to learn all you can about advance healthcare directives before you decide to make one. Once you have decided to make an advance directive then you should:-

- Discuss your wishes with your family members, friends, doctor and maybe even your attorney. Getting others to understand and respect your wishes is the first step in ensuring that they are carried out.

- Decide whether you wish to make a living will, a healthcare power of attorney, a DNR Order and/or another form of advance healthcare directive.

- Choose a state form from the back of this book and complete it in the required manner. Many states require advance directives to be substantially in the same format as those samples in the back of this book. As such, it is not recommended that you use a completely fresh document (such as that contained in Appendix B) without checking your state's laws. That said, most states and medical facilities will try to honor advance directives written in generic form such as that in Appendix B.

- Alternatively, contact your attorney and instruct him or her to prepare the relevant form for you.

- Decide what instructions you want to give in your advance directive. It's important to be clear on matters such as the receipt of blood transfusions, hydration, nutrition, CPR, kidney dialysis, artificial respiration, surgical procedures and so on. If the state form does not fully meet your requirements, complete the Addendum in Appendix F and attach it to your state document. Remember to have it signed and witnessed also.

- Decide who you want as your healthcare agent or proxy (if required). Choose this person carefully.

- Have one or more witnesses sign your advance directive. Make sure you comply with the requirements set out in your state.

- While not required in every case, you could also sign the self proving affidavit contained in Appendix E. This will reduce the possibility that people will challenge the authenticity of your advance directive at a later date. You and your witnesses will need to sign the self proving affidavit in front of a notary.

- Give a copy of your advance directive to your healthcare agent or proxy and ask him or her to keep it in a safe place where it can be found quickly if needed.

- Ask your doctor, physician and healthcare providers to place a copy of your advance directive on your medical records.

- Keep a copy of your advance directive in a safe place at home. Make sure that someone close to you knows where it's kept. Consider storing a copy of your document with a service such as Legal Vaults™ (www.legalvaults.com).

APPENDIX A:
STATE SPECIFIC LIVING WILL FORMS

CD-ROM & Downloadable Forms

Blank copies of all of the forms contained in this book are available on the CD-ROM which accompanies this book. Alternatively all forms can be downloaded from the enodare website.

Web: http://www.enodare.com/downloadarea/

Unlock Code: XYZ10412

enodare

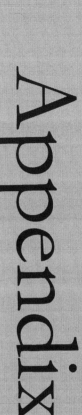

Appendix A

APPENDIX A

STATE SPECIFIC LIVING WILL FORMS

Alabama State Forms

ADVANCE DIRECTIVE FOR HEALTH CARE

(Living Will and Health Care Proxy)

This form may be used in the State of Alabama to make your wishes known about what medical treatment or other care you would or would not want if you become too sick to speak for yourself. You are not required to have an advance directive. If you do have an advance directive, be sure that your doctor, family, and friends know you have one and know where it is located.

SECTION 1 - LIVING WILL

I, _____, being of sound mind and at least 19 years old, would like to make the following wishes known. I direct that my family, my doctors and health care workers, and all others follow the directions I am writing down. I know that at any time I can change my mind about these directions by tearing up this form and writing a new one. I can also do away with these directions by tearing them up and by telling someone at least 19 years of age of my wishes and asking him or her to write them down.

I understand that these directions will only be used if I am not able to speak for myself.

IF I BECOME TERMINALLY ILL OR INJURED:

Terminally ill or injured is when my doctor and another doctor decide that I have a condition that cannot be cured and that I will likely die in the near future from this condition.

Life sustaining treatment—Life sustaining treatment includes drugs, machines, or medical procedures that would keep me alive but would not cure me. I know that even if I choose not to have life sustaining treatment, I will still get medicines and treatments that ease my pain and keep me comfortable.

Place your initials by either "**yes**" or "**no**":

I want to have life sustaining treatment if I am terminally ill or injured.

_____ Yes _____ No

Artificially provided food and hydration (Food and water through a tube or an IV)—I understand that if I am terminally ill or injured I may need to be given food and water through a tube or an IV to keep me alive if I can no longer chew or swallow on my own or with someone helping me.

Place your initials by either "yes" or "no":

I want to have food and water provided through a tube or an IV if I am terminally ill or injured.
_____ Yes _____ No

IF I BECOME PERMANENTLY UNCONSCIOUS:

Permanent unconsciousness is when my doctor and another doctor agree that within a reasonable degree of medical certainty I can no longer think, feel anything, knowingly move, or be aware of being alive. They believe this condition will last indefinitely without hope for improvement and have watched me long enough to make that decision. I understand that at least one of these doctors must be qualified to make such a diagnosis.

Life sustaining treatment—Life sustaining treatment includes drugs, machines, or other medical procedures that would keep me alive but would not cure me. I know that even if I choose not to have life sustaining treatment, I will still get medicines and treatments that ease my pain and keep me comfortable.

Place your initials by either "yes" or "no":

I want to have life-sustaining treatment if I am permanently unconscious.

_____ Yes _____No

Artificially provided food and hydration (Food and water through a tube or an IV)—I understand that if I become permanently unconscious, I may need to be given food and water through a tube or an IV to keep me alive if I can no longer chew or swallow on my own or with someone helping me.

Place your initials by either "yes" or "no":

I want to have food and water provided through a tube or an IV if I am permanently unconscious. _____ Yes _____ No

OTHER DIRECTIONS:

Please list any other things you want done or not done.

In addition to the directions I have listed on this form, I also want the following:

_____

_____

_____

If you do not have other directions, place your initials here: _____ No, I do not have any other directions.

SECTION 2 - IF I NEED SOMEONE TO SPEAK FOR ME

This form can be used in the State of Alabama to name a person you would like to make medical or other decisions for you if you become too sick to speak for yourself. This person is called a health care proxy. You do not have to name a health care proxy. The directions in this form will be followed even if you do not name a health care proxy.

Place your initials by only one answer:

_____ I do not want to name a health care proxy. (If you check this answer, go to Section 3)

_____ I do want the person listed below to be my health care proxy. I have talked with this person about my wishes.

First choice for proxy: _____Relationship to me:
Address: _____City: _____ State: _____ Zip:
Day-time phone number: _____ Night-time phone number: _____

If this person is not able, not willing, or not available to be my health care proxy, this is my next choice:

Second choice for prxy:_____Relationship to me:
Address: _____City: _____ State: _____ Zip:
Day-time phone number: _____ Night-time phone number: _____

Instructions for Proxy

Place your initials by either "**yes**" or "**no**":

I want my health care proxy to make decisions about whether to give me food and water through a tube or an IV. _____ Yes _____ No

Place your initials by only one of the following:

_____ I want my health care proxy to follow only the directions as listed on this form.

_____ I want my health care proxy to follow my directions as listed on this form and to make any decisions about things I have not covered in the form.

_____ I want my health care proxy to make the final decision, even though it could mean doing something different from what I have listed on this form.

SECTION 3 - THE THINGS LISTED ON THIS FORM ARE WHAT I WANT

I understand the following:

If my doctor or hospital does not want to follow the directions I have listed, they must see that I get to a doctor or hospital who will follow my directions.

If I am pregnant, or if I become pregnant, the choices I have made on this form will not be followed until after the birth of the baby.

If the time comes for me to stop receiving life sustaining treatment or food and water through a tube or an IV, I direct that my doctor talk about the good and bad points of doing this, along with my wishes, with my health care proxy, if I have one, and with the following people:

_____

_____

SECTION 4 - MY SIGNATURE

Your name: _____ The month, day, and year of your birth:

Your signature: _____ Date

signed: _____

SECTION 5 - WITNESSES

(need two witnesses to sign)

I am witnessing this form because I believe this person to be of sound mind. I did not sign the person's signature, and I am not the health care proxy. I am not related to the person by blood, adoption, or marriage and not entitled to any part of his or her estate. I am at least 19 years of age and am not directly responsible for paying for his or her medical care.

Name of first witness: _____ Signature:

Date: _____ Name of second witness:

Signature: _____

Date: _____

SECTION 6 - SIGNATURE OF PROXY

I, _____, am willing to serve as the health care proxy.

Signature: _____ Date:

Signature of Second Choice for Proxy:

I, _____, am willing to serve as the health care proxy if the first choice cannot serve.

Signature: _____ Date: _____

Alaska State Forms

ADVANCE HEALTH CARE DIRECTIVE

Explanation

You have the right to give instructions about your own health care to the extent allowed by law. You also have the right to name someone else to make health care decisions for you to the extent allowed by law.

This form lets you do either or both of these things. It also lets you express your wishes regarding the designation of your health care provider. If you use this form, you may complete or modify all or any part of it. You are free to use a different form if the form complies with the requirements of A.S. 13.52.

Part 1 of this form is a durable power of attorney for health care. A durable power of attorney for health care means the designation of an agent to make health care decisions for you. Part 1 lets you name another individual as an agent to make health care decisions for you if you do not have the capacity to make your own decisions or if you want someone else to make those decisions for you now even though you still have the capacity to make those decisions. You may name an alternate agent to act for you if your first choice is not willing, able, or reasonably available to make decisions for you. Unless related to you, your agent may not be an owner, operator, or employee of a health care institution where you are receiving care.

Unless the form you sign limits the authority of your agent, your agent may make all health care decisions for you that you could legally make for yourself. This form has a place for you to limit the authority of your agent. You do not have to limit the authority of your agent if you wish to rely on your agent for all health care decisions that may have to be made. If you choose not to limit the authority of your agent, your agent will have the right, to the extent allowed by law, to

(a) consent or refuse consent to any care, treatment, service, or procedure to maintain, diagnose, or otherwise affect a physical or mental condition, including the administration or discontinuation of psychotropic medication;

(b) select or discharge health care providers and institutions;

(c) approve or disapprove proposed diagnostic tests, surgical procedures, and programs of medication;

(d) direct the provision, withholding, or withdrawal of artificial nutrition and hydration and all other forms of health care; and

(e) make an anatomical gift following your death.

Part 2 of this form lets you give specific instructions for any aspect of your health care to the extent allowed by law, except you may not authorize mercy killing, assisted suicide, or euthanasia. Choices are provided for you to express your wishes regarding the provision, withholding, or withdrawal of treatment to keep you alive, including the provision of artificial nutrition and hydration, as well as the provision of pain relief medication. Space is provided for you to add to the choices you have made or for you to write out any additional wishes.

Part 3 of this form lets you express an intention to make an anatomical gift following your death.

Part 4 of this form lets you make decisions in advance about certain types of mental health treatment.

Part 5 of this form lets you designate a physician to have primary responsibility for your health care.

After completing this form, sign and date the form at the end and have the form witnessed by one of the two alternative methods listed below. Give a copy of the signed and completed form to your physician, to any other health care providers you may have, to any health care institution at which you are receiving care, and to any health care agents you have named. You should talk to the person you have named as your agent to make sure that the person understands your wishes and is willing to take the responsibility.

You have the right to revoke this advance health care directive or replace this form at any time, except that you may not revoke this declaration when you are determined not to be competent by a court, by two physicians, at least one of whom shall be a psychiatrist, or by both a physician and a professional mental health clinician. In this advance health care directive, "competent" means that you have the capacity

(1)   to assimilate relevant facts and to appreciate and understand your situation with regard to those facts; and

(2)   to participate in treatment decisions by means of a rational thought process.

ADVANCE HEALTH CARE DIRECTIVE

PART 1
DURABLE POWER OF ATTORNEY FOR HEALTH CARE DECISIONS

(1)   **DESIGNATION OF AGENT**

I designate the following individual as my agent to make health care decisions for me:

_____

(name of individual you choose as agent)

_____

(address)   (city)   (state)   (zip code)

_____

(home telephone)   (work telephone)

OPTIONAL: If I revoke my agent's authority or if my agent is not willing, able, or reasonably available to make a health care decision for me, I designate as my first alternate agent

_____

(name of individual you choose as first alternate agent)

_____

(address)   (city)   (state)   (zip code)

_____

(home telephone)   (work telephone)

OPTIONAL: If I revoke the authority of my agent and first alternate agent or if neither is willing, able, or reasonably available to make a health care decision for me, I designate as my second alternate agent

_____

(name of individual you choose as second alternate agent)

_____

(address)   (city)   (state)   (zip code)

_____

(home telephone)   (work telephone)

(2)   AGENT'S AUTHORITY

My agent is authorized and directed to follow my individual instructions and my other wishes to the extent known to the agent in making all health care decisions for me. If these are not known, my agent is authorized to make these decisions in accordance with my best interest, including decisions to provide, withhold, or withdraw artificial hydration and nutrition and other forms of health care to keep me alive, except as I state here:

_____

_____

_____

(Add additional sheets if needed.)

Under this authority, "best interest" means that the benefits to you resulting from a treatment outweigh the burdens to you resulting from that treatment after assessing

(A)   the effect of the treatment on your physical, emotional, and cognitive functions;

(B)   the degree of physical pain or discomfort caused to you by the treatment or the withholding or withdrawal of the treatment;

(C)   the degree to which your medical condition, the treatment, or the withholding or withdrawal of treatment, results in a severe and continuing impairment;

(D)   the effect of the treatment on your life expectancy;

(E)   your prognosis for recovery, with and without the treatment;

(F)   the risks, side effects, and benefits of the treatment or the withholding of treatment; and

(G)   your religious beliefs and basic values, to the extent that these may assist in determining benefits and burdens.

(3)   **WHEN AGENT'S AUTHORITY BECOMES EFFECTIVE**

Except in the case of mental illness, my agent's authority becomes effective when my primary physician determines that I am unable to make my own health care decisions unless I mark the following box. In the case of mental illness, unless I mark the following box, my agent's authority becomes effective when a court determines I am unable to make my own decisions, or, in an emergency, if my primary physician or another health care provider determines I am unable to make my own decisions. _____ If I mark this box, my agent's authority to make health care decisions for me takes effect immediately.

(4)   **AGENT'S OBLIGATION**

My agent shall make health care decisions for me in accordance with this durable power of attorney for health care, any instructions I give in Part 2 of this form, and my other wishes to the extent known to my agent. To the extent my wishes are unknown, my agent shall make health care decisions for me in accordance with what my agent determines to be in my best interest. In determining my best interest, my agent shall consider my personal values to the extent known to my agent.

(5)   **NOMINATION OF GUARDIAN**

If a guardian of my person needs to be appointed for me by a court, I nominate the agent designated in this form. If that agent is not willing, able, or reasonably available to act as guardian, I nominate the alternate agents whom I have named under (1) above, in the order designated.

PART 2
INSTRUCTIONS FOR HEALTH CARE

If you are satisfied to allow your agent to determine what is best for you in making health care decisions, you do not need to fill out this part of the form. If you do fill out this part of the form, you may strike any wording you do not want. There is a state protocol that governs the use of do not resuscitate orders by physicians and other health care providers. You may obtain a copy of the protocol from the Alaska Department of Health and Social Services. A "do not resuscitate order" means a directive from a licensed physician that emergency cardiopulmonary resuscitation should not be administered to you.

(6) END-OF-LIFE DECISIONS

Except to the extent prohibited by law, I direct that my health care providers and others involved in my care provide, withhold, or withdraw treatment in accordance with the choice I have marked below:

(Check only one box.)

(A) ___ Choice To Prolong Life

I want my life to be prolonged as long as possible within the limits of generally accepted health care standards; OR

(B) ___ Choice Not To Prolong Life

I want comfort care only and I do not want my life to be prolonged with medical treatment if, in the judgment of my physician, I have

(check all choices that represent your wishes)

___ (i) a condition of permanent unconsciousness: a condition that, to a high degree of medical certainty, will last permanently without improvement; in which, to a high degree of medical certainty, thought, sensation, purposeful action, social interaction, and awareness of myself and the environment are absent; and for which, to a high degree of medical certainty, initiating or continuing life-sustaining procedures for me, in light of my medical outcome, will provide only minimal medical benefit for me; or

____ (ii) a terminal condition: an incurable or irreversible illness or injury that without the administration of life-sustaining procedures will result in my death in a short period of time, for which there is no reasonable prospect of cure or recovery, that imposes severe pain or otherwise imposes an inhumane burden on me, and for which, in light of my medical condition, initiating or continuing life-sustaining procedures will provide only minimal medical benefit.

____ Additional instructions: _____
_____

(C) Artificial Nutrition and Hydration

If I am unable to safely take nutrition, fluids, or nutrition and fluids (check your choices or write your instructions),

____ I wish to receive artificial nutrition and hydration indefinitely;

____ I wish to receive artificial nutrition and hydration indefinitely, unless it clearly increases my suffering and is no longer in my best interest;

____ I wish to receive artificial nutrition and hydration on a limited trial basis to see if I can improve;

____ In accordance with my choices in (6)(B) above, I do not wish to receive artificial nutrition and hydration.

____ Other instructions: _____
_____
_____

(D) Relief from Pain

____ I direct that adequate treatment be provided at all times for the sole purpose

of the alleviation of pain or discomfort; or

____ I give these instructions: _____
_____

(E) Should I become unconscious and I am pregnant, I direct that _____

___ ___ ___ ___ ___ ___ ___ ___ ___ ___ ___ ___ ___ ___ ___ ___

_____

(7) OTHER WISHES

(If you do not agree with any of the optional choices above and wish to write your own, or if you wish to add to the instructions you have given above, you may do so here.) I direct that _____

_____

_____

_____

Conditions or limitations: _____

_____

_____

_____ (Add additional sheets if needed.)

PART 3
(OPTIONAL)
ANATOMICAL GIFT AT DEATH

If you are satisfied to allow your agent to determine whether to make an anatomical gift at your death, you do not need to fill out this part of the form.

(8)   Upon my death: (mark applicable box)

(A) ___ I give any needed organs, tissues, or other body parts, OR

(B) ___ I give the following organs, tissues, or other body parts only _____

_____

_____

(C) ___ My gift is for the following purposes (mark any of the following you want):

    ___ (i) transplant;

    ___ (ii) therapy;

____ (iii) research;

____ (iv) education.

(D) ____ I refuse to make an anatomical gift.

PART 4 - MENTAL HEALTH TREATMENT

This part of the declaration allows you to make decisions in advance about mental health treatment. The instructions that you include in this declaration will be followed only if a court, two physicians that include a psychiatrist, or a physician and a professional mental health clinician believe that you are not competent and cannot make treatment decisions. Otherwise, you will be considered to be competent and to have the capacity to give or withhold consent for the treatments.

If you are satisfied to allow your agent to determine what is best for you in making these mental health decisions, you do not need to fill out this part of the form. If you do fill out this part of the form, you may strike any wording you do not want.

(9)   PSYCHOTROPIC MEDICATIONS

If I do not have the capacity to give or withhold informed consent for mental health treatment, my wishes regarding psychotropic medications are as follows:

_____ I consent to the administration of the following medications: _____
_____
_____

_____ I do not consent to the administration of the following medications: _____
_____
_____

Conditions or limitations: _____
_____
_____

(10)   ELECTROCONVULSIVE TREATMENT

If I do not have the capacity to give or withhold informed consent for mental health treatment, my wishes regarding electroconvulsive treatment are as follows:

_____ I consent to the administration of electroconvulsive treatment.

_____ I do not consent to the administration of electroconvulsive treatment.

Conditions or limitations: _____

_____

_____ . _____

(11) ADMISSION TO AND RETENTION IN FACILITY

If I do not have the capacity to give or withhold informed consent for mental health treatment, my wishes regarding admission to and retention in a mental health facility for mental health treatment are as follows:

_____ I consent to being admitted to a mental health facility for mental health treatment for up to _____ days. (The number of days not to exceed 17.)

_____ I do not consent to being admitted to a mental health facility for mental health treatment.

Conditions or limitations: _____

_____

_____

OTHER WISHES OR INSTRUCTIONS

_____

_____

_____

_____

Conditions

_____

_____

PART 5
PRIMARY PHYSICIAN
(OPTIONAL)

(12) I designate the following physician as my primary physician:

_____

(name of physician)

_____

(address)   (city)   (state)   (zip code)

_____

(telephone)

OPTIONAL: If the physician I have designated above is not willing, able, or reasonably available to act as my primary physician, I designate the following physician as my primary physician:

_____

(name of physician)

_____

(address)   (city)   (state)   (zip code)

_____

(13)   **EFFECT OF COPY**

A copy of this form has the same effect as the original.

(14)   **SIGNATURES**

Sign and date the form here:

_____(date)

   (sign your name)

_____

(print your name)

_____

(address)   (city)   (state)   (zip code)

(15)   **WITNESSES**

This advance care health directive will not be valid for making health care decisions unless it is

(A)   signed by two qualified adult witnesses who are personally known to you and who are present when you sign or acknowledge your signature; the witnesses may not be a health care provider employed at the health care institution or health care facility where you are receiving health care, an employee of the health care provider who is providing health care to you, an employee of the health care institution or health care facility where you are receiving health care, or the person appointed as your agent by this document; at least one of the two witnesses may not be related to you by blood, marriage, or adoption or entitled to a portion of your estate upon your death under your will or codicil; or

(B)   acknowledged before a notary public in the state.

ALTERNATIVE NO. 1

Witness Who is Not Related to or a Devisee of the Principal

I swear under penalty of perjury under AS 11.56.200 that the principal is personally known to me, that the principal signed or acknowledged this durable power of attorney for health care in my presence, that the principal appears to be of sound mind and under no duress, fraud, or undue influence, and that I am not

(1)   a health care provider employed at the health care institution or health care facility where the principal is receiving health care;

(2)   an employee of the health care provider providing health care to the principal;

(3)   an employee of the health care institution or health care facility where the principal is receiving health care;

(4)   the person appointed as agent by this document;

(5)   related to the principal by blood, marriage, or adoption; or

(6)   entitled to a portion of the principal's estate upon the principal's death under a will or codicil.

_____

_____(date)   (signature of witness)

_____

_____(printed name of witness)

_____

(address)   (city)   (state)   (zip code)

Witness Who May be Related to or a Devisee of the Principal

I swear under penalty of perjury under AS 11.56.200 that the principal is personally known to me, that the principal signed or acknowledged this durable power of attorney for health care in my presence, that the principal appears to be of sound mind and under no duress, fraud, or undue influence, and that I am not

(1)   a health care provider employed at the health care institution or health care facility where the principal is receiving health care;

(2)   an employee of the health care provider who is providing health care to the principal;

(3)   an employee of the health care institution or health care facility where the principal is receiving health care; or

(4)   the person appointed as agent by this document.

_____   _____
(date)   (signature of witness)

_____

_____
(printed name of witness)

_____
(address)   (city)   (state)   (zip code)

ALTERNATIVE NO. 2

State of Alaska

_____ Judicial District

On this _____ day of _____, in the year _____, before me, _____ (insert name of notary public) appeared _____ , personally known to me (or proved to me on the basis of satisfactory evidence) to be the person whose name is subscribed to this instrument, and acknowledged that the person executed it.

Notary Seal

_____ (signature of notary public)

Arizona State Forms

HEALTH CARE POWER OF ATTORNEY

1. <u>Health Care Power of Attorney</u>

I, _____, as principal, designate _____
_____ as my agent for all matters
relating to my health care, including, without limitation, full power to give or refuse consent to
all medical, surgical, hospital and related health care. This power of attorney is effective on my
inability to make or communicate health care decisions. All of my agent's actions under this power
during any period when I am unable to make or communicate health care decisions or when there
is uncertainty whether I am dead or alive have the same effect on my heirs, devisees and personal
representatives as if I were alive, competent and acting for myself.

If my agent is unwilling or unable to serve or continue to serve, I hereby appoint _____
_____ as my agent.

I have _____ I have not _____ completed and attached a living will for purposes of providing
specific direction to my agent in situations that may occur during any period when I am unable to
make or communicate health care decisions or after my death. My agent is directed to implement
those choices I have initialed in the living will.

I have _____ I have not _____ completed a prehospital medical directive pursuant to § 36-3251,
Arizona Revised Statutes.

This health care directive is made under § 36-3221, Arizona Revised Statutes, and continues in
effect for all who may rely on it except those to whom I have given notice of its revocation.

2. <u>Autopsy</u> (under Arizona law, an autopsy may be required)

If you wish to do so, reflect your desires below:

_____ 1. I <u>do not</u> consent to an autopsy.

_____ 2. I <u>consent</u> to an autopsy.

_____ 3. My agent <u>may</u> give consent to an autopsy.

3. <u>Organ Donation</u> (Optional)

(Under Arizona law, you may make a gift of all or part of your body to a bank or storage facility or a hospital, physician or medical or dental school for transplantation, therapy, medical or dental evaluation or research or for the advancement of medical or dental science. You may also authorize your agent to do so or a member of your family to make a gift unless you give them notice that you do not want a gift made. In the space below you may make a gift yourself or state that you do not want to make a gift. If you do not complete this section, your agent will have the authority to make a gift of a part of your body pursuant to law. Note: The donation elections you make in this health care power of attorney survive your death.)

If any of the statements below reflects your desire, initial on the line next to that statement. You do not have to initial any of the statements.

If you do not check any of the statements, your agent and your family will have the authority to make a gift of all or part of your body under Arizona law.

_____ I do not want to make an organ or tissue donation and do not want my agent or family to do so.

_____ I have already signed a written agreement or donor card regarding organ and tissue donation with the following individual or institution:_____

_____ Pursuant to Arizona law, I hereby give, effective on my death

[ ] Any needed organ or parts.

[ ] The following part or organs listed:

_____

_____

for (check one):

[ ] Any legally authorized purpose.

[ ] Transplant or therapeutic purposes only.

4. <u>Physician Affidavit</u> (Optional)

(Before initialing any choices above you may wish to ask questions of your physician regarding a particular treatment alternative. If you do speak with your physician it is a good idea to ask your physician to complete this affidavit and keep a copy for his file.)

I, Dr. _____, have reviewed this guidance document and have discussed with _____
___ any questions regarding the probable medical consequences of the treatment choices provided above. This discussion with the principal occurred on _____(date). I have agreed to comply with the provisions of this directive.

_____

Signature of physician

5. <u>Living Will</u> (Optional)

(Some general statements concerning your health care options are outlined below. If you agree with one of the statements, you should initial that statement. **Read all of these statements carefully before you initial your selection.** You can also write your own statement concerning life-sustaining treatment and other matters relating to your health care. You may initial any combination of paragraphs 1, 2, 3 and 4, but if you initial paragraph 5 the others should not be initialed.)

_____ 1.   If I have a terminal condition I **do not** want my life to be prolonged and I **do not** want life-sustaining treatment, beyond comfort care, that would serve

only to artificially delay the moment of my death.

_____ 2.   If I am in a terminal condition or an irreversible coma or a persistent vegetative state that my doctors reasonably feel to be irreversible or incurable, I **do** want the medical treatment necessary to provide care that would keep me comfortable, but I **do not** want the following:

_____ (a)   Cardiopulmonary resuscitation, for example, the use of drugs, electric shock and artificial breathing.

_____ (b)   Artificially administered food and fluids.

_____ (c)   To be taken to a hospital if at all avoidable.

_____ 3.   Notwithstanding my other directions, if I am known to be pregnant, I do not want life-sustaining treatment withheld or withdrawn if it is possible that the embryo/fetus will develop to the point of live birth with the continued application of life-sustaining treatment.

_____ 4.   Notwithstanding my other directions I **do** want the use of all medical care necessary to treat my condition until my doctors reasonably conclude that my condition is terminal or is irreversible and incurable or I am in a persistent vegetative state.

_____ 5.   I **want** my life to be prolonged to the greatest extent possible.

Other or additional statement of desires

I have _____ I have not _____ attached additional special provisions or limitations to this document to be honored in the absence of my being able to give health care directions.

_____

Signature of Principal

Witness:_____ Date:_____

_____Time:_____

Address:_____

_____

_____Address of Agent

_____

_____

Witness:_____

Address:_____

_____

Telephone of Agent_____

(Note: This document may be notarized instead of being witnessed.)

State of Arizona_____)

County of _____)

On this _____ day of _____, _____ before me, personally appeared _____ (name of principal), who is personally known to me or provided _____ as identification, and acknowledged that he or she executed it.

[NOTARY SEAL]

_____

(signature of notary public)

Arkansas State Forms

DECLARATION

Initial and complete one or both of the following:

_____ If I should have an incurable or irreversible condition that will cause my death within a relatively short time, and I am no longer able to make decisions regarding my medical treatment, I direct my attending physician, pursuant to Arkansas Rights of the Terminally Ill or Permanently Unconscious Act, to (initial one)

_____ Withhold or withdraw treatment that only prolongs the process of dying and is not necessary to my comfort or to alleviate pain

_____ Follow the instructions of _____, whom I appoint as my health care proxy to decide whether life-sustaining treatment should be withheld or withdrawn.

_____ If I should become permanently unconscious I direct my attending physician, pursuant to Arkansas Rights ofthe Terminally Ill or Permanently Unconscious Act, to (initial one)

_____ Withhold or withdraw treatment that only prolongs the process of dying and is not necessary to my comfort or to alleviate pain

_____ Follow the instructions of _____, whom I appoint as my health care proxy to decide whether life-sustaining treatment should be withheld or withdrawn].

Initial and complete one of the following:

_____ It is my specific directive that nutrition may be withheld after consultation with my attending physician.

_____ It is my specific directive that nutrition may not be withheld.

Initial and complete one of the following:

_____ It is my specific directive that hydration may be withheld after consultation with my attending physician.

_____ It is my specific directive that hydration may not be withheld.

Signed this _____ day of _____, 20___.

Signature _____

Address _____

_____

The declarant voluntarily signed this writing in my presence.

Witness _____   Witness _____

Address _____   Address _____

_____   _____

_____   _____

_____   _____

California State Forms

ADVANCE HEALTH CARE DIRECTIVE

(California Probate Code Section 4701)

Explanation

You have the right to give instructions about your own health care. You also have the right to name someone else to make health care decisions for you. This form lets you do either or both of these things. It also lets you express your wishes regarding donation of organs and the designation of your primary physician. If you use this form, you may complete or modify all or any part of it. You are free to use a different form.

Part 1 of this form is a power of attorney for health care. Part 1 lets you name another individual as agent to make health care decisions for you if you become incapable of making your own decisions or if you want someone else to make those decisions for you now even though you are still capable. You may also name an alternate agent to act for you if your first choice is not willing, able, or reasonably available to make decisions for you. (Your agent may not be an operator or employee of a community care facility or a residential care facility where you are receiving care, or your supervising health care provider or employee of the health care institution where you are receiving care, unless your agent is related to you or is a coworker.)

Unless the form you sign limits the authority of your agent, your agent may make all health care decisions for you. This form has a place for you to limit the authority of your agent. You need not limit the authority of your agent if you wish to rely on your agent for all health care decisions that may have to be made. If you choose not to limit the authority of your agent, your agent will have the right to:

(a)   Consent or refuse consent to any care, treatment, service, or procedure to maintain, diagnose, or otherwise affect a physical or mental condition.

(b)   Select or discharge health care providers and institutions.

(c)   Approve or disapprove diagnostic tests, surgical procedures, and programs of medication.

(d)   Direct the provision, withholding, or withdrawal of artificial nutrition and hydration and all other forms of health care, including cardiopulmonary resuscitation.

(e)   Make anatomical gifts, authorize an autopsy, and direct disposition of remains.

Part 2 of this form lets you give specific instructions about any aspect of your health care, whether or not you appoint an agent. Choices are provided for you to express your wishes regarding the provision, withholding, or withdrawal of treatment to keep you alive, as well as the provision of pain relief. Space is also provided for you to add to the choices you have made or for you to write out any additional wishes. If you are satisfied to allow your agent to determine what is best for you in making end-of-life decisions, you need not fill out Part 2 of this form.

Part 3 of this form lets you express an intention to donate your bodily organs and tissues following your death.

Part 4 of this form lets you designate a physician to have primary responsibility for your health care.

After completing this form, sign and date the form at the end. The form must be signed by two qualified witnesses or acknowledged before a notary public. Give a copy of the signed and completed form to your physician, to any other health care providers you may have, to any health care institution at which you are receiving care, and to any health care agents you have named. You should talk to the person you have named as agent to make sure that he or she understands your wishes and is willing to take the responsibility.

You have the right to revoke this advance health care directive or replace this form at any time.

* * * * * * * * * * * * * * * *

PART 1

POWER OF ATTORNEY FOR HEALTH CARE

(1.1) **DESIGNATION OF AGENT**: I designate the following individual as my agent to make health care decisions for me: _____

_____

(name of individual you choose as agent)

(address)   (city)   (state)   (ZIP Code)

(home phone)   (work phone)

OPTIONAL: If I revoke my agent's authority or if my agent is not willing, able, or reasonably available to make a health care decision for me, I designate as my first alternate agent:

(name of individual you choose as first alternate agent)

(address)   (city)   (state)   (ZIP Code)

(home phone)   (work phone)

OPTIONAL: If I revoke the authority of my agent and first alternate agent or if neither is willing, able, or reasonably available to make a health care decision for me, I designate as my second alternate agent:

(name of individual you choose as second alternate agent)

(address)   (city)   (state)   (ZIP Code)

(home phone)   (work phone)

(1.2) **AGENT'S AUTHORITY**: My agent is authorized to make all health care decisions for me, including decisions to provide, withhold, or withdraw artificial nutrition and hydration and all other forms of health care to keep me alive, except as I state here:

_____

_____

_____

(Add additional sheets if needed.)

(1.3) **WHEN AGENT'S AUTHORITY BECOMES EFFECTIVE**: My agent's authority becomes effective when my primary physician determines that I am unable to make my own health care decisions, unless I mark the following box.

If I mark this box ( ), my agent's authority to make health care decisions for me takes effect immediately.

(1.4) **AGENT'S OBLIGATION**: My agent shall make health care decisions for me in accordance with this power of attorney for health care, any instructions I give in Part 2 of this form, and my other wishes to the extent known to my agent. To the extent my wishes are unknown, my agent shall make health care decisions for me in accordance with what my agent determines to be in my best interest. In determining my best interest, my agent shall consider my personal values to the extent known to my agent.

(1.5) **AGENT'S POSTDEATH AUTHORITY**: My agent is authorized to make anatomical gifts, authorize an autopsy, and direct disposition of my remains, except as I state here or in Part 3 of this form:

_____

_____

_____

(Add additional sheets if needed.)

(1.6) **NOMINATION OF CONSERVATOR**: If a conservator of my person needs to be appointed for me by a court, I nominate the agent designated in this form. If that agent is not willing, able, or reasonably available to act as conservator, I nominate the alternate agents whom I have named, in the order designated.

PART 2

INSTRUCTIONS FOR HEALTH CARE

If you fill out this part of the form, you may strike any wording you do not want.

(2.1) **END-OF-LIFE DECISIONS**: I direct that my health care providers and others involved in my care provide, withhold, or withdraw treatment in accordance with the choice I have marked below:

[ ]   (a) Choice Not To Prolong Life

I do not want my life to be prolonged if (1) I have an incurable and irreversible condition that will result in my death within a relatively short time, (2) I become unconscious and, to a reasonable degree of medical certainty, I will not regain consciousness, or (3) the likely risks and burdens of treatment would outweigh the expected benefits, OR

[ ]   (b) Choice To Prolong Life

I want my life to be prolonged as long as possible within the limits of generally accepted health care standards.

(2.2) **RELIEF FROM PAIN**: Except as I state in the following space, I direct that treatment for alleviation of pain or discomfort be provided at all times, even if it hastens my death:

_____

_____

_____

(Add additional sheets if needed.)

(2.3) **OTHER WISHES**: (If you do not agree with any of the optional choices above and wish to write your own, or if you wish to add to the instructions you have given above, you may do so here.) I direct that:

(Add additional sheets if needed.)

PART 3

DONATION OF ORGANS AT DEATH (OPTIONAL)

(3.1)   Upon my death (mark applicable box):

[ ]   (a) I give any needed organs, tissues, or parts, OR

[ ]   (b) I give the following organs, tissues, or parts only.

_____

_____

_____

_____

[ ]   (c)   My gift is for the following purposes (strike any of the following you do not want):

(1) Transplant

(2) Therapy

(3) Research

(4) Education

PART 4

PRIMARY PHYSICIAN (OPTIONAL)

_____

(name of physician)

_____

(address)   (city)   (state)   (ZIP Code)

_____

(phone)

OPTIONAL: If the physician I have designated above is not willing, able, or reasonably available to act as my primary physician, I designate the following physician as my primary physician:

_____

(name of physician)

_____

(address)   (city)   (state)   (ZIP Code)

_____

(phone)

PART 5

(5.1)   **EFFECT OF COPY**: A copy of this form has the same effect as the original.

(5.2)   **SIGNATURE**: Sign and date the form here:

_____   _____

(date)   (sign your name)

_____   _____

(address)   (print your name)

_____

(city)

_____

(state)

(5.3)   **STATEMENT OF WITNESSES**: I declare under penalty of perjury under the laws of California (1) that the individual who signed or acknowledged this advance health care directive is personally known to me, or that the individual's identity was proven to me by convincing evidence (2) that the individual signed or acknowledged this advance directive in my presence, (3) that the individual appears to be of sound mind and under no duress, fraud, or undue influence, (4) that I am not a person appointed as agent by this advance directive, and (5) that I am not the individual's health care provider, an employee of the individual's health care provider, the operator of a community care facility, an employee of an operator of a community care facility, the operator of a residential care facility for the elderly, nor an employee of an operator of a residential care facility for the elderly.

_____	_____
First witness	Second witness
_____	_____
(print name)	(print name)
_____	_____
(address)	(address)
_____	_____
(city) (state)	(city) (state)
_____	_____
(signature of witness)	(signature of witness)
_____	_____
(date)	(date)

(5.4)   **ADDITIONAL STATEMENT OF WITNESSES**: At least one of the above witnesses must also sign the following declaration: _____

_____

_____

_____

I further declare under penalty of perjury under the laws of California that I am not related to the individual executing this advance health care directive by blood, marriage, or adoption, and to the best of my knowledge, I am not entitled to any part of the individual's estate upon his or her death under a will now existing or by operation of law.

_____   _____
(signature of witness)   (signature of witness)

PART 6

SPECIAL WITNESS REQUIREMENT

(6.1)   The following statement is required only if you are a patient in a skilled nursing facility or a health care facility that provides the following basic services: skilled nursing care and supportive care to patients whose primary need is for availability of skilled nursing care on an extended basis. The patient advocate or ombudsman must sign the following statement:

STATEMENT OF PATIENT ADVOCATE OR OMBUDSMAN

I declare under penalty of perjury under the laws of California that I am a patient advocate or ombudsman as designated by the State Department of Aging and that I am serving as a witness as required by Section 4675 of the Probate Code.

_____   _____
(date)   (sign your name)

_____   _____
(address)   (print your name)

_____   _____
(city)   (state)

_____   _____

Colorado State Forms

DECLARATION AS TO MEDICAL OR SURGICAL TREATMENT

I,_____, being of sound mind and at least eighteen years of age, direct that my life shall not be artificially prolonged under the circumstances set forth below and hereby declare that:

1.   If at any time my attending physician and one other qualified physician certify in writing that:

        1.   I have an injury, disease or illness which is not curable or reversible and which, in their judgment, is a terminal condition, and

        2.   For a period of seven consecutive days or more, I have been unconscious, comatose or otherwise incompetent so as to be unable to make or communicate responsible decisions concerning my person, then

I direct that, in accordance with Colorado law, life sustaining procedures shall be withdrawn and withheld pursuant to the terms of this declaration, it being understood that life-sustaining procedures shall not include any medical procedure or intervention for nourishment considered necessary by the attending physician to provide comfort or alleviate pain. However, I may specifically direct, in accordance with Colorado law, that artificial nourishment be withdrawn or withheld pursuant to the terms of this declaration.

2.   In the event that the only procedure I am being provided is artificial nourishment, I direct that one of the following actions be taken:

    _____   a. Artificial nourishment shall not be continued when it is the only procedure being provided; or

    _____   b. Artificial nourishment shall be continued for ____ days when it is the only procedure being provided; or

    _____   c. Artificial nourishment shall be continued when it is the only procedure being provided.

3.   I execute this declaration, as my free and voluntary act, this ____ day of _____, 20____.

_____

Declarant

The foregoing instrument was signed and declared by _____to be his/her declaration, in the presence of us, who, in his/her presence, in the presence of each other, and at his/her request, have signed our names below as witnesses, and we declare that, at the time of the execution of this instrument, the declarant, according to our best knowledge and belief, was of sound mind and under no constraint or undue influence.

Dated at _____, Colorado, this _____ day of_____, 20___.

_____   _____
Name   Name

_____   _____

_____   _____
Address   Address

STATE OF COLORADO   )

) ss.

COUNTY OF _____   )

SUBSCRIBED and sworn to before me by _____, the declarant, and _____ and _____, witnesses, as the voluntary act and deed of the declarant this _____ day of _____, 20___.

_____

Witness my hand and seal.

My Commission expires:

Connecticut State Forms

DOCUMENT CONCERNING WITHHOLDING OR WITHDRAWAL OF LIFE SUPPORT SYSTEMS

If the time comes when I am incapacitated to the point when I can no longer actively take part in decisions for my own life, and am unable to direct my physician as to my own medical care, I wish this statement to stand as a statement of my wishes.

I, _____, the author of this document, request that, if my condition is deemed terminal or if I am determined to be permanently unconscious, I be allowed to die and not be kept alive through life support systems.

By terminal condition, I mean that I have an incurable or irreversible medical condition which, without the administration of life support systems, will, in the opinion of my attending physician, result in death within a relatively short time. By permanently unconscious I mean that I am in a permanent coma or persistent vegetative state which is an irreversible condition in which I am at no time aware of myself or the environment and show no behavioural response to the environment.

Specific Instructions

Listed below are my instructions regarding particular types of life support systems. This list is not all-inclusive. My general statement that I not be kept alive through life support systems provided to me is limited only where I have indicated that I desire a particular treatment to be provided.

	Provide	Withhold
Cardiopulmonary Resuscitation	_____	_____
Artificial Respiration (including a respirator)	_____	_____
Artificial means of providing nutrition and hydration	_____	_____

Other specific requests: _____

_____

_____

_____

_____

I do want sufficient pain medication to maintain my physical comfort. I do not intend any direct taking of my life, but only that my dying not be unreasonably prolonged.

This request is made, after careful reflection, while I am of sound mind.

_____ / _____ / _____ (Date) X_____

WITNESSES' STATEMENTS

This document was signed in our presence by _____ the author of this document, who appeared to be eighteen years of age or older, of sound mind and able to understand the nature and consequences of health care decisions at the time this document was signed. The author appeared to be under no improper influence. We have subscribed this document in the author's presence and at the author's request and in the presence of each other.

(Witness)   _____
(Number and Street)   _____
(City, State and Zip Code)   _____
                                  _____
                                  _____

(Witness)   _____
(Number and Street)   _____
(City, State and Zip Code)   _____
                                  _____
                                  _____

Health Care Instructions

THESE ARE MY HEALTH CARE INSTRUCTIONS, MY APPOINTMENT OF A HEALTH CARE AGENT, MY APPOINTMENT OF AN ATTORNEY-IN-FACT FOR HEALTH CARE DECISIONS, THE DESIGNATION OF MY CONSERVATOR OF THE PERSON FOR MY FUTURE INCAPACITY AND MY DOCUMENT OF ANATOMICAL GIFT

To any physician who is treating me: These are my health care instructions including those concerning the withholding or withdrawal of life support systems, together with the appointment of my health care agent and my attorney-in-fact for health care decisions, the designation of my conservator of the person for future incapacity and my document of anatomical gift. As my physician, you may rely on any decision made by my health care agent, attorney-in-fact for health care decisions or conservator of my person, if I am unable to make a decision for myself.

I, _____, the author of this document, request that, if my condition is deemed terminal or if I am determined to be permanently unconscious, I be allowed to die and not be kept alive through life support systems. By terminal condition, I mean that I have an incurable or irreversible medical condition which, without the administration of life support systems, will, in the opinion of my attending physician, result in death within a relatively short time. By permanently unconscious I mean that I am in a permanent coma or persistent vegetative state which is an irreversible condition in which I am at no time aware of myself or the environment and show no behavioral response to the environment. The life support systems which I do not want include, but are not limited to: Artificial respiration, cardiopulmonary resuscitation and artificial means of providing nutrition and hydration. I do want sufficient pain medication to maintain my physical comfort. I do not intend any direct taking of my life, but only that my dying not be unreasonably prolonged.

I appoint _____ to be my health care agent and my attorney-in-fact for health care decisions. If my attending physician determines that I am unable to understand and appreciate the nature and consequences of health care decisions and unable to reach and communicate an informed decision regarding treatment, my health care agent and attorney-in-fact for health care decisions is authorized to:

(1)   Convey to my physician my wishes concerning the withholding or removal of life

support systems;

(2)   Take whatever actions are necessary to ensure that any wishes are given effect;

(3)   Consent, refuse or withdraw consent to any medical treatment as long as such action is consistent with my wishes concerning the withholding or removal of life support systems; and

(4)   Consent to any medical treatment designed solely for the purpose of maintaining physical comfort.

If _____ is unwilling or unable to serve as my health care agent and my attorney-in-fact for health care decisions, I appoint _____ to be my alternative health care agent and my attorney-in-fact for health care decisions. If a conservator of my person should need to be appointed, I designate _____ be appointed my conservator. If _____ is unwilling or unable to serve as my conservator, I designate _____. No bond shall be required of either of them in any jurisdiction.

I hereby make this anatomical gift, if medically acceptable, to take effect upon my death.

I give: (check one)

    [ ]   (1) any needed organs or parts

    [ ]   (2) only the following organs or parts _____

    _____

    to be donated for: (check one)

    (1)   [ ] any of the purposes stated in subsection (a) of section 19a-279f of the general statutes

    (2)   [ ] these limited purposes _____
    _____
    _____

These requests, appointments, and designations are made after careful reflection, while I am of sound mind. Any party receiving a duly executed copy or facsimile of this document may rely upon it unless such party has received actual notice of my revocation of it.

Date _____, 20__.

_____

Signature

This document was signed in our presence by _____ the author of this document, who appeared to be eighteen years of age or older, of sound mind and able to understand the nature and consequences of health care decisions at the time this document was signed. The author appeared to be under no improper influence. We have subscribed this document in the author's presence and at the author's request and in the presence of each other.

_____(Witness)
_____(Number and Street)
_____ (City, State and Zip Code)

_____(Witness)
_____(Number and Street)
_____ (City, State and Zip Code)

STATE OF CONNECTICUT   )

) ss_____

COUNTY OF _____   )

We, the subscribing witnesses, being duly sworn, say that we witnessed the execution of these health care instructions, the appointments of a health care agent and an attorney-in-fact, the designation of a conservator for future incapacity and a document of anatomical gift by the author of this document; that the author subscribed, published and declared the same to be the author's instructions, appointments and designation in our presence; that we thereafter subscribed the document as witnesses in the author's presence, at the author's request, and in the presence of each other; that at the time of the execution of said document the author appeared to us to be eighteen years of age or older, of sound mind, able to understand the nature and consequences of said document, and under no improper influence, and we make this affidavit at the author's request this ___ day of _____ 20__.

_____   _____

(Signature of Witness)   (Signature of Witness)

_____   _____
(Name of Witness)   (Name of Witness

SUBSCRIBED and sworn to before me this _____ day of _____, 20___.

Commissioner of the Superior Court
Notary Public

My commission expires: _____

Delaware State Forms

ADVANCE HEALTH-CARE DIRECTIVE

EXPLANATION

You have the right to give instructions about your own health care. You also have the right to name someone else to make health-care decisions for you. This form lets you do either or both of these things. It also lets you express your wishes regarding anatomical gifts and the designation of your primary physician. If you use this form, you may complete or modify all or any part of it. You are free to use a different form.

Part 1 of this form is a power of attorney for health care. Part 1 lets you name another individual as agent to make health-care decisions for you if you become incapable of making your own decisions. You may also name an alternate agent to act for you if your first choice is not willing, able or reasonably available to make decisions for you. Unless related to you, an agent may not have a controlling interest in or be an operator or employee of a residential long-term health-care institution at which you are receiving care.

If you do not have a qualifying condition (terminal illness/injury or permanent unconsciousness), your agent may make all health-care decisions for you except for decisions providing, withholding or withdrawing of a life sustaining procedure. Unless you limit the agent's authority, your agent will have the right to:

(a)   Consent or refuse consent to any care, treatment, service or procedure to maintain, diagnose or otherwise affect a physical or mental condition unless it's a life-sustaining procedure or otherwise required by law.

(b)   Select or discharge health-care providers and health-care institutions;

If you have a qualifying condition, your agent may make all health-care decisions for you, including, but not limited to:

(c)   The decisions listed in (a) and (b).

(d)   Consent or refuse consent to life sustaining procedures, such as, but not limited to, cardiopulmonary resuscitation and orders not to resuscitate.

(e)   Direct the providing, withholding or withdrawal of artificial nutrition and hydration and all other forms of health care.

Part 2 of this form lets you give specific instructions about any aspect of your health care. Choices are provided for you to express your wishes regarding the provision, withholding or withdrawal of treatment to keep you alive, including the provision of artificial nutrition and hydration as well as the provision of pain relief. Space is also provided for you to add to the choices you have made or for you to write out any additional instructions for other than end of life decisions.

Part 3 of this form lets you express an intention to donate your bodily organs and tissues following your death.

Part 4 of this form lets you designate a physician to have primary responsibility for your health care.

After completing this form, sign and date the form at the end. It is required that 2 other individuals sign as witnesses. Give a copy of the signed and completed form to your physician, to any other health-care providers you may have, to any health-care institution at which you are receiving care and to any health-care agents you have named. You should talk to the person you have named as agent to make sure that the person understands your wishes and is willing to take the responsibility.

You have the right to revoke this advance health-care directive or replace this form at any time.

PART 1: POWER OF ATTORNEY FOR HEALTH CARE

(1)   **DESIGNATION OF AGENT**: I designate the following individual as my agent to make health-care decisions for me:

_____

(name of individual you choose as agent)

_____

(address) (city) (state) (zip code)

_____

(home phone) (work phone)

OPTIONAL: If I revoke my agent's authority or if my agent is not willing, able, or reasonably available to make a health-care decision for me, I designate as my first alternate agent:

_____

(name of individual you choose as first alternate agent)

_____

(address) (city) (state) (zip code)

_____

(home phone) (work phone)

OPTIONAL: If I revoke the authority of my agent and first alternate agent or if neither is willing, able, or reasonably available to make a health-care decision for me, I designate as my second alternate agent:

_____

(name of individual you choose as second alternate agent)

_____

(address) (city) (state) (zip code)

_____

(home phone) (work phone)

(2) **AGENT'S AUTHORITY**: If I am not in a qualifying condition my agent is authorized to make all health-care decisions for me, except decisions about life-sustaining procedures and as I state here; and if I am in a qualifying condition, my agent is authorized to make all health-care decisions for me, except as I state here:

_____

_____

_____

(Add additional sheets if necessary.)

(3) **WHEN AGENT'S AUTHORITY BECOMES EFFECTIVE**: My agent's authority becomes effective when my primary physician determines I lack the capacity to make my own health-care decisions. As to decisions concerning the providing, withholding and withdrawal of life-sustaining procedures my agent's authority becomes effective

when my primary physician determines I lack the capacity to make my own health-care decisions and my primary physician and another physician determine I am in a terminal condition or permanently unconscious.

(4)   **AGENT'S OBLIGATION**: My agent shall make health-care decisions for me in accordance with this power of attorney for health care, any instructions I give in Part 2 of this form, and my other wishes to the extent known to my agent. To the extent my wishes are unknown, my agent shall make health-care decisions for me in accordance with what my agent determines to be in my best interest. In determining my best interest, my agent shall consider my personal values to the extent known to my agent.

(5)   **NOMINATION OF GUARDIAN**: If a guardian of my person needs to be appointed for me by a court, (please check one):

   [ ]   I nominate the agent(s) whom I named in this form in the order designated to act as guardian.

   [ ]   I nominate the following to be guardian in the order designated:

   _____

   _____

   _____

   [ ]   I do not nominate anyone to be guardian.

PART 2: INSTRUCTIONS FOR HEALTH CARE

If you are satisfied to allow your agent to determine what is best for you in making end-of-life decisions, you need not fill out this part of the form. If you do fill out this part of the form, you may strike any wording you do not want.

(6)   **END-OF-LIFE DECISIONS**: If I am in a qualifying condition, I direct that my health-care providers and others involved in my care provide, withhold, or withdraw treatment in accordance with the choice I have marked below:

Choice Not To Prolong Life

I do not want my life to be prolonged if: (please check all that apply)

   _____ (i)   I have a terminal condition (an incurable condition causednby injury, disease, or illness which, to a reasonable degree of medical certainty, makes death imminent and from which, despite the application of life-sustaining procedures, there can be no recovery) and regarding artificial nutrition and hydration, I make the following specific directions:

I want used I do not want used

Artificial nutrition through
a conduit   _____ _____

Hydration through a conduit _____ _____

_____ (ii) I become permanently unconscious (a medical condition that has been diagnosed in accordance with currently accepted medical standards that has lasted at least 4 weeks and with reasonable medical certainty as total and irreversible loss of consciousness and capacity for interaction with the environment. The term includes, without limitation, a persistent vegetative state or irreversible coma) and regarding artificial nutrition and hydration, I make the following specific directions:

I want used I do not want used

Artificial nutrition through
a conduit   _____ _____

Hydration through a conduit _____ _____

Choice To Prolong Life

_____ I want my life to be prolonged as long as possible within the limits of generally accepted health-care standards.

RELIEF FROM PAIN: Except as I state in the following space, I direct treatment for alleviation of pain or discomfort be provided at all times, even if it hastens my death:

_____

_____

(7)   **OTHER MEDICAL INSTRUCTIONS**: (If you do not agree with any of the optional choices above and wish to write your own, or if you wish to add to the instructions you have given above, you may do so here.) I direct that:

_____

_____

_____

(Add additional sheets if necessary.)

PART 3: ANATOMICAL GIFTS AT DEATH

(OPTIONAL)

(8)   I am mentally competent and 18 years or more of age. I hereby make this anatomical gift to take effect upon my death. The marks in the appropriate squares and words filled into the blanks below indicate my desires.

I give: [ ]   my body;
        [ ]   any needed organs or parts;
        [ ]   the following organs or parts

_____

_____

_____

to the following person or institutions

        [ ]   the physician in attendance at my death;
        [ ]   the hospital in which I die;
        [ ]   the following named physician, hospital, storage bank or other medical institution;
        [ ]   the following individual for treatment;

for the following purposes:

        [ ]   any purpose authorized by law;
        [ ]   transplantation;
        [ ]   therapy;
        [ ]   research;

[ ]   medical education.

PART 4: PRIMARY PHYSICIAN

(OPTIONAL)

(9)   I designate the following physician as my primary physician:

_____

(name of physician)

_____

(address) (city) (state) (zip code)

_____

(phone)

OPTIONAL: If the physician I have designated above is not willing, able or reasonably available to act as my primary physician, I designate the following physician as my primary physician:

_____(name of physician)

_____(address) (city)

(state) (zip code)

_____ (phone)

Primary Physician shall mean a physician designated by an individual or the individual's agent or guardian, to have primary responsibility for the individual's health care or, in the absence of a designation or if the designated physician is not reasonably available, a physician who undertakes the responsibility.

(10)   **EFFECT OF COPY**: A copy of this form has the same effect as the original.

(11)   **SIGNATURE**: Sign and date the form here: I understand the purpose and effect of this document.

_____   _____

(date)   (sign your name)

_____   _____

(address)   (print your name)

_____

(city)   (state)   (zip code)

(12)   **SIGNATURES OF WITNESSES:**

Statement Of Witnesses

SIGNED AND DECLARED by the above-named declarant as and for the declarant's written declaration under 16 Del.C. §§ 2502 and 2503, in our presence, who in the declarant's presence, at the declarant's request, and in the presence of each other, have hereunto subscribed our names as witnesses, and state:

A.   That the Declarant is mentally competent.

B.   That neither of them:

   1.   Is related to the declarant by blood, marriage or adoption;

   2.   Is entitled to any portion of the estate of the declarant under any will of the declarant or codicil thereto then existing nor, at the time of the executing of the advance health care directive, is so entitled by operation of law then existing;

   3.   Has, at the time of the execution of the advance health-care directive, a present or inchoate claim against any portion of the estate of the declarant;

   4.   Has a direct financial responsibility for the declarant's medical care;

   5.   Has a controlling interest in or is an operator or an employee of a residential long-term health-care institution in which the declarant is a resident; or

   6.   Is under eighteen years of age.

C.   That if the declarant is a resident of a sanitarium, rest home, nursing home, boarding home or related institution, one of the witnesses, _____, is at the time of the execution of the advance health-care directive, a patient advocate or ombudsman designated by the Division of Services for Aging and Adults with Physical Disabilities or the Public Guardian.

First witness   **Second Witness**

_____   _____
(print name)   (print name)

_____   _____
(address) (city, state, zip code)   (address) (city, state, zip code)

_____   _____
(signature of witness) (date)   (signature of witness) (date)

I am not prohibited by § 2503 of   I am not prohibited by § 2503 of
Title 16 of the Delaware Code   Title 16 of the Delaware Code from being a witness.
from being a witness.

(Notary)

District of Columbia State Forms

DISTRICT OF COLUMBIA LIVING WILL DECLARATION

Declaration made this _____ day of _____ (month, year).

I, _____ of _____, being of sound mind, wilfully and voluntarily make known my desires that my dying shall not be artificially prolonged under the circumstances set forth below, do declare:

If at any time I should have an incurable injury, disease, or illness certified to be a terminal condition by 2 physicians who have personally examined me, one of whom shall be my attending physician, and the physicians have determined that my death will occur whether or not life-sustaining procedures are utilized and where the application of life-sustaining procedures would serve only to artificially prolong the dying process, I direct that such procedures be withheld or withdrawn, and that I be permitted to die naturally with only the administration of medication or the performance of any medical procedure deemed necessary to provide me with comfort care or to alleviate pain.

In the absence of my ability to give directions regarding the use of such life-sustaining procedures, it is my intention that this declaration shall be honored by my family and physician(s) as the final expression of my legal right to refuse medical or surgical treatment and accept the consequences from such refusal.

I understand the full import of this declaration and I am emotionally and mentally competent to make this declaration.

Signed   _____
Address   _____
              _____
              _____

I believe the declarant to be of sound mind. I did not sign the declarant's signature above for or at the direction of the declarant. I am at least 18 years of age and am not related to the declarant by blood, marriage, or domestic partnership, entitled to any portion of the estate of the declarant according to the laws of intestate succession of the District of Columbia or under any will of the declarant or codicil thereto, or directly financially responsible for declarant's medical care. I am not the declarant's attending physician, an employee of the attending physician, or an employee of the health facility in which the declarant is a patient.

Witness _____   _____
        Name of witness   Signature of witness

Witness _____   _____
        Name of witness   Signature of witness

DISTRICT OF COLUMBIA POWER OF ATTORNEY FOR HEALTH CARE

INFORMATION ABOUT THIS DOCUMENT

THIS IS AN IMPORTANT LEGAL DOCUMENT. BEFORE SIGNING THIS DOCUMENT, IT IS VITAL FOR YOU TO KNOW AND UNDERSTAND THESE FACTS: THIS DOCUMENT GIVES THE PERSON YOU NAME AS YOUR ATTORNEY IN FACT THE POWER TO MAKE HEALTH-CARE DECISIONS FOR YOU IF YOU CANNOT MAKE THE DECISIONS FOR YOURSELF.

AFTER YOU HAVE SIGNED THIS DOCUMENT, YOU HAVE THE RIGHT TO MAKE HEALTH-CARE DECISIONS FOR YOURSELF IF YOU ARE MENTALLY COMPETENT TO DO SO. IN ADDITION, AFTER YOU HAVE SIGNED THIS DOCUMENT, NO TREATMENT MAY BE GIVEN TO YOU OR STOPPED OVER YOUR OBJECTION IF YOU ARE MENTALLY COMPETENT TO MAKE THAT DECISION.

YOU MAY STATE IN THIS DOCUMENT ANY TYPE OF TREATMENT THAT YOU DO NOT DESIRE AND ANY THAT YOU WANT TO MAKE SURE YOU RECEIVE. YOU HAVE THE RIGHT TO TAKE AWAY THE AUTHORITY OF YOUR ATTORNEY IN FACT, UNLESS YOU HAVE BEEN ADJUDICATED INCOMPETENT, BY NOTIFYING YOUR ATTORNEY IN FACT OR HEALTH-CARE PROVIDER EITHER ORALLY OR IN WRITING. SHOULD YOU REVOKE THE AUTHORITY OF YOUR ATTORNEY IN FACT, IT IS ADVISABLE TO REVOKE IN WRITING AND TO PLACE COPIES OF THE REVOCATION WHEREVER THIS DOCUMENT IS LOCATED.

IF THERE IS ANYTHING IN THIS DOCUMENT THAT YOU DO NOT UNDERSTAND, YOU SHOULD ASK A SOCIAL WORKER, LAWYER, OR OTHER PERSON TO EXPLAIN IT TO YOU.

* * * * *

YOU SHOULD KEEP A COPY OF THIS DOCUMENT AFTER YOU HAVE SIGNED IT. GIVE A COPY TO THE PERSON YOU NAME AS YOUR ATTORNEY IN FACT. IF YOU ARE IN A HEALTH- CARE FACILITY, A COPY OF THIS DOCUMENT SHOULD BE INCLUDED IN YOUR MEDICAL RECORD.

I, _____, hereby appoint:

_____

name

_____

home address

_____

home telephone number

_____

work telephone number

as my attorney in fact to make health-care decisions for me if I become unable to make my own health-care decisions. This gives my attorney in fact the power to grant, refuse, or withdraw consent on my behalf for any health-care service, treatment or procedure. My attorney in fact also has the authority to talk to health-care personnel, get information and sign forms necessary to carry out these decisions.

If the person named as my attorney in fact is not available or is unable to act as my attorney in fact, I appoint the following person to serve in the order listed below:

1.   _____

        name

        _____

        home address

        _____

        home telephone number

        _____

        work telephone number

2.   _____

        name

        _____

        home address

        _____

        home telephone number

        _____

        work telephone number

With this document, I intend to create a power of attorney for health care, which shall take effect if I become incapable of making my own health-care decisions and shall continue during that incapacity.

My attorney in fact shall make health-care decisions as I direct below or as I make known to my attorney in fact in some other way.

(a) STATEMENT OF DIRECTIVES CONCERNING LIFE-PROLONGING CARE, TREATMENT, SERVICES, AND PROCEDURES:

_____

_____

_____

_____

_____

_____

(b) SPECIAL PROVISIONS AND LIMITATIONS:

_____

_____

_____

_____

_____

BY MY SIGNATURE I INDICATE THAT I UNDERSTAND THE PURPOSE AND EFFECT OF THIS DOCUMENT.

I sign my name to this form on _____ (date) at: _____ _____(address).

_____ (Signature)

WITNESSES

I declare that the person who signed or acknowledged this document is personally known to me, that the person signed or acknowledged this durable power of attorney for health care in my presence, and that the person appears to be of sound mind and under no duress, fraud, or undue influence. I am not the person appointed as the attorney in fact by this document, nor am I the health-care provider of the principal or an employee of the health-care provider of the principal.

First Witness
Signature: _____
Home Address: _____
Print Name: _____
Date: _____

Second Witness
Signature: _____
Home Address: _____
Print Name: _____
Date: _____
(AT LEAST ONE OF THE WITNESSES LISTED ABOVE SHALL ALSO SIGN THE FOLLOWING DECLARATION.)

I further declare that I am not related to the principal by blood, marriage or adoption, and, to the best of my knowledge, I am not entitled to any part of the estate of the principal under a currently existing will or by operation of law.

Signature: _____

Signature: _____

Florida State Forms

LIVING WILL DECLARATION

Declaration made this _____ day of _____, (year) , I, _____, willfully and voluntarily make known my desire that my dying not be artificially prolonged under the circumstances set forth below, and I do hereby declare that, if at any time I am incapacitated and (*Initial one of the options below*)

[   ] I have a terminal condition

       or

[   ] I have an end-stage condition

       or

[   ] I am in a persistent vegetative state

and if my attending or treating physician and another consulting physician have determined that there is no reasonable medical probability of my recovery from such condition, I direct that life-prolonging procedures be withheld or withdrawn when the application of such procedures would serve only to prolong artificially the process of dying, and that I be permitted to die naturally with only the administration of medication or the performance of any medical procedure deemed necessary to provide me with comfort care or to alleviate pain.

It is my intention that this declaration be honored by my family and physician as the final expression of my legal right to refuse medical or surgical treatment and to accept the consequences for such refusal.

In the event that I have been determined to be unable to provide express and informed consent regarding the withholding, withdrawal, or continuation of life-prolonging procedures, I wish to designate, as my surrogate to carry out the provisions of this declaration:

Name: _____

Address: _____

               _____

Zip Code: _____

Phone: _____

Additional Instructions (optional): _____

_____

_____

_____

I understand the full import of this declaration, and I am emotionally and mentally competent to make this declaration.

Signed: _____

Witness #1
Name: _____
Address: _____

_____

Zip Code: _____
Phone: _____

Witness #2
Name: _____
Address: _____

_____

Zip Code: _____
Phone: _____

DESIGNATION OF HEALTH CARE SURROGATE

Name: _____ (Last) _____ (First)_____(Middle Initial)_____

In the event that I have been determined to be incapacitated to provide informed consent for medical treatment and surgical and diagnostic procedures, I wish to designate as my surrogate for health care decisions:

Name: _____
Address: _____
_____
Zip Code: _____
Phone: _____

If my surrogate is unwilling or unable to perform his or her duties, I wish to designate as my alternate surrogate:

Name: _____
Address: _____
_____
Zip Code: _____
Phone: _____

I fully understand that this designation will permit my designee to make health care decisions and to provide, withhold, or withdraw consent on my behalf; to apply for public benefits to defray the cost of health care; and to authorize my admission to or transfer from a health care facility.

Additional Instructions (optional): _____
_____
_____
_____

I further affirm that this designation is not being made as a condition of treatment or admission to a health care facility. I will notify and send a copy of this document to the following persons other than my surrogate, so they may know who my surrogate is.

Name: _____

Name: _____

Signed: _____

Date: _____

Witness #1

Name: _____

Address: _____

_____

Zip Code: _____

Phone: _____

Witness #2

Name: _____

Address: _____

_____

Zip Code: _____

Phone: _____

Georgia State Forms

LIVING WILL

Living will made this _____ day of _____ (month, year).

I, _____, being of sound mind, willfully and voluntarily make known my desire that my life shall not be prolonged under the circumstances set forth below and do declare:

1.   If at any time I should (check each option desired):

        [ ]   have a terminal condition,

        [ ]   become in a coma with no reasonable expectation of regaining consciousness, or

        [ ]   become in a persistent vegetative state with no reasonable expectation of regaining significant cognitive function, as defined in and established in accordance with the procedures set forth in paragraphs (2), (9), and (13) of Code Section 31-32-2 of the Official Code of Georgia Annotated,

      I direct that the application of life-sustaining procedures to my body (check the option desired):

        [ ]   including nourishment and hydration,

        [ ]   including nourishment but not hydration, or

        [ ]   excluding nourishment and hydration,

      be withheld or withdrawn and that I be permitted to die;

2.   In the absence of my ability to give directions regarding the use of such life-sustaining procedures, it is my intention that this living will shall be honored by my family and physician(s) as the final expression of my legal right to refuse medical or surgical treatment and accept the consequences from such refusal;

3.   I understand that I may revoke this living will at any time;

4.   I understand the full import of this living will, and I am at least 18 years of age and am emotionally and mentally competent to make this living will; and

5.   If I am a female and I have been diagnosed as pregnant, this living will shall have no force and effect unless the fetus is not viable and I indicate by initialing after this sentence that I want this living will to be carried out. _____ (Initial)

Signed _____

_____(City), _____(County), and _____(State of Residence).

I hereby witness this living will and attest that:

(1)   The declarant is personally known to me and I believe the declarant to be at least 18 years of age and of sound mind;

(2)   I am at least 18 years of age;

(3)   To the best of my knowledge, at the time of the execution of this living will, I:

   (A)   Am not related to the declarant by blood or marriage;

   (B)   Would not be entitled to any portion of the declarant´s estate by any will or by operation of law under the rules of descent and distribution of this state;

   (C)   Am not the attending physician of declarant or an employee of the attending physician or an employee of the hospital or skilled nursing facility in which declarant is a patient;

   (D)   Am not directly financially responsible for the declarant´s medical care; and

   (E)   Have no present claim against any portion of the estate of the declarant;

(4)   Declarant has signed this document in my presence as above instructed, on the date above first shown.

Witnesses: Addresses:

_____   _____

                                _____

                                _____

_____   _____

                                _____

                                _____

Additional witness required when living will is signed in a hospital or skilled nursing facility.

I hereby witness this living will and attest that I believe the declarant to be of sound mind and to have made this living will willingly and voluntarily.

Witness: _____

Medical director of skilled nursing facility or staff physician not participating in care of the patient or chief of the hospital medical staff or staff physician or hospital designee not participating in care of the patient.'

DURABLE POWER OF ATTORNEY FOR HEALTH CARE

NOTICE: THE PURPOSE OF THIS POWER OF ATTORNEY IS TO GIVE THE PERSON YOU DESIGNATE (YOUR AGENT) BROAD POWERS TO MAKE HEALTH CARE DECISIONS FOR YOU, INCLUDING POWER TO REQUIRE, CONSENT TO, OR WITHDRAW ANY TYPE OF PERSONAL CARE OR MEDICAL TREATMENT FOR ANY PHYSICAL OR MENTAL CONDITION AND TO ADMIT YOU TO OR DISCHARGE YOU FROM ANY HOSPITAL, HOME, OR OTHER INSTITUTION; BUT NOT INCLUDING PSYCHOSURGERY, STERILIZATION, OR INVOLUNTARY HOSPITALIZATION OR TREATMENT COVERED BY TITLE 37 OF THE OFFICIAL CODE OF GEORGIA ANNOTATED. THIS FORM DOES NOT IMPOSE A DUTY ON YOUR AGENT TO EXERCISE GRANTED POWERS; BUT, WHEN A POWER IS EXERCISED, YOUR AGENT WILL HAVE TO USE DUE CARE TO ACT FOR YOUR BENEFIT AND IN ACCORDANCE WITH THIS FORM. A COURT CAN TAKE AWAY THE POWERS OF YOUR AGENT IF IT FINDS THE AGENT IS NOT ACTING PROPERLY. YOU MAY NAME COAGENTS AND SUCCESSOR AGENTS UNDER THIS FORM, BUT YOU MAY NOT NAME A HEALTH CARE PROVIDER WHO MAY BE DIRECTLY OR INDIRECTLY INVOLVED IN RENDERING HEALTH CARE TO YOU UNDER THIS POWER. UNLESS YOU EXPRESSLY LIMIT THE DURATION OF THIS POWER IN THE MANNER PROVIDED BELOW OR UNTIL YOU REVOKE THIS POWER OR A COURT ACTING

ON YOUR BEHALF TERMINATES IT, YOUR AGENT MAY EXERCISE THE POWERS GIVEN IN THIS POWER THROUGHOUT YOUR LIFETIME, EVEN AFTER YOU BECOME DISABLED, INCAPACITATED, OR INCOMPETENT.

THE POWERS YOU GIVE YOUR AGENT, YOUR RIGHT TO REVOKE THOSE POWERS, AND THE PENALTIES FOR VIOLATING THE LAW ARE EXPLAINED MORE FULLY IN CODE SECTIONS 31-36-6, 31-36-9, AND 31-36-10 OF THE GEORGIA "DURABLE POWER OF ATTORNEY FOR HEALTH CARE ACT" OF WHICH THIS FORM IS A PART (SEE THE BACK OF THIS FORM). THAT ACT EXPRESSLY PERMITS THE USE OF ANY DIFFERENT FORM OF POWER OF ATTORNEY YOU MAY DESIRE. IF THERE IS ANYTHING ABOUT THIS FORM THAT YOU DO NOT UNDERSTAND, YOU SHOULD ASK A LAWYER TO EXPLAIN IT TO YOU.

GEORGIA DURABLE POWER OF ATTORNEY FOR HEALTHCARE

DURABLE POWER OF ATTORNEY made this _____ day of _____, _____.

1.   I, _____

(insert name and address of principal)

hereby appoint _____

insert name and address of agent)

as my attorney in fact (my agent) to act for me and in my name in any way I could act in person to make any and all decisions for me concerning my personal care, medical treatment, hospitalization, and health care and to require, withhold, or withdraw any type of medical treatment or procedure, even though my death may ensue. My agent shall have the same access to my medical records that I have, including the right to disclose the contents to others. My agent shall also have full power to make a disposition of any part or all of my body for medical purposes, authorize an autopsy of my body, and direct the disposition of my remains.

THE ABOVE GRANT OF POWER IS INTENDED TO BE AS BROAD AS POSSIBLE SO THAT YOUR AGENT WILL HAVE AUTHORITY TO MAKE ANY DECISION YOU COULD MAKE TO OBTAIN OR TERMINATE ANY TYPE OF HEALTH CARE, INCLUDING WITHDRAWAL OF NOURISHMENT AND FLUIDS AND OTHER LIFE-SUSTAINING OR DEATH-DELAYING MEASURES, IF YOUR AGENT BELIEVES SUCH ACTION WOULD BE CONSISTENT WITH YOUR INTENT AND DESIRES. IF YOU WISH TO LIMIT THE SCOPE OF YOUR AGENT´S POWERS OR PRESCRIBE SPECIAL RULES TO LIMIT THE POWER TO MAKE AN ANATOMICAL GIFT, AUTHORIZE AUTOPSY, OR DISPOSE OF REMAINS, YOU MAY DO SO IN THE FOLLOWING PARAGRAPHS.

2.   The powers granted above shall not include the following powers or shall be subject to the following rules or limitations (here you may include any specific limitations you deem appropriate, such as your own definition of when life-sustaining or death-delaying measures should be withheld; a direction to continue nourishment and fluids or other life-sustaining or death-delaying treatment in all events; or instructions to refuse any specific types of treatment that are inconsistent with your religious beliefs or unacceptable to you for any other reason, such as blood transfusion, electroconvulsive

therapy, or amputation):

_____

_____

_____

THE SUBJECT OF LIFE-SUSTAINING OR DEATH-DELAYING TREATMENT IS OF PARTICULAR IMPORTANCE. FOR YOUR CONVENIENCE IN DEALING WITH THAT SUBJECT, SOME GENERAL STATEMENTS CONCERNING THE

WITHHOLDING OR REMOVAL OF LIFE-SUSTAINING OR DEATH-DELAYING TREATMENT ARE SET FORTH BELOW. IF YOU AGREE WITH ONE OF THESE STATEMENTS, YOU MAY INITIAL THAT STATEMENT, BUT DO NOT INITIAL MORE THAN ONE:

I do not want my life to be prolonged nor do I want life-sustaining or death-delaying treatment to be provided or continued if my agent believes the burdens of the treatment outweigh the expected benefits. I want my agent to consider the relief of suffering, the expense involved, and the quality as well as the possible extension of my life in making decisions concerning life sustaining or death-delaying treatment.

Initialled _____

I want my life to be prolonged and I want life-sustaining or death-delaying treatment to be provided or continued unless I am in a coma, including a persistent vegetative state, which my attending physician believes to be irreversible, in accordance with reasonable medical standards at the time of reference. If and when I have suffered such an irreversible coma, I want life sustaining or death-delaying treatment to be withheld or discontinued.

Initialled _____

I want my life to be prolonged to the greatest extent possible without regard to my condition, the chances I have for recovery, or the cost of the procedures.

Initialled _____

THIS POWER OF ATTORNEY MAY BE AMENDED OR REVOKED BY YOU AT ANY TIME AND IN ANY MANNER WHILE YOU ARE ABLE TO DO SO. IN THE ABSENCE OF AN AMENDMENT OR REVOCATION, THE AUTHORITY GRANTED IN THIS POWER OF ATTORNEY WILL BECOME EFFECTIVE AT THE TIME THIS POWER IS SIGNED AND WILL CONTINUE UNTIL YOUR DEATH AND WILL CONTINUE BEYOND YOUR DEATH IF ANATOMICAL GIFT, AUTOPSY, OR DISPOSITION OF REMAINS IS AUTHORIZED, UNLESS A LIMITATION ON THE BEGINNING DATE

OR DURATION IS MADE BY INITIALING AND COMPLETING EITHER OR BOTH OF THE FOLLOWING:

3. [ ]   This power of attorney shall become effective on _____ (insert a future date or event during your lifetime, such as court determination of your disability, incapacity, or incompetency, when you want this power to first take effect).

4. [ ]   This power of attorney shall terminate on _____ (insert a future date or event, such as court determination of your disability, incapacity, or incompetency, when you want this power to terminate prior to your death).

IF YOU WISH TO NAME SUCCESSOR AGENTS, INSERT THE NAMES AND ADDRESSES OF SUCH SUCCESSORS IN THE FOLLOWING PARAGRAPH:

5.   If any agent named by me shall die, become legally disabled, incapacitated, or incompetent, or resign, refuse to act, or be unavailable, I name the following (each to act successively in the order named) as successors to such agent:

_____

_____

IF YOU WISH TO NAME A GUARDIAN OF YOUR PERSON IN THE EVENT A COURT DECIDES THAT ONE SHOULD BE APPOINTED, YOU MAY, BUT ARE NOT REQUIRED TO, DO SO BY INSERTING THE NAME OF SUCH GUARDIAN IN THE FOLLOWING PARAGRAPH. THE COURT WILL APPOINT THE PERSON NOMINATED BY YOU IF THE COURT FINDS THAT SUCH APPOINTMENT WILL SERVE YOUR BEST INTERESTS AND WELFARE. YOU MAY, BUT ARE NOT REQUIRED TO, NOMINATE AS YOUR GUARDIAN THE SAME PERSON NAMED IN THIS FORM AS YOUR AGENT.

6.   If a guardian of my person is to be appointed, I nominate the following to serve as such guardian: _____ _____ _____(insert name and address of nominated guardian of the person)

7.   I am fully informed as to all the contents of this form and understand the full import of this grant of powers to my agent.

Signed _____
(Principal)

The principal has had an opportunity to read the above form and has signed the above form in our presence. We, the undersigned, each being over 18 years of age, witness the principal's signature at the request and in the presence of the principal, and in the presence of each other, on the day and year above set out.

Witnesses: Addresses:

_____   _____

                                _____

                                _____

_____   _____

                                _____

                                _____

Additional witness required when health care agency is signed in a hospital or skilled nursing facility.

I hereby witness this health care agency and attest that I believe the principal to be of sound mind and to have made this health care agency willingly and voluntarily.

Witness: Address:

_____   _____

Attending Physician   _____

                                _____

                                _____

YOU MAY, BUT ARE NOT REQUIRED TO, REQUEST YOUR AGENT AND SUCCESSOR AGENTS TO PROVIDE SPECIMEN SIGNATURES BELOW. IF YOU INCLUDE SPECIMEN SIGNATURES IN THIS POWER OF ATTORNEY, YOU MUST COMPLETE THE CERTIFICATION OPPOSITE THE SIGNATURES OF THE AGENTS.

Specimen signatures of   I certify that the signature of
agent and successor(s)   my agent and successor(s) correct.

_____   _____(Agent)
      (Principal)

_____   _____(Successor agent)
      (Principal)

_____   _____(Successor agent)
      (Principal)

Hawaii State Forms

ADVANCE HEALTH-CARE DIRECTIVE

Explanation

You have the right to give instructions about your own health care. You also have the right to name someone else to make health-care decisions for you. This form lets you do either or both of these things. It also lets you express your wishes regarding the designation of your health-care provider. If you use this form, you may complete or modify all or any part of it. You are free to use a different form.

Part 1 of this form is a power of attorney for health care. Part 1 lets you name another individual as agent to make health-care decisions for you if you become incapable of making your own decisions or if you want someone else to make those decisions for you now even though you are still capable. You may name an alternate agent to act for you if your first choice is not willing, able, or reasonably available to make decisions for you. Unless related to you, your agent may not be an owner, operator, or employee of a health-care institution where you are receiving care.

Unless the form you sign limits the authority of your agent, your agent may make all health-care decisions for you. This form has a place for you to limit the authority of your agent. You need not limit the authority of your agent if you wish to rely on your agent for all health-care decisions that may have to be made. If you choose not to limit the authority of your agent, your agent will have the right to:

(1)   Consent or refuse consent to any care, treatment, service, or procedure to maintain, diagnose, or otherwise affect a physical or mental condition;

(2)   Select or discharge health-care providers and institutions;

(3)   Approve or disapprove diagnostic tests, surgical procedures, programs of medication, and orders not to resuscitate; and

(4)   Direct the provision, withholding, or withdrawal of artificial nutrition and hydration and all other forms of health care.

Part 2 of this form lets you give specific instructions about any aspect of your health care.

Choices are provided for you to express your wishes regarding the provision, withholding, or withdrawal of treatment to keep you alive, including the provision of artificial nutrition and hydration, as well as the provision of pain relief medication. Space is provided for you to add to the choices you have made or for you to write out any additional wishes.

Part 4 of this form lets you designate a physician to have primary responsibility for your health care.

After completing this form, sign and date the form at the end and have the form witnessed by one of the two alternative methods listed below. Give a copy of the signed and completed form to your physician, to any other health-care providers you may have, to any health-care institution at which you are receiving care, and to any health-care agents you have named. You should talk to the person you have named as agent to make sure that he or she understands your wishes and is willing to take the responsibility.

You have the right to revoke this advance health-care directive or replace this form at any time.

PART 1 - DURABLE POWER OF ATTORNEY FOR HEALTH-CARE DECISIONS

(1) **DESIGNATION OF AGENT**: I designate the following individual as my agent to make health-care decisions for me:

_____

(name of individual you choose as agent)

_____

(address) (city) (state) (zip code)

_____

(home phone) (work phone)

OPTIONAL: If I revoke my agent's authority or if my agent is not willing, able, or reasonably available to make a health-care decision for me, I designate as my first alternate agent:

_____

(name of individual you choose as first alternate agent)

_____

(address) (city) (state) (zip code)

_____

(home phone) (work phone)

OPTIONAL: If I revoke the authority of my agent and first alternate agent or if neither is willing, able, or reasonably available to make a health-care decision for me, I designate as my second alternate agent:

_____

(name of individual you choose as second alternate agent)

_____

(address) (city) (state) (zip code)

_____

(home phone) (work phone)

(2)   **AGENT'S AUTHORITY**: My agent is authorized to make all health-care decisions for me, including decisions to provide, withhold, or withdraw artificial nutrition and hydration, and all other forms of health care to keep me alive, except as I state here:

_____

_____

_____

(Add additional sheets if needed.)

(3)   **WHEN AGENT'S AUTHORITY BECOMES EFFECTIVE**: My agent's authority becomes effective when my primary physician determines that I am unable to make my own health-care decisions unless I mark the following box. If I mark this box [ ], my agent's authority to make health-care decisions for me takes effect immediately.

(4)   **AGENT'S OBLIGATION**: My agent shall make health-care decisions for me in accordance with this power of attorney for health care, any instructions I give in Part 2 of this form, and my other wishes to the extent known to my agent. To the extent my wishes are unknown, my agent shall make health-care decisions for me in accordance with what my agent determines to be in my best interest. In determining my best interest, my agent shall consider my personal values to the extent known to my agent.

(5)   **NOMINATION OF GUARDIAN**: If a guardian needs to be appointed for me by a court, I nominate the agent designated in this form. If that agent is not willing, able, or reasonably available to act as guardian, I nominate the alternate agents whom I have named, in the order designated.

PART 2 - INSTRUCTIONS FOR HEALTH CARE

If you are satisfied to allow your agent to determine what is best for you in making end-of-life decisions, you need not fill out this part of the form. If you do fill out this part of the form, you may strike any wording you do not want.

(6)   **END-OF-LIFE DECISIONS**: I direct that my health-care providers and others involved in my care provide, withhold, or withdraw treatment in accordance with the choice I have marked below: (Check only one box.)

[ ]   (a) <u>Choice Not To Prolong Life</u>

I do not want my life to be prolonged if (i) I have an incurable and irreversible condition that will result in my death within a relatively short time, (ii) I become unconscious and, to a reasonable degree of medical certainty, I will not regain consciousness, or (iii) the likely risks and burdens of treatment would outweigh the expected benefits, OR

[ ]   (b) <u>Choice To Prolong Life</u>

I want my life to be prolonged as long as possible within the limits of generally accepted health-care standards.

(7)   **ARTIFICIAL NUTRITION AND HYDRATION**: Artificial nutrition and hydration must be provided, withheld or withdrawn in accordance with the choice I have made in paragraph (6) unless I mark the following box. If I mark this box [ ], artificial nutrition and hydration must be provided regardless of my condition and regardless of the choice I have made in paragraph (6).

(8)   **RELIEF FROM PAIN**: If I mark this box [ ], I direct that treatment to alleviate pain or discomfort should be provided to me even if it hastens my death.

(9)   **OTHER WISHES**: (If you do not agree with any of the optional choices above and wish to write your own, or if you wish to add to the instructions you have given above, you may do so here.) I direct that:

_____

_____

_____

_____

(Add additional sheets if needed.)

PART 3 - DONATION OF ORGANS AT DEATH

(OPTIONAL)

(10)   Upon my death: (mark applicable box)

[ ]   (a) I give any needed organs, tissues, or parts,

OR

[ ]   (b) I give the following organs, tissues, or parts only

_____

_____

[ ]   (c) My gift is for the following purposes (strike any of the following you do not want)

  (i)   Transplant

  (ii)   Therapy

  (iii)   Research

  (iv)   Education

PART 4 - PRIMARY PHYSICIAN

(OPTIONAL)

(11)   I designate the following physician as my primary physician:

_____

(name of physician)

_____

(address) (city) (state) (zip code)

_____

(phone)

OPTIONAL: If the physician I have designated above is not willing, able, or reasonably available to act as my primary physician, I designate the following physician as my primary physician:

_____

(name of physician)

_____

(address) (city) (state) (zip code)

_____

(phone)

(12)   **EFFECT OF COPY**: A copy of this form has the same effect as the original.

(13)   **SIGNATURES**: Sign and date the form here:

_____	_____
(date)	(sign your name)
_____	_____
(address)	(print your name)
_____	_____
(city)	(state)

(14)   **WITNESSES**: This power of attorney will not be valid for making health-care decisions unless it is either (a) signed by two qualified adult witnesses who are personally known to you and who are present when you sign or acknowledge your signature; or (b) acknowledged before a notary public in the State.

ALTERNATIVE NO. 1
Witness

I declare under penalty of false swearing pursuant to section 710-1062, Hawaii Revised Statutes, that the principal is personally known to me, that the principal signed or acknowledged this power of attorney in my presence, that the principal appears to be of sound mind and under no duress, fraud, or undue influence, that I am not the person appointed as agent by this document, and that I am not a health-care provider, nor an employee of a health-care provider or facility. I am not related to the principal by blood, marriage, or adoption, and to the best of my knowledge, I am not entitled to any part of the estate of the principal upon the death of the principal under a will now existing or by operation of law.

_____   _____(date)

(signature of witness)

_____   _____

(address)   (printed name of witness)

_____

(city)

_____

(state

Witness

I declare under penalty of false swearing pursuant to section 710-1062, Hawaii Revised Statutes, that the principal is personally known to me, that the principal signed or acknowledged this power of attorney in my presence, that the principal appears to be of sound mind and under no duress, fraud, or undue influence, that I am not the person appointed as agent by this document, and that I am not a health-care provider, nor an employee of a health-care provider or facility.

_____   _____(date)

(signature of witness)

_____   _____

(address)   (printed name of witness)

_____

(city)

_____

(state)

ALTERNATIVE NO. 2

State of Hawaii   County of _____

On this _____ day of _____, in the year _____, before me, _____ (insert name of notary public) appeared _____, personally known to me (or proved to me on the basis of satisfactory evidence) to be the person whose name is subscribed to this instrument, and acknowledged that he or she executed it.

Notary Seal

_____

(Signature of Notary Public)

Idaho State Forms

LIVING WILL AND DURABLE POWER OF ATTORNEY FOR HEALTH CARE

Date of Directive: _____

Name of person executing Directive: _____

Address of person executing Directive: _____

A LIVING WILL

A Directive to Withhold or to Provide Treatment

1.   I willfully and voluntarily make known my desire that my life shall not be prolonged artificially under the circumstances set forth below. This Directive shall only be effective if I am unable to communicate my instructions and:

    a.   I have an incurable or irreversible injury, disease, illness or condition, and a medical doctor who has examined me has certified:

        1.   That such injury, disease, illness or condition is terminal; and

        2.   That the application of artificial life-sustaining procedures would serve only to prolong artificially my life; and

        3.   That my death is imminent, whether or not artificial life-sustaining procedures are utilized; or

    b.   I have been diagnosed as being in a persistent vegetative state.

In such event, I direct that the following marked expression of my intent be followed, and that I receive any medical treatment or care that may be required to keep me free of pain or distress.

Check <u>one</u> box and initial the line after such box:

[ ] _____   I direct that all medical treatment, care and procedures necessary to restore my health and sustain my life be provided to me. Nutrition and hydration, whether artificial or non-artificial, shall not be withheld or withdrawn from me if I would likely die primarily from malnutrition or dehydration rather than from my injury, disease, illness or condition.

OR

[ ] _____   I direct that all medical treatment, care and procedures, including artificial life-sustaining procedures, be withheld or withdrawn, except that nutrition and hydration, whether artificial or non-artificial shall not be withheld or withdrawn from me if, as a result, I would likely die primarily from malnutrition or dehydration rather than from my injury, disease, illness or condition, as follows: (If none of the following boxes are checked and initialed, then both nutrition and hydration, of any nature, whether artificial or non-artificial, shall be administered.)

Check one box and initial the line after such box:

A.   [ ] _____   Only hydration of any nature, whether artificial or non-artificial, shall be administered;

B.   [ ] _____   Only nutrition, of any nature, whether artificial or non-artificial, shall be administered;

C.   [ ] _____   Both nutrition and hydration, of any nature, whether artificial or non-artificial shall be administered.

OR

[ ] _____   I direct that all medical treatment, care and procedures be withheld or withdrawn, including withdrawal of the administration of artificial nutrition and hydration.

2.   If I have been diagnosed as pregnant, this Directive shall have no force during the course of my pregnancy.

3.   I understand the full importance of this Directive and am mentally competent to make this Directive. No participant in the making of this Directive or in its being carried into effect shall be held responsible in any way for complying with my directions.

4.   Check one box and initial the line after such box:

[ ] _____   I have discussed these decisions with my physician and have also completed a Physician Orders for Scope of Treatment (POST) form that contains directions that may be more specific than, but are compatible with, this Directive. I hereby approve of those orders and incorporate them herein as if fully set forth.

OR

[ ] _____   I have not completed a Physician Orders for Scope of Treatment (POST) form. If a POST form is later signed by my physician, then this living will shall be deemed modified to be compatible with the terms of the POST form.

A DURABLE POWER OF ATTORNEY FOR HEALTH CARE

1.   DESIGNATION OF HEALTH CARE AGENT

None of the following may be designated as your agent: (1) your treating health care provider; (2) a nonrelative employee of your treating health care provider; (3) an operator of a community care facility; or (4) a nonrelative employee of an operator of a community care facility. If the agent or an alternate agent designated in this Directive is my spouse, and our marriage is thereafter dissolved, such designation shall be thereupon revoked.

I do hereby designate and appoint the following individual as my attorney in fact (agent) to make health care decisions for me as authorized in this Directive. (Insert name, address and telephone number of one individual only as your agent to make health care decisions for you.)

Name of Health Care Agent: _____
Address of Health Care Agent: _____
Telephone Number of Health Care Agent: _____

For the purposes of this Directive, "health care decision" means consent, refusal of consent, or withdrawal of consent to any care, treatment, service or procedure to maintain, diagnose or treat an individual's physical condition.

2. CREATION OF DURABLE POWER OF ATTORNEY FOR HEALTH CARE

By this portion of this Directive, I create a durable power of attorney for health care. This power of attorney shall not be affected by my subsequent incapacity. This power shall be effective only when I am unable to communicate rationally.

3. GENERAL STATEMENT OF AUTHORITY GRANTED

I hereby grant to my agent full power and authority to make health care decisions for me to the same extent that I could make such decisions for myself if I had the capacity to do so. In exercising this authority, my agent shall make health care decisions that are consistent with my desires as stated in this Directive or otherwise made known to my agent including, but not limited to, my desires concerning obtaining or refusing or withdrawing artificial life-sustaining care, treatment, services and procedures, including such desires set forth in a living will, Physician Orders for Scope of Treatment (POST) form, or similar document executed by me, if any. (If you want to limit the authority of your agent to make health care decisions for you, you can state the limitations in paragraph 4 ("Statement of Desires, Special Provisions, and Limitations") below. You can indicate your desires by including a statement of your desires in the same paragraph.)

4. STATEMENT OF DESIRES, SPECIAL PROVISIONS, AND LIMITATIONS

(Your agent must make health care decisions that are consistent with your known desires. You can, but are not required to, state your desires in the space provided below. You should consider whether you want to include a statement of your desires concerning artificial life-sustaining care, treatment, services and procedures. You can also include a statement of your desires concerning other matters relating to your health care, including a list of one or more persons whom you designate to be able to receive medical information about you and/or to be allowed to visit you in a medical institution. You can also make your desires known to your agent by discussing your desires with your agent or by some other means. If there are any types of treatment that you do not want to be used, you should state them in the space below. If you want to limit in any other way the authority given your agent by this Directive, you should state the limits in the space below. If you do not state any limits, your agent will have broad powers to make health care decisions for you, except to the extent that there are limits provided by law.) In exercising the authority under this durable power of attorney for health care, my agent shall act consistently with my desires as stated below and is subject to the special provisions and limitations stated in my Physician Orders for Scope of Treatment (POST) form, a living will, or similar document executed by me, if any. Additional statement of desires, special provisions, and limitations: _____

_____

_____

_____

_____ You may attach additional pages or documents if you need more space to complete your statement.)

5. **INSPECTION AND DISCLOSURE OF INFORMATION RELATING TO MY PHYSICAL OR MENTAL HEALTH**

    A.   <u>General Grant of Power and Authority</u>

    Subject to any limitations in this Directive, my agent has the power and authority to do all of the following: (1) Request, review and receive any information, verbal or written, regarding my physical or mental health including, but not limited to, medical and hospital records; (2) Execute on my behalf any releases or other documents that may be required in order to obtain this information; (3) Consent to the disclosure of this information; and (4) Consent to the donation of any of my organs for medical purposes. (If you want to limit the authority of your agent to receive and disclose information relating to your health, you must state the limitations in paragraph 4 ("Statement of Desires, Special Provisions, and Limitations") above.)

    B.   <u>HIPAA Release Authority</u>

    My agent shall be treated as I would be with respect to my rights regarding the use and disclosure of my individually identifiable health information or other medical records. This release authority applies to any information governed by the Health Insurance Portability and Accountability Act of 1996 (HIPAA), 42 U.S.C. 1320d and 45 CFR 160 through 164. I authorize any physician, health care professional, dentist, health plan, hospital, clinic, laboratory, pharmacy, or other covered health care provider, any insurance company, and the Medical Information Bureau, Inc. or other health care clearinghouse that has provided treatment or services to me, or that has paid for or is seeking payment from me for such services, to give, disclose and release to my agent, without restriction, all of my individually identifiable health information and medical records regarding any past, present or future medical or mental health condition, including all information relating to the diagnosis of HIV/AIDS, sexually transmitted diseases, mental illness, and drug or alcohol abuse. The authority given my agent shall supersede any other agreement that I may have made with my health care providers to restrict access to or disclosure of my individually identifiable health information. The authority given my agent has no expiration date and shall expire only in the event that I revoke the authority in writing and deliver it to my health care provider.

6. **SIGNING DOCUMENTS, WAIVERS AND RELEASES**

Where necessary to implement the health care decisions that my agent is authorized by this Directive to make, my agent has the power and authority to execute on my behalf all of the following: (a) Documents titled, or purporting to be, a "Refusal to Permit Treatment" and/or a "Leaving Hospital Against Medical Advice"; and (b) Any necessary waiver or release from liability required by a hospital or physician.

7. **DESIGNATION OF ALTERNATE AGENTS**

(You are not required to designate any alternate agents but you may do so. Any alternate agent you designate will be able to make the same health care decisions as the agent you designated in paragraph 1 above, in the event that agent is unable or ineligible to act as your agent. If an alternate agent you designate is your spouse, he or she becomes ineligible to act as your agent if your marriage is thereafter dissolved.) If the person designated as my agent in paragraph 1 is not available or becomes ineligible to act as my agent to make a health care decision for me or loses the mental capacity to make health care decisions for me, or if I revoke that person's appointment or authority to act as my agent to make health care decisions for me, then I designate and appoint the following persons to serve as my agent to make health care decisions for me as authorized in this Directive, such persons to serve in the order listed below:

A.   First Alternate Agent:

      Name: _____

      Address: _____

                  _____

                  _____

      Telephone Number: _____

B.   Second Alternate Agent:

      Name: _____

      Address: _____

                   _____

                  _____

      Telephone Number: _____

C.   Third Alternate Agent:

Name: _____

Address: _____

_____

_____

Telephone Number: _____

8.   PRIOR DESIGNATIONS REVOKED

I revoke any prior durable power of attorney for health care.

DATE AND SIGNATURE OF PRINCIPAL

(You must date and sign this Living Will and Durable Power of Attorney for Health Care.)

I sign my name to this Statutory Form Living Will and Durable Power of Attorney for Health Care on the date set forth at the beginning of this Form at _____

_____ (City, State)   _____.

_____

Signature

Illinois State Forms

LIVING WILL DECLARATION

This declaration is made this _____ day of _____ (month, year).

I, _____, being of sound mind, willfully and voluntarily make known my desires that my moment of death shall not be artificially postponed.

If at any time I should have an incurable and irreversible injury, disease, or illness judged to be a terminal condition by my attending physician who has personally examined me and has determined that my death is imminent except for death delaying procedures, I direct that such procedures which would only prolong the dying process be withheld or withdrawn, and that I be permitted to die naturally with only the administration of medication, sustenance, or the performance of any medical procedure deemed necessary by my attending physician to provide me with comfort care.

In the absence of my ability to give directions regarding the use of such death delaying procedures, it is my intention that this declaration shall be honored by my family and physician as the final expression of my legal right to refuse medical or surgical treatment and accept the consequences from such refusal.

Signed _____

City, County and State of Residence _____

_____

The declarant is personally known to me and I believe him or her to be of sound mind. I saw the declarant sign the declaration in my presence (or the declarant acknowledged in my presence that he or she had signed the declaration) and I signed the declaration as a witness in the presence of the declarant. I did not sign the declarant's signature above for or at the direction of the declarant. At the date of this instrument, I am not entitled to any portion of the estate of the declarant according to the laws of intestate succession or, to the best of my knowledge and belief, under any will of declarant or other instrument taking effect at declarant's death, or directly financially responsible for declarant's medical care.

Witnesses: Addresses:

_____   _____

                                             _____

_____
_____

_____   _____
                                   _____
                                   _____
                                   _____

Illinois Statutory Short Form Power of Attorney for Health Care

Notice: The purpose of this Power of Attorney for Health Care is to give the person you designate (your "agent") broad powers to make health care decisions for you, including power to require, consent to or withdraw any type of personal care or medical treatment for any physical or mental condition and to admit you to or discharge you from any hospital, home or other institution. This form does not impose a duty on your agent to exercise granted powers; but when powers are exercised, your agent will have to use due care to act for your benefit and in accordance with this form and keep a record of receipts, disbursements and significant actions taken as agent. A court can take away the powers of your agent if it finds the agent is not acting properly. You may name successor agents under this form but not co-agents, and no healthcare provider may be named. Unless you expressly limit the duration of this power in the manner provided below, until you revoke this power or a court acting on your behalf terminates it, your agent may exercise the powers given here throughout your lifetime, even after you become disabled. The powers you give your agent, your right to revoke those powers and the penalties for violating the law are explained more fully in Section 4-5, 4-6, 4-9 and 4-10(b) of the Illinois "Powers of Attorney for Health Care Law" of which this form is a part (see pages 3-6 of this form). That law expressly permits the use of any different form of power of attorney you may desire. (If there is anything about this form that you do not understand, you should ask a lawyer to explain it to you.)

POWER OF ATTORNEY made this _____ day of _____ (month, year).

1.   I, _____
                        (insert name of principal)
        of _____
                        (insert address of principal)
        hereby appoint: _____
                        (insert name of agent)
        of _____
                        (insert address of agent)

as my attorney-in-fact (my "agent") to act for me and in my name (in any way I could act in person) to make any and all decisions for me concerning my personal care, medical treatment, hospitalization and health care and to require, withhold or withdraw any type of medical treatment or   procedure, even though my death may ensue. My agent shall have the same access to my medical records that I have, including the right to disclose the contents to others. My agent shall also have the full power to authorize an autopsy and direct the disposition of my remains. Effective upon my death, my agent has the full power to make an anatomical gift of the following: **(initial one)**

_____ Any organs, tissues or eyes suitable for transplantation or used for research or education.

_____ Specific organs: _____

(The above grant of power is intended to be as broad as possible so that your agent will have authority to make any decision you could make to obtain or terminate any type of health care, including withdrawal of food and water and other life-sustaining measures, if your agent believes such action would be consistent with your intent and desires. If you wish to limit the scope of your agent's powers or prescribe special rules or limit the power to make an anatomical gift, authorize autopsy or dispose of remains, you may do so in the following paragraphs).

2.   The powers granted above shall not include the following powers or shall be subject to the following rules or limitations (here you may include any specific limitations you deem appropriate, such as: your own definition of when life-sustaining measures should be withheld; a direction to continue food and fluids or life-sustaining treatment in all events; or instructions to refuse any specific types of treatment that are inconsistent with your religious beliefs or unacceptable to you for any other reason, such as blood transfusion, electro-convulsive therapy, amputation, psychosurgery, voluntary admission to a mental institution, etc.):

_____

_____

_____

_____

(The subject of life-sustaining treatment is of particular importance. For your convenience in dealing with that subject, some general statements concerning the withholding or removal of life-sustaining treatment are set forth below. If you agree with one of these statements, you may initial that statement; **do not** initial more than one):

_____ I do not want my life to be prolonged nor do I want life-sustaining treatment to be provided or continued if my agent believes the burdens of the treatment outweigh the expected benefits. I want my agent to consider the relief of suffering, the expense involved and the quality as well as the possible extension of my life in making decisions concerning lifesustaining treatment.

_____ I want my life to be prolonged, and I want life-sustaining treatment to be provided or continued unless I am in a coma which my attending physician believes to be irreversible, in accordance with reasonable medical standards at the time of reference. If and when I have suffered irreversible coma, I want life-sustaining treatment to be withheld or discontinued.

_____ I want my life to be prolonged to the greatest extent possible without regard to my condition, the chances I have for recovery or the cost of the procedures. (This power of attorney may be amended or revoked by you in the manner provided in Section 4-6 of the Illinois "Powers of Attorney for Health Care Law" (see page 3-4 of this document). Absent amendment or revocation, the authority granted in this power of attorney will become effective at the time this power is signed and will continue until your death, and beyond if anatomical gift, autopsy or disposition of remains is authorized, unless a limitation on the beginning date or duration is made by initialing and completing either (or both) of the following:

3.   [ ] This power of attorney shall become effective on _____

_____

(insert a future date or event during your lifetime, such as court determination of your disability, when you want this power to first take effect)

4.   [ ] This power of attorney shall terminate
on_____.
(insert a future date or event, such as court determination of your
disability, when you want this power to terminate prior to your death)

(If you wish to name successor agents, insert the names and addresses of such successors in the following paragraph.)

5.   If any agent named by me shall die, become incompetent, resign, refuse to accept the office of agent or be unavailable, I name the following (each to act alone and successively, in the order named) as successors to such agent:

_____

_____

_____

For purposes of this paragraph 5, a person shall be considered to be incompetent if and while the person is a minor or an adjudicated incompetent or disabled person or the person is unable to give prompt and intelligent consideration to health care matters, as certified by a licensed physician.

(If you wish to name your agent as guardian of your person, in the event a court decides that one should be appointed, you may, but are not required to, do so by retaining the following paragraph. The court will appoint your agent if the court finds that such appointment will serve your best interests and welfare. Strike out paragraph 6 if you do not want your agent to act as guardian.)

6.   If a guardian of my person is to be appointed, I nominate the agent acting under this power of attorney as such guardian, to serve without bond or security.

7.   I am fully informed as to all the contents of this form and understand the full import of this grant of powers to my agent.

Signed: _____
(Principal)

The principal has had an opportunity to read the above form and has signed the form or acknowledged his or her signature or mark on the form in my presence.

Witness: _____
Residing at:

_____

OPTIONAL

State of _____)

) SS.

County of _____)

The undersigned, a notary public in and for the above state and county, certifies that _____ _____, known to me to be the same person whose name is subscribed as principal to the foregoing power of attorney, appeared in person before me and the additional witness and acknowledged signing and delivering the instrument as the free and voluntary act of the principal, for the uses and purposes therein set forth (and certified to the correctness of the signatures of the agent and successors).

        Dated: _____ (SEAL)

                               _____
                                      (Notary Public)

        My commission expires _____ .

(You may, but are not required to, request your agent and successor agents to provide specimen signatures below. If you include specimen signatures in this power of attorney, you must complete the certification opposite the signatures of the agents).

Specimen signatures of   I certify that the signature of

agent and successor(s):   my agent and successor(s) correct.

_____   _____
(Agent)   (Principal)

_____   _____
(Successor agent)   (Principal)

_____   _____
(Successor agent)   (Principal)

Indiana State Forms

LIVING WILL DECLARATION

Declaration made this _____ day of _____ (month, year). I, _____, being at least eighteen (18) years of age and of sound mind, willfully and voluntarily make known my desires that my dying shall not be artificially prolonged under the circumstances set forth below, and I declare:

If at any time my attending physician certifies in writing that: (1) I have an incurable injury, disease, or illness; (2) my death will occur within a short time; and (3) the use of life prolonging procedures would serve only to artificially prolong the dying process, I direct that such procedures be withheld or withdrawn, and that I be permitted to die naturally with only the performance or provision of any medical procedure or medication necessary to provide me with comfort care or to alleviate pain, and, if I have so indicated below, the provision of artificially supplied nutrition and hydration. (Indicate your choice by initialling or making your mark before signing this declaration):

_____ I wish to receive artificially supplied nutrition and hydration, even if the effort to sustain life is futile or excessively burdensome to me.

_____ I do not wish to receive artificially supplied nutrition and hydration, if the effort to sustain life is futile or excessively burdensome to me.

_____ I intentionally make no decision concerning artificially supplied nutrition and hydration, leaving the decision to my health care representative appointed under IC 16-36-1-7 or my attorney in fact with health care powers under IC 30-5-5.

In the absence of my ability to give directions regarding the use of life prolonging procedures, it is my intention that this declaration be honored by my family and physician as the final expression of my legal right to refuse medical or surgical treatment and accept the consequences of the refusal.

I understand the full import of this declaration.

Signed _____

_____

City, County, and State of Residence

The declarant has been personally known to me, and I believe (him/her) to be of sound mind. I did not sign the declarant's signature above for or at the direction of the declarant. I am not a parent, spouse, or child of the declarant. I am not entitled to any part of the declarant's estate or directly financially responsible for the declarant's medical care. I am competent and at least eighteen (18) years of age.

Witness _____ Date _____

Witness _____ Date _____

LIFE PROLONGING PROCEDURES DECLARATION

Declaration made this _____ day of _____ (month, year). I, _____, being at least eighteen (18) years of age and of sound mind, willfully and voluntarily make known my desire that if at any time I have an incurable injury, disease, or illness determined to be a terminal condition I request the use of life prolonging procedures that would extend my life. This includes appropriate nutrition and hydration, the administration of medication, and the performance of all other medical procedures necessary to extend my life, to provide comfort care, or to alleviate pain.

In the absence of my ability to give directions regarding the use of life prolonging procedures, it is my intention that this declaration be honored by my family and physician as the final expression of my legal right to request medical or surgical treatment and accept the consequences of the request.

I understand the full import of this declaration.

Signed _____

_____
City, County, and State of Residence

The declarant has been personally known to me, and I believe (him/her) to be of sound mind. I am competent and at least eighteen (18) years of age.

Witness _____ Date _____
Witness _____ Date _____

Iowa State Forms

LIVING WILL DECLARATION

If I should have an incurable or irreversible condition that will result either in death within a relatively short period of time or a state of permanent unconsciousness from which, to a reasonable degree of medical certainty, there can be no recovery, it is my desire that my life not be prolonged by the administration of life-sustaining procedures. If I am unable to participate in my health care decisions, I direct my attending physician to withhold or withdraw life-sustaining procedures that merely prolong the dying process and are not necessary to my comfort or freedom from pain.

Signed this_____ of _____.

_____
Signature of Person Making Declaration (Declarant)

_____
(Type or Print Name of Declarant)

_____
Street Address

_____
State Zip Code City

This Declaration must be witnessed by two persons or be notarized.

STATE OF IOWA, _____ **COUNTY**, ss: _____

On this _____ day of _____,_____, before me, the Undersigned, a Notary Public in and for the State of Iowa, personally appeared to me known to be the person named in and who executed the foregoing instrument as Declarant, and acknowledged that (he) (she) executed the same as (his) (her) voluntary act and deed.

_____
Notary Public in and for said State

By signing this form I declare that I signed this form in the presence of the other witness and the Declarant and I witnessed the signing by the Declarant or by another person acting on behalf of and at the Declarant's direction.

_____   _____
Signature of 1st Witness   Signature of 2nd Witness

_____   _____
(Type or Print Name of Witness)   (Type or Print Name of Witness)

_____   _____
Street Address   Street Address

_____   _____
Zip Code State City   Zip Code State City

DURABLE POWER OF ATTORNEY FOR HEALTH CARE

1.   I hereby designate _____ of_____ _____
_____ as my attorney in fact (my agent) and give to my
agent the power to make health care decisions for me. This power exists only when I am
unable, in the judgment of my attending physician, to make those health care decisions.
The attorney in fact must act consistently with my desires as stated in this document or
otherwise made known.

Except as otherwise specified in this document, this document gives my agent the power,
where otherwise consistent with the law of this state, to consent to my physician not
giving health care or stopping health care which is necessary to keep me alive.

This document gives my agent power to make health care decisions on my behalf,
including to consent, to refuse to consent, or to withdraw consent to the provision
of any care, treatment, service, or procedure to maintain, diagnose, or treat a physical
or mental condition. This power is subject to any statement of my desires and any
limitations included in this document.

My agent has the right to examine my medical records and to consent to disclosure of
such records.

2.   In addition to the foregoing, the principal may provide specific instructions in the
document conferring the durable power of attorney for health care, consistent with the
provisions of this chapter.

3.   The principal may include a statement indicating that the designated attorney in fact has
been notified of and consented to the designation.

4.   A durable power of attorney for health care may designate one or more alternative
attorneys in fact.

I, _____, the principal, sign
my name to this instrument this _____ day of _____, 20 _____, and being first duly
sworn, do hereby declare to the undersigned that I am eighteen years of age or older, of sound
mind, and under no undue constraint or influence.

_____

(principal)

WITNESS STATEMENT

I declare that the person who signed or acknowledged this document is personally known to me, that he/she signed or acknowledged this durable power of attorney in my presence, and that he/she appears to be of sound mind and under no duress, fraud or undue influence. I am not the person designated as attorney in fact by this document, nor am I the principal's healthcare provider or an employee of the principal's healthcare provider. I am at least eighteen years of age.

<u>Witness #1</u>

_____   _____
(date)   (signature of witness)

_____   _____
(address)   (printed name of witness)

_____   _____
(city)   (telephone number)

_____
(state)

<u>Witness #2</u>

_____   _____
(date)   (signature of witness)

_____   _____
(address)   (printed name of witness)

_____   _____
(city)   (telephone number)

_____
(state)

I further declare that I am not a relative of the principal by blood, marriage or adoption (within the third degree of consanguinity).

_____

(witness' signature)

- OR -

NOTARY

The state of Iowa   )

) ss.

The County of _____   )

Signed and sworn to before me by _____, the principal, this _____
day of _____, 20____.

SEAL _____
(notary public)

Kansas State Forms

LIVING WILL DECLARATION

Declaration made this _____ day of _____ (month, year) I, _____ being of sound mind, willfully and voluntarily make known my desire that my dying shall not be artificially prolonged under the circumstances set forth below, do hereby declare:

If at any time I should have an incurable injury, disease, or illness certified to be a terminal condition by two physicians who have personally examined me, one of whom shall be my attending physician, and the physicians have determined that my death will occur whether or not life-sustaining procedures are utilized and where the application of life-sustaining procedures would serve only to artificially prolong the dying process, I direct that such procedures be withheld or withdrawn, and that I be permitted to die naturally with only the administration of medication or the performance of any medical procedure deemed necessary to provide me with comfort care.

In the absence of my ability to give directions regarding the use of such life-sustaining procedures, it is my intention that this declaration shall be honored by my family and physician(s) as the final expression of my legal right to refuse medical or surgical treatment and accept the consequences from such refusal.

I understand the full import of this declaration and I am emotionally and mentally competent to make this declaration.

Signed: _____
City, County and State of Residence: _____

The declarant has been personally known to me and I believe him or her to be of sound mind. I did not sign the declarant's signature above for or at the direction of the declarant. I am not related to the declarant by blood or marriage, entitled to any portion of the estate of the declarant according to the laws of intestate succession of under any will of declarant or codicil thereto, or directly financially responsible for declarant's medical care.

Witness _____

Witness _____

DURABLE POWER OF ATTORNEY FOR HEALTH CARE DECISIONS GENERAL STATEMENT OF AUTHORITY GRANTED

I, _____ of _____ designate and appoint:

Name _____

Address _____

Telephone Number _____

to be my agent for health care decisions and pursuant to the language stated below, on behalf to:

(1)   consent, refuse consent, or withdraw consent to any care, treatment, service or procedure to maintain, diagnose or treat a physical or mental condition, and to make decisions about organ donation, autopsy and disposition of the body;

(2)   make all necessary arrangements at any hospital, psychiatric hospital or psychiatric treatment facility, hospice, nursing home or similar institution; to employ or discharge health care personnel to include physicians, psychiatrists, psychologists, dentists, nurses, therapists or any other person who is licensed, certified or otherwise authorized or permitted by the laws of this state to administer health care as the agent shall deem necessary for my physical, mental and emotional well-being; and

(3)   request, receive and review any information, verbal or written, regarding my personal affairs or physical or mental health including medical and hospital records and to execute any releases of other documents that may be required in order to obtain such information.

In exercising the grant of authority set forth above my agent for health care shall: _____
_____
_____
_____
_____

(Here may be inserted any special instructions or statement of the principal's desired to be followed by the agent in exercising the authority granted.)

LIMITATIONS OF AUTHORITY

(1)   The powers of the agent herein shall be limited to the extent set out in writing in this durable power of attorney for health care decisions, and shall not include the power to revoke or invalidate any previously existing declaration made in accordance with the natural death act.

(2)   The agent shall be prohibited from authorizing consent for the following items:

_____

_____

_____

_____

(3)   This durable power of attorney for health care decisions shall be subject to the additional following limitations:

_____

_____

_____

_____

EFFECTIVE TIME

This power of attorney for health care decisions shall become effective immediately and shall not be affected by my subsequent disability or incapacity or upon the occurrence of my disability or incapacity.

REVOCATION

Any durable power of attorney for health care decisions I have previously made is thereby revoked. (This durable power of attorney for health care decisions shall be revoked by an instrument in writing executed, witnessed or acknowledged in the same manner as required herein or set out in another manner of revocation, if desired.)

EXECUTION

Executed this _____ day of _____, 20___ at _____, Kansas.

_____

(Principal)

This document must be: (1) witnessed by two individuals of lawful age who are not the agent, not related to the principal by blood, marriage or adoption, not entitled to any portion of principal's estate and not financially responsible for principal's health care: OR (2) acknowledged by a notary public.

Witness: _____

Address: _____

(or)

STATE OF _____) **COUNTY OF** _____)

This instrument was acknowledged before me on

_____

(date)

by _____

(name of person)

_____

(signature of notary public)

(Seal, if any)

My appointment expires: _____ Copies

Kentucky State Forms

LIVING WILL DIRECTIVE

My wishes regarding life-prolonging treatment and artificially provided nutrition and hydration to be provided to me if I no longer have decisional capacity, have a terminal condition, or become permanently unconscious have been indicated by checking and initialing the appropriate lines below. By checking and initialing the appropriate lines, I specifically:

[ ] _____   Designate _____ as my health care surrogate(s) to make health care decisions for me in accordance with this directive when I no longer have decisional capacity. If _____ refuses or is not able to act for me, I designate _____ as my health care surrogate(s).

Any prior designation is revoked.

If I do not designate a surrogate, the following are my directions to my attending physician. If I have designated a surrogate, my surrogate shall comply with my wishes as indicated below:

[ ] _____   Direct that treatment be withheld or withdrawn, and that I be permitted to die naturally with only the administration of medication or the performance of any medical treatment deemed necessary to alleviate pain.

[ ] _____   DO NOT authorize that life-prolonging treatment be withheld or withdrawn.

[ ] _____   Authorize the withholding or withdrawal of artificially provided food, water, or other artificially provided nourishment or fluids.

[ ] _____   DO NOT authorize the withholding or withdrawal of artificially provided food, water, or other artificially provided nourishment or fluids.

[ ] _____   Authorize my surrogate, designated above, to withhold or withdraw artificially provided nourishment or fluids, or other treatment if the surrogate determines that withholding or withdrawing is in my best interest; but I do not mandate that withholding or withdrawing.

[ ] _____   Authorize the giving of all or any part of my body upon death for any purpose

specified in KRS 311.185.

[ ] _____   DO NOT authorize the giving of all or any part of my body upon death.

In the absence of my ability to give directions regarding the use of life-prolonging treatment and artificially provided nutrition and hydration, it is my intention that this directive shall be honored by my attending physician, my family, and any surrogate designated pursuant to this directive as the final expression of my legal right to refuse medical or surgical treatment and I accept the consequences of the refusal.

If I have been diagnosed as pregnant and that diagnosis is known to my attending physician, this directive shall have no force or effect during the course of my pregnancy.

I understand the full import of this directive and I am emotionally and mentally competent to make this directive.

Signed this _____ day of _____, 20___.

_____

Signature and address of the grantor

In our joint presence, the grantor, who is of sound mind and eighteen (18) years of age, or older, voluntarily dated and signed this writing or directed it to be dated and signed for the grantor.

_____

Signature and address of witness.

_____

Signature and address of witness.

OR

STATE OF KENTUCKY)

)

_____ **County**)

Before me, the undersigned authority, came the grantor who is of sound mind and eighteen (18) years of age, or older, and acknowledged that he voluntarily dated and signed this writing or directed it to be signed and dated as above.

Done this _____day of _____, 20___.

Signature of Notary Public or other officer.

Date commission expires:.............

Louisiana State Forms

DECLARATION

Declaration made this _____ day of _____, _____ (month, year).

I, _____, being of sound mind, willfully and voluntarily make known my desire that my dying shall not be artificially prolonged under the circumstances set forth below and do hereby declare:

If at any time I should have an incurable injury, disease or illness, or be in a continual profound comatose state with no reasonable chance of recovery, certified to be a terminal and irreversible condition by two physicians who have personally examined me, one of whom shall be my attending physician, and the physicians have determined that my death will occur whether or not life-sustaining procedures are utilized and where the application of life-sustaining procedure would serve only to prolong artificially the dying process, I direct (initial one only):

_____ That all life-sustaining procedures, including nutrition and hydration, be withheld or withdrawn so that food and water will not be administered invasively.

_____ That life-sustaining procedures, except nutrition and hydration, be withheld or withdrawn so that food and water can be administered invasively.

I further direct that I be permitted to die naturally with only the administration of medication or the performance of any medical procedure deemed necessary to provide me with comfort care.

In the absence of my ability to give directions regarding the use of such life-sustaining procedures, it is my intention that this declaration shall be honored by my family and physician(s) as the final expression of my legal right to refuse medical or surgical treatment and accept the consequences from such refusal.

I understand the full import of this declaration and I am emotionally and mentally competent to make this declaration.

Signed _____

City, Parish, and State of Residence _____

The declarant has been personally known to me and I believe him or her to be of sound mind.

Witness_____

Witness_____

Maine State Forms

ADVANCE HEALTH-CARE DIRECTIVE

Explanation

You have the right to give instructions about your own health care. You also have the right to name someone else to make health-care decisions for you. This form lets you do either or both of these things. It also lets you express your wishes regarding donation of organs and the designation of your primary physician. If you use this form, you may complete or modify all or any part of it. You are free to use a different form.

Part 1 of this form is a power of attorney for health care. Part 1 lets you name another individual as agent to make health-care decisions for you if you become incapable of making your own decisions or if you want someone else to make those decisions for you now even though you are still capable. You may also name an alternate agent to act for you if your first choice is not willing, able or reasonably available to make decisions for you. Unless related to you, your agent may not be an owner, operator or employee of a residential long-term health-care institution at which you are receiving care.

Unless the form you sign limits the authority of your agent, your agent may make all health-care decisions for you. This form has a place for you to limit the authority of your agent. You need not limit the authority of your agent if you wish to rely on your agent for all health-care decisions that may have to be made. If you choose not to limit the authority of your agent, your agent will have the right to:

(a)   Consent or refuse consent to any care, treatment, service or procedure to maintain, diagnose or otherwise affect a physical or mental condition;

(b)   Select or discharge health-care providers and institutions;

(c)   Approve or disapprove diagnostic tests, surgical procedures, programs of medication and orders not to resuscitate; and

(d)   Direct the provision, withholding or withdrawal of artificial nutrition and hydration and all other forms of health care, including life-sustaining treatment.

Part 2 of this form lets you give specific instructions about any aspect of your health care. Choices are provided for you to express your wishes regarding the provision, withholding or withdrawal of treatment to keep you alive, including the provision of artificial nutrition and hydration, as well as the provision of pain relief. Space is also provided for you to add to the choices you have made or for you to write out any additional wishes.

Part 3 of this form lets you express an intention to donate your bodily organs and tissues following your death.

Part 4 of this form lets you designate a physician to have primary responsibility for your health care.

After completing this form, sign and date the form at the end. You must have 2 other individuals sign as witnesses. Give a copy of the signed and completed form to your physician, to any other health-care providers you may have, to any health-care institution at which you are receiving care and to any health-care agents you have named. You should talk to the person you have named as agent to make sure that he or she understands your wishes and is willing to take the responsibility.

You have the right to revoke this advance health-care directive or replace this form at any time.

* * * * * * * * * * * * * * * * * *

LIVING WILL AND ADVANCE HEALTH CARE DIRECTIVE

PART 1 - POWER OF ATTORNEY FOR HEALTH CARE

(1)   **DESIGNATION OF AGENT**: I designate the following individual as my agent to make health-care decisions for me:

_____

(name of individual you choose as agent)

_____

(address) (city) (state) (zip code)

_____

(home phone) (work phone)

OPTIONAL: If I revoke my agent's authority or if my agent is not willing, able or reasonably available to make a health-care decision for me, I designate as my first alternate agent:

_____

(name of individual you choose as first alternate agent)

_____

(address) (city) (state) (zip code)

_____

(home phone) (work phone)

OPTIONAL: If I revoke the authority of my agent and first alternate agent or if neither is willing, able or reasonably available to make a health-care decision for me, I designate as my second alternate agent:

_____

(name of individual you choose as second alternate agent)

_____

(address) (city) (state) (zip code)

_____

(home phone) (work phone)

(2)   **AGENT'S AUTHORITY**: My agent is authorized to make all health-care decisions

for me, including decisions to provide, withhold or withdraw artificial nutrition and hydration and all other forms of health care to keep me alive, except as I state here:

_____

_____

_____

(Add additional sheets if needed.)

(3) **WHEN AGENT'S AUTHORITY BECOMES EFFECTIVE**: My agent's authority becomes effective when my primary physician determines that I am unable to make my own health-care decisions unless I mark the following box. If I mark this box [ ], my agent's authority to make health-care decisions for me takes effect immediately.

(4) **AGENT'S OBLIGATION**: My agent shall make health-care decisions for me in accordance with this power of attorney for health care, any instructions I give in Part 2 of this form and my other wishes to the extent known to my agent. To the extent my wishes are unknown, my agent shall make health-care decisions for me in accordance with what my agent determines to be in my best interest. In determining my best interest, my agent shall consider my personal values to the extent known to my agent.

(5) **NOMINATION OF GUARDIAN**: If a guardian of my person needs to be appointed for me by a court, I nominate the agent designated in this form. If that agent is not willing, able or reasonably available to act as guardian, I nominate the alternate agents whom I have named, in the order designated.

PART 2 - INSTRUCTIONS FOR HEALTH CARE

If you are satisfied to allow your agent to determine what is best for you in making end-of-life decisions, you need not fill out this part of the form. If you do fill out this part of the form, you may strike any wording you do not want.

(6) **END-OF-LIFE DECISIONS**: I direct that my health-care providers and others involved in my care provide, withhold or withdraw treatment in accordance with the choice I have marked below:

[ ]   (a)   <u>Choice Not To Prolong Life</u>

I do not want my life to be prolonged if (i) I have an incurable and irreversible condition that will result in my death within a relatively short time, (ii) I become unconscious and, to a reasonable degree of medical certainty, I will not regain consciousness, or (iii) the likely risks and burdens of treatment would outweigh the expected benefits, OR

[ ]   (b)   <u>Choice To Prolong Life</u>

I want my life to be prolonged as long as possible within the limits of generally accepted health-care standards.

(7)   **ARTIFICIAL NUTRITION AND HYDRATION**: Artificial nutrition and hydration must be provided, withheld or withdrawn in accordance with the choice I have made in paragraph (6) unless I mark the following box. If I mark this box [ ], artificial nutrition and hydration must be provided regardless of my condition and regardless of the choice I have made in paragraph (6).

(8)   **RELIEF FROM PAIN**: Except as I state in the following space, I direct that treatment for alleviation of pain or discomfort be provided at all times, even if it hastens my death:

_____
_____

(9)   **OTHER WISHES**: (If you do not agree with any of the optional choices above and wish to write your own, or if you wish to add to the instructions you have given above, you may do so here.) I direct that:

_____
_____
_____

(Add additional sheets if needed)

PART 3 - DONATION OF ORGANS AT DEATH

(OPTIONAL)

(10)   Upon my death (mark applicable box)

[ ]   (a) I give any needed organs, tissues or parts, OR

[ ]   (b) I give the following organs, tissues or parts only

_____

(c) My gift is for the following purposes (strike any of the following you do not want)

    (i)   Transplant

    (ii)   Therapy

    (iii)   Research

    (iv)   Education

PART 4 PRIMARY PHYSICIAN

(OPTIONAL)

(11)   I designate the following physician as my primary physician:

_____

(name of physician)

_____

(address) (city) (state) (zip code)

_____

(phone)

OPTIONAL: If the physician I have designated above is not willing, able or reasonably available to act as my primary physician, I designate the following physician as my primary physician:

_____

(name of physician)

_____

(address) (city) (state) (zip code)

_____

(phone)

(12)   **EFFECT OF COPY**: A copy of this form has the same effect as the original.

(13)   **SIGNATURES**: Sign and date the form here:

_____

_____
(date) (sign your name)

_____
(address) (print your name)

(city) (state)

SIGNATURES OF WITNESSES:

First witness   *Second witness*

_____   _____
(print name)   (print name)

_____   _____
(address)   (address)

_____   _____
(city) (state)   (city) (state)

_____   _____
(signature of witness)   (signature of witness)

_____   _____
(date)   (date)

Maryland State Forms

Maryland Advance Directive:

Planning for Future Health Care Decisions

By: _____

(Print Name)

Date of Birth: _____

(Month/Day/Year)

Using this advance directive form to do health care planning is completely optional. Other forms are also valid in Maryland. No matter what form you use, talk to your family and others close to you about your wishes.

This form has two parts to state your wishes, and a third part for needed signatures. Part I of this form lets you answer this question: If you cannot (or do not want to) make your own health care decisions, who do you want to make them for you? The person you pick is called your health care agent. Make sure you talk to your health care agent (and any back-up agents) about this important role. Part II lets you write your preferences about efforts to extend your life in three situations: terminal condition, persistent vegetative state, and end-stage condition. In addition to your health care planning decisions, you can choose to become an organ donor after your death by filling out the form for that too.

You can fill out Parts I and II of this form, or only Part I, or only Part II. Use the form to reflect your wishes, then sign in front of two witnesses (Part III). If your wishes change, make a new advance directive.

Make sure you give a copy of the completed form to your health care agent, your doctor, and others who might need it. Keep a copy at home in a place where someone can get it if needed. Review what you have written periodically.

PART I: SELECTION OF HEALTH CARE AGENT

A.   Selection of Primary Agent

Select the following individual as my agent to make health care decisions for me:

Name: _____

Address: _____

                _____

                _____

Telephone Numbers: _____
(home and cell)

B.   Selection of Back-up Agents

(Optional; form valid if left blank)

1.   If my primary agent cannot be contacted in time or for any reason is unavailable or unable or unwilling to act as my agent, then I select the following person to act in this capacity:

Name: _____

Address: _____

                _____

Telephone Numbers: _____
(home and cell)

2.   If my primary agent and my first back-up agent cannot be contacted in time or for any reason are unavailable or unable or unwilling to act as my agent, then I select the following person to act in this capacity:

Name: _____

Address: _____

                _____

Telephone Numbers: _____
(home and cell)

C.   Powers and Rights of Health Care Agent

I want my agent to have full power to make health care decisions for me, including the power to:

1. Consent or not consent to medical procedures and treatments which my doctors offer, including things that are intended to keep me alive, like ventilators and feeding tubes;

2. Decide who my doctor and other health care providers should be; and

3. Decide where I should be treated, including whether I should be in a hospital, nursing home, other medical care facility, or hospice program.

I also want my agent to:

1. Ride with me in an ambulance if ever I need to be rushed to the hospital; and

2. Be able to visit me if I am in a hospital or any other health care facility.

THIS ADVANCE DIRECTIVE DOES NOT MAKE MY AGENT RESPONSIBLE FOR ANY OF THE COSTS OF MY CARE.

This power is subject to the following conditions or limitations:

(Optional; form valid if left blank)

_____

_____

_____

D. <u>How My Agent Is To Decide Specific Issues</u>

I trust my agent's judgment. My agent should look first to see if there is anything in Part II of this advance directive that helps decide the issue. Then, my agent should think about the conversations we have had, my religious or other beliefs and values, my personality, and how I handled medical and other important issues in the past. If what I would decide is still unclear, then my agent is to make decisions for me that my agent believes are in my best interest. In doing so, my agent should consider the benefits, burdens, and risks of the choices presented by my doctors.

E. <u>People My Agent Should Consult</u>

(Optional; form valid if left blank)

In making important decisions on my behalf, I encourage my agent to consult with the following people. By filling this in, I do not intend to limit the number of people with whom my agent might want to consult or my agent's power to make these decisions.

Name(s)   Telephone Number(s)

_____

_____

_____

_____

_____

F.   In Case of Pregnancy

(Optional, for women of child-bearing years only; form valid if left blank)

If I am pregnant, my agent shall follow these specific instructions:

_____

_____

_____

_____

G.   Access to My Health Information - Federal Privacy Law (HIPAA) Authorization

1.   If, prior to the time the person selected as my agent has power to act under this document, my doctor wants to discuss with that person my capacity to make my own health care decisions, I authorize my doctor to disclose protected health information which relates to that issue.

2.   Once my agent has full power to act under this document, my agent may request, receive, and review any information, oral or written, regarding my physical or mental health, including, but not limited to, medical and hospital records and other protected health information, and consent to disclosure of this information.

3.   For all purposes related to this document, my agent is my personal representative under the Health Insurance Portability and Accountability Act (HIPAA). My agent may sign, as my personal representative, any release forms or other HIPAA-related materials.

H.   Effectiveness of This Part

(Read both of these statements carefully. Then, initial one only.)
My agent's power is in effect:

1.   Immediately after I sign this document, subject to my right to make any decision
         about my health care if I want and am able to. _____

         _____

((or))

2.   Whenever I am not able to make informed decisions about my health care,
         either because the doctor in charge of my care (attending physician) decides that
         I have lost this ability temporarily, or my attending physician and a consulting
         doctor agree that I have lost this ability permanently.

         _____

         If the only thing you want to do is select a health care agent, skip Part II. Go
         to Part III to sign and have the advance directive witnessed. If you also want to
         write your treatment preferences, use Part II. Also consider becoming an organ
         donor, using the separate form for that.

PART II: TREATMENT PREFERENCES ("LIVING WILL")

A.   Statement of Goals and Values

(Optional; form valid if left blank)

I want to say something about my goals and values, and especially what's most important
to me during the last part of my life:

_____
_____
_____
_____
_____

B.   Preference in Case of Terminal Condition

(If you want to state your preference, initial one only. If you do not want to state a preference here, cross through the whole section.)

1.   Keep me comfortable and allow natural death to occur. I do not want any medical interventions used to try to extend my life. I do not want to receive nutrition and fluids by tube or other medical means.

        _____

        ((or))

2.   Keep me comfortable and allow natural death to occur. I do not want medical interventions used to try to extend my life. If I am unable to take enough nourishment by mouth, however, I want to receive nutrition and fluids by tube or other medical means.

        _____

        ((or))

3.   Try to extend my life for as long as possible, using all available interventions that in reasonable medical judgment would prevent or delay my death. If I am unable to take enough nourishment by mouth, I want to receive nutrition and fluids by tube or other medical means.

        _____

        C.   Preference in Case of Persistent Vegetative State

(If you want to state your preference, initial one only. If you do not want to state a preference here, cross through the whole section.)

If my doctors certify that I am in a persistent vegetative state, that is, if I am not conscious and am not aware of myself or my environment or able to interact with others, and there is no reasonable expectation that I will ever regain consciousness:

1.   Keep me comfortable and allow natural death to occur. I do not want any medical interventions used to try to extend my life. I do not want to receive nutrition and fluids by tube or other medical means.

        _____

        ((or))

2.   Keep me comfortable and allow natural death to occur. I do not want medical interventions used to try to extend my life. If I am unable to take enough nourishment by mouth, however, I want to receive nutrition and fluids by tube

or other medical means.

_____

((or))

3.   Try to extend my life for as long as possible, using all available interventions that in reasonable medical judgment would prevent or delay my death. If I am unable to take enough nourishment by mouth, I want to receive nutrition and fluids by tube or other medical means.

_____

D.   <u>Preference in Case of End-Stage Condition</u>

(If you want to state your preference, initial one only. If you do not want to state a preference here, cross through the whole section.)

If my doctors certify that I am in an end-stage condition, that is, an incurable condition that will continue in its course until death and that has already resulted in loss of capacity and complete physical dependency:

1.   Keep me comfortable and allow natural death to occur. I do not want any medical interventions used to try to extend my life. I do not want to receive nutrition and fluids by tube or other medical means.

_____

((or))

2.   Keep me comfortable and allow natural death to occur. I do not want medical interventions used to try to extend my life. If I am unable to take enough nourishment by mouth, however, I want to receive nutrition and fluids by tube or other medical means.

_____

((or))

3.   Try to extend my life for as long as possible, using all available interventions that in reasonable medical judgment would prevent or delay my death. If I am unable to take enough nourishment by mouth, I want to receive nutrition and fluids by tube or other medical means.

_____

E.   Pain Relief

No matter what my condition, give me the medicine or other treatment I need to relieve pain.

_____

F.   In Case of Pregnancy

(Optional, for women of child-bearing years only; form valid if left blank)

If I am pregnant, my decision concerning life-sustaining procedures shall be modified as follows:

_____ _____

_____ _____

_____ _____

_____ _____

G.   Effect of Stated Preferences

(Read both of these statements carefully. Then, initial one only.)

1.   I realize I cannot foresee everything that might happen after I can no longer decide for myself. My stated preferences are meant to guide whoever is making decisions on my behalf and my health care providers, but I authorize them to be flexible in applying these statements if they feel that doing so would be in my best interest.

_____

((or))

2.   I realize I cannot foresee everything that might happen after I can no longer decide for myself. Still, I want whoever is making decisions on my behalf and my health care providers to follow my stated preferences exactly as written, even if they think that some alternative is better.

_____

PART III: SIGNATURE AND WITNESSES

By signing below as the Declarant, I indicate that I am emotionally and mentally competent to make this advance directive and that I understand its purpose and effect. I also understand that this document replaces any similar advance directive I may have completed before this date.

_____   _____
(Signature of Declarant)   (Date)

The declarant signed or acknowledged signing this document in my presence and,

based upon personal observation, appears to be emotionally and mentally competent to make this advance directive.

_____   _____
(Signature of Witness)   (Date)

_____
Telephone Number(s)

_____   _____
(Signature of Witness)   (Date)

_____
Telephone Number(s)

(Note: Anyone selected as a health care agent in Part I may not be a witness. Also, at least one of the witnesses must be someone who will not knowingly inherit anything from the declarant or otherwise knowingly gain a financial benefit from the declarant's death. Maryland law does not require this document to be notarized.)

AFTER MY DEATH
(This form is optional. Fill out only what reflects your wishes.)

By: _____   (Print Name)
Date of Birth:_____   (Month/Day/Year)

PART I: ORGAN DONATION

(Initial the ones that you want.)
Upon my death I wish to donate:
Any needed organs, tissues, or eyes.   _____

Only the following organs, tissues, or eyes: _____

_____

_____

_____

I authorize the use of my organs, tissues, or eyes:

For transplantation   _____

For therapy   _____

For research   _____

For medical education   _____

For any purpose authorized by law   _____

I understand that no vital organ, tissue, or eye may be removed for transplantation until after I have been pronounced dead under legal standards. This document is not intended to change anything about my health care while I am still alive. After death, I authorize any appropriate support measures to maintain the viability for transplantation of my organs, tissues, and eyes until organ, tissue, and eye recovery has been completed. I understand that my estate will not be charged for any costs related to this donation.

PART II: DONATION OF BODY

After any organ donation indicated in Part I, I wish my body to be donated for use in a medical study program. _____

PART III: DISPOSITION OF BODY AND FUNERAL ARRANGEMENTS

I want the following person to make decisions about the disposition of my body and my funeral arrangements:

(Either initial the first or fill in the second.)

The health care agent who I named in my advance directive. _____

((or))

This person:

Name: _____

Address: _____

_____

_____

Telephone Numbers: _____
(home and cell)

If I have written my wishes below, they should be followed. If not, the person I have named should decide based on conversations we have had, my religious or other beliefs and values, my personality, and how I reacted to other peoples' funeral arrangements. My wishes about the disposition of my body and my funeral arrangements are:

_____

_____

_____

PART IV: SIGNATURE AND WITNESSES

By signing below, I indicate that I am emotionally and mentally competent to make this donation and that I understand the purpose and effect of this document.

_____   _____
(Signature of Donor)   (Date)

The Donor signed or acknowledged signing this donation document in my presence and, based upon personal observation, appears to be emotionally and mentally competent to make this donation.

_____   _____
(Signature of Witness)   (Date)

_____
Telephone Number(s)

_____   _____
(Signature of Witness)   (Date)

_____
Telephone Number(s)

Minnesota State Forms

HEALTH CARE LIVING WILL

Notice:

This is an important legal document. Before signing this document, you should know these important facts:

(a)   This document gives your health care providers or your designated proxy the power and guidance to make health care decisions according to your wishes when you are in a terminal condition and cannot do so. This document may include what kind of treatment you want or do not want and under what circumstances you want these decisions to be made. You may state where you want or do not want to receive any treatment.

(b)   If you name a proxy in this document and that person agrees to serve as your proxy, that person has a duty to act consistently with your wishes. If the proxy does not know your wishes, the proxy has the duty to act in your best interests. If you do not name a proxy, your health care providers have a duty to act consistently with your instructions or tell you that they are unwilling to do so.

(c)   This document will remain valid and in effect until and unless you amend or revoke it. Review this document periodically to make sure it continues to reflect your preferences. You may amend or revoke the living will at any time by notifying your health care providers.

(d)   Your named proxy has the same right as you have to examine your medical records and to consent to their disclosure for purposes related to your health care or insurance unless you limit this right in this document.

(e)   If there is anything in this document that you do not understand, you should ask for professional help to have it explained to you.

TO MY FAMILY, DOCTORS, AND ALL THOSE CONCERNED WITH MY CARE:

I, _____ born on _____ (birthdate), being an adult of sound mind, willfully and voluntarily make this statement as a directive to be followed if I am in a terminal condition and become unable to participate in decisions regarding my health care. I understand that my health care providers are legally bound to act consistently with my wishes, within the limits of reasonable medical practice and other applicable law. I also understand that I have the right to make medical and health care decisions for myself as long as I am able to do so and to revoke this living will at any time.

(1)   The following are my feelings and wishes regarding my health care (you may state the circumstances under which this living will applies):

_____

_____

_____

_____

(2)   I particularly want to have all appropriate health care that will help in the following ways (you may give instructions for care you do want):

_____

_____

_____

_____

(3)   I particularly do not want the following (you may list specific treatment you do not want in certain circumstances):

_____

_____

_____

_____

(4)   I particularly want to have the following kinds of life-sustaining treatment if I am diagnosed to have a terminal condition (you may list the specific types of life-sustaining treatment that you do want if you have a terminal condition):

_____

_____

_____

_____

(5)   I particularly do not want the following kinds of life-sustaining treatment if I am diagnosed to have a terminal condition (you may list the specific types of life-sustaining treatment that you do not want if you have a terminal condition):

_____

_____

_____

_____

(6)   I recognize that if I reject artificially administered sustenance, then I
        may die of dehydration or malnutrition rather than from my illness or injury. The
        following are my feelings and wishes regarding artificially administered sustenance
        should I have a terminal condition (you may indicate whether you wish to receive food
        and fluids given to you in some other way than by mouth if you have a terminal
        condition):

_____

_____

_____

_____

(7)   Thoughts I feel are relevant to my instructions. (You may, but need not, give your
        religious beliefs, philosophy, or other personal values that you feel are important. You
        may also state preferences concerning the location of your care.)

_____

_____

_____

_____

(8)   Proxy Designation. (If you wish, you may name someone to see that your wishes
        are carried out, but you do not have to do this. You may also name a proxy without
        including specific instructions regarding your care. If you name a proxy, you should
        discuss your wishes with that person.)

If I become unable to communicate my instructions, I designate the following person(s) to act
on my behalf consistently with my instructions, if any, as stated in this document. Unless I write
instructions that limit my proxy's authority, my proxy has full power and authority to make health
care decisions for me. If a guardian is to be appointed for me, I nominate my proxy named in
this document to act as my guardian.

        Name: _____
        Address: _____
                   _____
                   _____
                   _____

Phone Number: _____

Relationship: (If any) _____

If the person I have named above refuses or is unable or unavailable to act on my behalf, or if I revoke that person's authority to act as my proxy, I authorize the following person to do so:

Name: _____

Address: _____

_____

_____

Phone Number: _____

Relationship: (If any) _____

I understand that I have the right to revoke the appointment of the persons named above to act on my behalf at any time by communicating that decision to the proxy or my health care provider.

(9) Organ Donation After Death. (If you wish, you may indicate whether you want to be an organ donor upon your death.) Initial the statement which expresses your wish:

_____ In the event of my death, I would like to donate my organs. I understand that to become an organ donor, I must be declared brain dead. My organ function may be maintained artificially on a breathing machine, (i.e., artificial ventilation), so that my organs can be removed.

Limitations or special wishes: (If any) _____

_____

_____

_____

I understand that, upon my death, my next of kin may be asked permission for donation. Therefore, it is in my best interests to inform my next of kin about my decision ahead of time and ask them to honor my request.

I (have) (have not) agreed in another document or on another form to donate some or all of my organs when I die.

_____ I do not wish to become an organ donor upon my death.

DATE: _____

SIGNED: _____

STATE OF: _____

COUNTY OF: _____

Subscribed, sworn to, and acknowledged before me by _____ on this _____ day of

_____, 20

NOTARY PUBLIC

OR

(Sign and date here in the presence of two adult witnesses, neither of whom is entitled to any part of your estate under a will or by operation of law, and neither of whom is your proxy.)

I certify that the declarant voluntarily signed this living will in my presence and that the declarant is personally known to me. I am not named as a proxy by the living will, and to the best of my knowledge, I am not entitled to any part of the estate of the declarant under a will or by operation of law.

Witness: _____

Address: _____

_____

_____

_____

Witness: _____

Address: _____

_____

_____

_____

Mississippi State Forms

ADVANCE HEALTH CARE DIRECTIVE

Explanation

You have the right to give instructions about your own health care. You also have the right to name someone else to make health care decisions for you. This form lets you do either or both of these things. It also lets you express your wishes regarding the designation of your primary physician. If you use this form, you may complete or modify all or any part of it. You are free to use a different form.

Part 1 of this form is a power of attorney for health care. Part 1 lets you name another individual as agent to make health care decisions for you if you become incapable of making your own decisions or if you want someone else to make those decisions for you now even though you are still capable. You may name an alternate agent to act for you if your first choice is not willing, able or reasonably available to make decisions for you. Unless related to you, your agent may not be an owner, operator, or employee of a residential long-term health care institution at which you are receiving care.

Unless the form you sign limits the authority of your agent, your agent may make all health care decisions for you. This form has a place for you to limit the authority of your agent. You need not limit the authority of your agent if you wish to rely on your agent for all health care decisions that may have to be made. If you choose not to limit the authority of your agent, your agent will have the right to:

(a)   Consent or refuse consent to any care, treatment, service, or procedure to maintain, diagnose, or otherwise affect a physical or mental condition;

(b)   Select or discharge health care providers and institutions;

(c)   Approve or disapprove diagnostic tests, surgical procedures, programs of medication, and orders not to resuscitate; and

(d)   Direct the provision, withholding, or withdrawal of artificial nutrition and hydration and all other forms of health care.

Part 2 of this form lets you give specific instructions about any aspect of your health care. Choices are provided for you to express your wishes regarding the provision, withholding, or withdrawal of treatment to keep you alive, including the provision of artificial nutrition and hydration, as well as the provision of pain relief. Space is provided for you to add to the choices you have made or for you to write out any additional wishes.

Part 3 of this form lets you designate a physician to have primary responsibility for your health care.

Part 4 of this form lets you authorize the donation of your organs at your death, and declares that this decision will supersede any decision by a member of your family.

After completing this form, sign and date the form at the end and have the form witnessed by one of the two alternative methods listed below. Give a copy of the signed and completed form to your physician, to any other health care providers you may have, to any health care institution at which you are receiving care, and to any health care agents you have named. You should talk to the person you have named as agent to make sure that he or she understands your wishes and is willing to take the responsibility.

You have the right to revoke this advance health care directive or replace this form at any time.

ADVANCE DIRECTIVE

PART 1 - POWER OF ATTORNEY FOR HEALTH CARE

(1) **DESIGNATION OF AGENT**: I designate the following individual as my agent to make health care decisions for me:

_____

(name of individual you choose as agent)

_____

(address) (city) (state) (zip code)

_____

(home phone) (work phone)

OPTIONAL: If I revoke my agent's authority or if my agent is not willing, able, or reasonably available to make a health care decision for me, I designate as my first alternate agent:

_____

(name of individual you choose as first alternate agent)

_____

(address) (city) (state) (zip code)

_____

(home phone) (work phone)

OPTIONAL: If I revoke the authority of my agent and first alternate agent or if neither is willing, able, or reasonably available to make a health care decision for me, I designate as my second alternate agent:

_____

(name of individual you choose as second alternate agent)

_____

(address) (city) (state) (zip code)

_____

(home phone) (work phone)

(2) **AGENT'S AUTHORITY**: My agent is authorized to make all health care decisions

for me, including decisions to provide, withhold, or withdraw artificial nutrition and hydration, and all other forms of health care to keep me alive, except as I state here:

_____

_____

_____

(Add additional sheets if needed.)

(3)   **WHEN AGENT'S AUTHORITY BECOMES EFFECTIVE**: My agent's authority becomes effective when my primary physician determines that I am unable to make my own health care decisions unless I mark the following box. If I mark this box [ ], my agent's authority to make health care decisions for me takes effect immediately.

(4)   **AGENT'S OBLIGATION**: My agent shall make health care decisions for me in accordance with this power of attorney for health care, any instructions I give in Part 2 of this form, and my other wishes to the extent known to my agent. To the extent my wishes are unknown, my agent shall make health care decisions for me in accordance with what my agent determines to be in my best interest. In determining my best interest, my agent shall consider my personal values to the extent known to my agent.

(5)   **NOMINATION OF GUARDIAN**: If a guardian of my person needs to be appointed for me by a court, I nominate the agent designated in this form. If that agent is not willing, able, or reasonably available to act as guardian, I nominate the alternate agents whom I have named, in the order designated.

PART 2 - INSTRUCTIONS FOR HEALTH CARE

If you are satisfied to allow your agent to determine what is best for you in making end-of-life decisions, you need not fill out this part of the form. If you do fill out this part of the form, you may strike any wording you do not want.

(6)   **END-OF-LIFE DECISIONS**: I direct that my health care providers and others involved in my care provide, withhold or withdraw treatment in accordance with the choice I have marked below:

[ ]   (a) <u>Choice Not To Prolong Life</u>

I do not want my life to be prolonged if (i) I have an incurable and irreversible condition that will result in my death within a relatively short time, (ii) I become unconscious and, to a reasonable degree of medical certainty, I will not regain consciousness, or (iii) the likely risks and burdens of treatment would outweigh the expected benefits, or

[ ]   (b) <u>Choice To Prolong Life</u>

I want my life to be prolonged as long as possible within the limits of generally accepted health care standards.

(7)   **ARTIFICIAL NUTRITION AND HYDRATION**: Artificial nutrition and hydration must be provided, withheld or withdrawn in accordance with the choice I have made in paragraph (6) unless I mark the following box. If I mark this box [ ], artificial nutrition and hydration must be provided regardless of my condition and regardless of the choice I have made in paragraph (6).

(8)   **RELIEF FROM PAIN**: Except as I state in the following space, I direct that treatment for alleviation of pain or discomfort be provided at all times, even if it hastens my death:

_____

_____

_____

(9)   **OTHER WISHES**: (If you do not agree with any of the optional choices above and wish to write your own, or if you wish to add to the instructions you have given above, you may do so here.) I direct that:

_____

_____

_____

(Add additional sheets if needed.)

PART 3 - PRIMARY PHYSICIAN

(OPTIONAL)

(10)   I designate the following physician as my primary physician:

_____

(name of physician)

_____

(address) (city) (state) (zip code)

_____

(phone)

OPTIONAL: If the physician I have designated above is not willing, able, or reasonably available to act as my primary physician, I designate the following physician as my primary physician:

_____

(name of physician)

_____

(address) (city) (state) (zip code)

_____

(phone)

(11)   **EFFECT OF COPY**: A copy of this form has the same effect as the original.

(12)   **SIGNATURES**: Sign and date the form here:

_____   _____

(date)   (sign your name)

_____   _____

(address)   (print your name)

_____

(city) (state)

PART 4 - CERTIFICATE OF AUTHORIZATION FOR ORGAN DONATION

(OPTIONAL)

I, the undersigned, this _____ day of _____, 20___, desire that my _____ organ(s) be made available after my demise for:

(a)   Any licensed hospital, surgeon or physician, for medical education, research, advancement of medical science, therapy or transplantation to individuals;

(b)   Any accredited medical school, college or university engaged in medical education or research, for therapy, educational research or medical science purposes or any accredited school of mortuary science;

(c) Any person operating a bank or storage facility for blood, arteries, eyes, pituitaries, or other human parts, for use in medical education, research, therapy or transplantation to individuals;

(d) The donee specified below, for therapy or transplantation needed by him or her, do donate my _____ for that purpose to _____ (name) at _____ (address).

I authorize a licensed physician or surgeon to remove and preserve for use my _____ for that purpose.

I specifically provide that this declaration shall supersede and take precedence over any decision by my family to the contrary.

Witnessed this _____ day of _____, 20_____.

_____ (donor)

_____

_____

_____

(address)

_____

(telephone)

_____

(witness)

_____

(witness)

(13) **WITNESSES**: This power of attorney will not be valid for making health care decisions unless it is either (a) signed by two (2) qualified adult witnesses who are personally known to you and who are present when you sign or acknowledge your signature; or (b) acknowledged before a notary public in the state.

ALTERNATIVE NO. 1

Witness

I declare under penalty of perjury pursuant to Section 97-9-61, Mississippi Code of 1972, that the principal is personally known to me, that the principal signed or acknowledged this power of attorney in my presence, that the principal appears to be of sound mind and under no duress, fraud or undue influence, that I am not the person appointed as agent by this document, and that I am not a health care provider, nor an employee of a health care provider or facility. I am not related to the principal by blood, marriage or adoption, and to the best of my knowledge, I am not entitled to any part of the estate of the principal upon the death of the principal under a will now existing or by operation of law.

_____   _____
(date)   (signature of witness)

_____   _____
(address)   (printed name of witness)

_____
(city) (state)

Witness

I declare under penalty of perjury pursuant to Section 97-9-61, Mississippi Code of 1972, that the principal is personally known to me, that the principal signed or acknowledged this power of attorney in my presence, that the principal appears to be of sound mind and under no duress, fraud or undue influence, that I am not the person appointed as agent by this document, and that I am not a health care provider, nor an employee of a health care provider or facility.

_____   _____
(date)   (signature of witness)

_____   _____
(address)   (printed name of witness)

_____
(city) (state)

ALTERNATIVE NO. 2

State of _____   County of _____

On this _____ day of _____, in the year _____, before me, _____ (insert name
of notary public) appeared _____, personally known to me (or proved to me on the basis
of satisfactory evidence) to be the person whose name is subscribed to this instrument, and
acknowledged that he or she executed it. I declare under the penalty of perjury that the person
whose name is subscribed to this instrument appears to be of sound mind and under no duress,
fraud or undue influence.

Notary Seal

_____

(Signature of Notary Public)

Missouri State Forms

DECLARATION

I have the primary right to make my own decisions concerning treatment that might unduly prolong the dying process. By this declaration I express to my physician, family and friends my intent. If I should have a terminal condition it is my desire that my dying not be prolonged by administration of death-prolonging procedures. If my condition is terminal and I am unable to participate in decisions regarding my medical treatment, I direct my attending physician to withhold or withdraw medical procedures that merely prolong the dying process and are not necessary to my comfort or to alleviate pain. It is not my intent to authorize affirmative or deliberate acts or omissions to shorten my life rather only to permit the natural process of dying.

Signed this _____ day of _____, 20_____.

_____   _____
Printed Name of Declarant   Signature of Declarant
Address: _____

                    _____

WITNESSETH

The declarant is known to me, is eighteen years of age or older, of sound mind and voluntarily signed this document in my presence.

Witness #1:   **Witness #2:**

_____   _____
Signature   Signature

_____   _____
Printed Name   Printed Name

_____   _____
Address, Line 1   Address, Line

_____   _____
Address, Line 2   Address, Line 2

_____   _____
Address, Line 3   Address, Line

_____   _____
Address, Line 4   Address, Line 4

Montana State Forms

Note: A declaration directing a physician or advanced practice registered nurse to withhold or withdraw life-sustaining treatment may but need not be in the following form:

DECLARATION

If I should have an incurable or irreversible condition that, without the administration of life-sustaining treatment, will, in the opinion of my attending physician or attending advanced practice registered nurse, cause my death within a relatively short time and I am no longer able to make decisions regarding my medical treatment, I direct my attending physician or attending advanced practice registered nurse, pursuant to the Montana Rights of the Terminally Ill Act, to withhold or withdraw treatment that only prolongs the process of dying and is not necessary to my comfort or to alleviate pain.

Signed this _____ day of _____, 20___.
Signature _____
City, County, and State of Residence _____

The declarant voluntarily signed this document in my presence.

Witness: _____
Address: _____
Witness: _____
Address: _____

Note: A declaration that designates another individual to make decisions governing the withholding or withdrawal of life-sustaining treatment may but need not be in the following form:

DECLARATION

If I should have an incurable and irreversible condition that, without the administration of life-sustaining treatment, will, in the opinion of my attending physician or attending advanced practice registered nurse, cause my death within a relatively short time and I am no longer able to make decisions regarding my medical treatment, I appoint _____ or, if that person is not reasonably available or is unwilling to serve, _____, to make decisions on my behalf regarding withholding or withdrawal of treatment that only prolongs the process of dying and is not necessary for my comfort or to alleviate pain, pursuant to the Montana Rights of the Terminally Ill Act.

If the individual I have appointed is not reasonably available or is unwilling to serve, I direct my attending physician or attending advanced practice registered nurse, pursuant to the Montana Rights of the Terminally Ill Act, to withhold or withdraw treatment that only prolongs the process of dying and is not necessary for my comfort or to alleviate pain.

Signed this _____ day of _____, 20___.

Signature _____
City, County, and State of Residence _____

The declarant voluntarily signed this document in my presence.

Witness: _____
Address: _____
Witness: _____
Address: _____

Nebraska State Forms

NEBRASKA LIVING WILL DECLARATION

If I should lapse into a persistent vegetative state or have an incurable and irreversible condition that, without the administration of life-sustaining treatment, will, in the opinion of my attending physician, cause my death within a relatively short time and I am no longer able to make decisions regarding my medical treatment, I direct my attending physician, pursuant to the Rights of the Terminally Ill Act, to withhold or withdraw life-sustaining treatment that is not necessary for my comfort or to alleviate pain.

Other directions:

_____

_____

_____

_____

Signed this _____ day of _____, 20___.

Signature _____

City, County, and State of Residence _____

The declarant voluntarily signed this document in my presence.

Witness: _____

Address: _____

Witness: _____

Address: _____

Or

The declarant voluntarily signed this writing in my presence.

_____

Notary Public

Nevada State Forms

(Form of declaration directing physician to withhold or withdraw life-sustaining treatment.)

DECLARATION

If I should have an incurable and irreversible condition that, without the administration of life-sustaining treatment, will, in the opinion of my attending physician, cause my death within a relatively short time, and I am no longer able to make decisions regarding my medical treatment, I direct my attending physician, pursuant to NRS 449.535 to 449.690, inclusive, to withhold or withdraw treatment that only prolongs the process of dying and is not necessary for my comfort or to alleviate pain.

If you wish to include this statement in this declaration, you must INITIAL the statement in the box provided: [_____]

Withholding or withdrawal of artificial nutrition and hydration may result in death by starvation or dehydration. Initial this box if you want to receive or continue receiving artificial nutrition and hydration by way of the gastrointestinal tract after all other treatment is withheld pursuant to this declaration.   [_____]

Signed this _____ day of _____, 20___.
Signature: _____
Address: _____

The declarant voluntarily signed this writing in my presence.

Witness: _____
Address: _____
Witness: _____
Address: _____

(Form of declaration designating another person to decide to withhold or withdraw life-sustaining treatment.)

DECLARATION

If I should have an incurable and irreversible condition that, without the administration of life-sustaining treatment, will, in the opinion of my attending physician, cause my death within a relatively short time, and I am no longer able to make decisions regarding my medical treatment, I appoint _____ or, if he or she is not reasonably available or is unwilling to serve, _____, to make decisions on my behalf regarding withholding or withdrawal of treatment that only prolongs the process of dying and is not necessary for my comfort or to alleviate pain, pursuant to NRS 449.535 to 449.690, inclusive. (If the person or persons I have so appointed are not reasonably available or are unwilling to serve, I direct my attending physician, pursuant to those sections, to withhold or withdraw treatment that only prolongs the process of dying and is not necessary for my comfort or to alleviate pain.)

Strike language in parentheses if you do not desire it.

If you wish to include this statement in this declaration, you must INITIAL the statement in the box provided:

Withholding or withdrawal of artificial nutrition and hydration may result in death by starvation or dehydration. Initial this box if you want to receive or continue receiving artificial nutrition and hydration by way of the gastrointestinal tract after all other treatment is withheld pursuant to this declaration.   [_____]

Signed this _____ day of _____, 20___.
Signature: _____.
Address: _____

The declarant voluntarily signed this writing in my presence.

Witness: _____
Address: _____
Witness: _____
Address: _____

Name and address of each designee.

Witness: _____
Address: _____

New York State Forms

NEW YORK LIVING WILL

I, _____, being of sound mind, make this statement as a directive to be followed if I become permanently unable to participate in decisions regarding my Medical care. These instructions reflect my firm and settled commitment to decline medical treatment under the circumstances indicated below.

I direct my attending physician and other medical personnel to withhold or withdraw treatment that serves only to prolong the process of my dying, if I should be in an incurable or irreversible mental or physical condition with no reasonable expectation of recovery.

These instructions apply if I am: a) in a terminal condition; b) permanently unconscious; or c) if I am conscious but have irreversible brain damage and will never regain the ability to make decisions and express my wishes.

I direct that treatment be limited to measures to keep me comfortable and to relieve pain, including any pain that might occur by withholding or withdrawing treatment. While I understand that I am not legally required to be specific about future treatments, if I am in the condition(s) described above, I feel especially strong about the following forms of treatment.

[ ]   I do not want cardiac resuscitation.
[ ]   I do not want mechanical respiration.
[ ]   I do not want tube feeding.
[ ]   I do not want antibiotics.
[ ]   I do want maximum pain relief.
[ ]   Other instructions (insert personal instructions): _____

_____

_____

I HEREBY APPOINT

Name: _____

Address: _____

             _____

             _____

Phone Number: _____

as my health care agent to make all health care decisions for me in conformity with the guidelines I have expressed in this document. I direct my agent to make health care decisions in accordance with my wishes and instructions as stated above or as otherwise known to him or her. I also direct my agent to abide by any limitations on his or her authority as stated above or as otherwise known to him or her.

In the event my health care agent is unable, unwilling, or unavailable to serve as such, then I appoint as my substitute health care agent (with the same powers that I have heretofore enumerated).

Name: _____
Address: _____
_____
_____

Phone Number: _____

I understand that unless I revoke it, this living will and health care proxy will remain in effect indefinitely.

These directions express my legal right to refuse treatment, under the laws of New York. Unless I have revoked this instrument or otherwise clearly and explicitly indicated that I have changed my mind, it is my unequivocal intent that my instructions as set forth in this document be faithfully carried out.

Signature: _____
Address: _____
_____
_____

Date: _____

Statement By Witnesses

(Must Be 18 or Older)

I declare that the person who signed this document is personally known to me and appears to be of sound mind and acting of his or her own free will. He or she signed (or asked another to sign for him or her) this document in my presence.

Witness: _____

Address: _____

_____

_____

Witness: _____

Address: _____

_____

_____

New Hampshire State Forms

DECLARATION

Declaration made this _____ day of _____ (month, year). I, _____, being of sound mind, willfully and voluntarily make known my desire that my dying shall not be artificially prolonged under the circumstances set forth below, do hereby declare:

If at any time I should have an incurable injury, disease, or illness certified to be a terminal condition or a permanently unconscious condition by 2 physicians who have personally examined me, one of whom shall be my attending physician, and the physicians have determined that my death will occur whether or not life-sustaining procedures are utilized or that I will remain in a permanently unconscious condition and where the application of life-sustaining procedures would serve only to artificially prolong the dying process, I direct that such procedures be withheld or withdrawn, and that I be permitted to die naturally with only the administration of medication, sustenance, or the performance of any medical procedure deemed necessary to provide me with comfort care. I realize that situations could arise in which the only way to allow me to die would be to discontinue artificial nutrition and hydration. In carrying out any instruction I have given under this section, I authorize that artificial nutrition and hydration not be started or, if started, be discontinued. (yes) (no) (Circle your choice and initial beneath it. If you do not choose ""yes," artificial nutrition and hydration will be provided and will not be removed.)

In the absence of my ability to give directions regarding the use of such life-sustaining procedures, it is my intention that this declaration shall be honored by my family and physicians as the final expression of my right to refuse medical or surgical treatment and accept the consequences of such refusal.

I understand the full import of this declaration, and I am emotionally and mentally competent to make this declaration.

Signed _____
State of _____   _____ County
We, the following witnesses, being duly sworn each declare to the notary public or justice of the peace or other official signing below as follows:

1.   The declarant signed the instrument as a free and voluntary act for the purposes expressed, or expressly directed another to sign for him.

2.   Each witness signed at the request of the declarant, in his presence, and in the presence of the other witness.

3.   To the best of my knowledge, at the time of the signing the declarant was at least 18 years of age, and was of sane mind and under no constraint or undue influence.

_____ Witness

_____ Witness

The affidavit shall be made before a notary public or justice of the peace or other official authorized to administer oaths in the place of execution, who shall not also serve as a witness, and who shall complete and sign a certificate in content and form substantially as follows:

Sworn to and signed before me by _____, declarant _____ and _____, witnesses on _____.

_____

Signature

_____

Official Capacity

New Jersey State Forms

COMBINED ADVANCE DIRECTIVE FOR HEALTH CARE

(Combined Proxy and Instruction Directive)

I understand that as a competent adult I have the right to make decisions about my health care. There may come a time when I am unable, due to physical or mental incapacity, to make my own health care decisions. In these circumstances, those caring for me will need direction concerning my care and will turn to someone who knows my values and health care wishes. I understand that those responsible for my care will seek to make health care decisions in my best interests, based upon what they know of my wishes. In order to provide the guidance and authority needed to make decisions on my behalf:

I, _____ hereby declare and make known my instructions and wishes for my future health care. This advance directive for health care shall take effect in the event I become unable to make my own health care decisions, as determined by the physician who has primary responsibility for my care, and any necessary confirming determinations. I direct that this document become part of my permanent medical records.

In completing Part One of this directive, you will designate an individual you trust to act as your legally recognized health care representative to make health care decisions for you in the event you are unable to make decisions for yourself.

In completing Part Two of this directive, you will provide instructions concerning your health care preferences and wishes to your health care representative and others who will be entrusted with responsibility for your care, such as your physician, family members and friends.

PART ONE: DESIGNATION OF A HEALTH CARE REPRESENTATIVE

A)   **CHOOSING A HEALTH CARE REPRESENTATIVE:**

I hereby designate:
Name: _____
Address: _____
City: _____
State: _____
Telephone: _____

as my health care representative to make any and all health decisions for me, including decisions to accept or to refuse any treatment, service or procedure used to diagnose or treat my physical or mental condition, and decisions to provide, withhold or withdraw life-sustaining measures. I direct my representative to make decisions on my behalf in accordance with my wishes as stated in this document, or as otherwise known to him or her. In the event my wishes are not clear, or a situation arises I did not anticipate, my health care representative is authorized to make decisions in my best interests, based upon what is known of my wishes.

I have discussed the terms of this designation with my health care representative and he or she has willingly agreed to accept the responsibility for acting on my behalf.

B) **ALTERNATE REPRESENTATIVES**: If the person I have designated above is unable, unwilling or unavailable to act as my health care representative, I hereby designate the following person(s) to act as my health care representative, in order of priority stated:

Name #1: _____
Address: _____
City: _____
State: _____

Telephone: _____

Name #2: _____
Address: _____
City: _____
State: _____
Telephone: _____

PART TWO: INSTRUCTION DIRECTIVE

In Part Two, you are asked to provide instructions concerning your future health care. This will require making important and perhaps difficult choices. Before completing your directive, you should discuss these matters with your health care representative, doctor, family members or others who may become responsible for your care.

In Sections C and D, you may state the circumstances in which various forms of medical treatment, including life-sustaining measures, should be provided, withheld or discontinued. If the options and choices below do not fully express your wishes, you should use Section E, and/

or attach a statement to this document which would provide those responsible for your care with additional information you think would help them in making decisions about your medical treatment. Please familiarize yourself with all sections of Part Two before completing your directive.

C)   **GENERAL INSTRUCTIONS**: To inform those responsible for my care of my specific wishes, I make the following statement of personal views regarding my health care:

Initial ONE of the following two statements with which you agree:

1. _____ I direct that all medically appropriate measures be provided to sustain my life, regardless of my physical or mental condition

2. _____ There are circumstances in which I would not want my life to be prolonged by further medical treatment. In these circumstances, life-sustaining measures should not be initiated and if they have been, they should be discontinued. I recognize that this is likely to hasten my death. In the following, I specify the circumstances in which I would choose to forego life-sustaining measures.

If you have initialed statement 2, on the following page please initial each of the statements (a, b, c) with which you agree:

a.   _____ I realize that there may come a time when I am diagnosed as having an incurable and irreversible illness, disease, or condition. If this occurs, and my attending physician and at least one additional physician who has personally examined me determine that my condition is terminal, I direct that life-sustaining measures which would serve only to artificially prolong my dying be withheld or discontinued. I also direct that I be given all medically appropriate care necessary to make me comfortable and to relieve pain.

In the space provided, write in the bracketed phrase with which you agree:

To me, terminal condition means that my physicians have determined that:

_____

_____

_____

[I will die within a few days]   [I will die within a few weeks]

[I have a life expectancy of approximately _____ or less (enter 6 months, or 1 year)]

b.   _____ If there should come a time when I become permanently unconscious, and it is determined by my attending physician and at least one additional physician with appropriate expertise who has personally examined me, that I have totally and irreversibly lost consciousness and my capacity for interaction with other people and my surroundings, I direct that life-sustaining measures be withheld or discontinued. I understand that I will not experience pain or discomfort in this condition, and I direct that I be given all medically appropriate care necessary to provide for my personal hygiene and dignity.

c.   _____ I realize that there may come a time when I am diagnosed as having an incurable and irreversible illness, disease, or condition which may not be terminal. My condition may cause me to experience severe and progressive physical or mental deterioration and/or a permanent loss of capacities and faculties I value highly. If, in the course of my medical care, the burdens of continued life with treatment become greater than the benefits I experience, I direct that life-sustaining measures be withheld or discontinued. I also direct that I be given all medically appropriate care necessary to make me comfortable and to relieve pain.

(Paragraph c. covers a wide range of possible situations in which you may have experienced partial or complete loss of certain mental and physical capacities you value highly. If you wish, in the space provided below you may specify in more detail the conditions in which you would choose to forego life-sustaining measures. You might include a description of the faculties or capacities, which, if irretrievably lost would lead you to accept death rather than continue living. You may want to express any special concerns you have about particular medical conditions or treatments, or any other considerations which would provide further guidance to those who may become responsible for your care. If necessary, you may attach a separate statement to this document or use Section E to provide additional instructions.)

Examples of conditions which I find unacceptable are:

_____

_____

_____

_____

D)   **SPECIFIC INSTRUCTIONS**: Artificially Provided Fluids and Nutrition; Cardiopulmonary Resuscitation (CPR). On page 3 you provided general instructions regarding life-sustaining measures. Here you are asked to give specific instructions regarding two types of life-sustaining measures-artificially provided fluids and nutrition and cardiopulmonary resuscitation.

In the space provided, write in the bracketed phrase with which you agree:

1.   In the circumstances I initialed on page 3, I also direct that artificially provided fluids and nutrition, such as by feeding tube or intravenous infusion,

_____

_____

_____   [be

withheld or withdrawn and that I be allowed to die]
        [be provided to the extent medically appropriate]

2.   In the circumstances I initialed on page 3, if I should suffer a cardiac arrest, I also direct that cardiopulmonary resuscitation (CPR)

_____

_____

_____

_____

[not be provided and that I be allowed to die]
[be provided to preserve my life, unless medically inappropriate or futile]

3.   If neither of the above statements adequately expresses your wishes concerning artificially provided fluids and nutrition or CPR, please explain your wishes below.

_____

_____

_____

_____

E) **ADDITIONAL INSTRUCTIONS**: (You should provide any additional information about your health care preferences which is important to you and which may help those concerned with your care to implement your wishes. You may wish to direct your health care representative, family members, or your health care providers to consult with others, or you may wish to direct that your care be provided by a particular physician, hospital, nursing home, or at home. If you are or believe you may become pregnant, you may wish to state specific instructions. If you need more space than is provided here you may attach an additional statement to this directive.)

_____

_____

_____

_____

F) **BRAIN DEATH**: (The State of New Jersey recognizes the irreversible cessation of all functions of the entire brain, including the brain stem (also known as whole brain death), as a legal standard for the declaration of death. However, individuals who cannot accept this standard because of their personal religious beliefs may request that it not be applied in determining their death.)

Initial the following statement only if it applies to you:

_____ To declare my death on the basis of the whole brain death standard would violate my personal religious beliefs. I therefore wish my death to be declared solely on the basis of the traditional criteria of irreversible cessation of cardiopulmonary (heartbeat and breathing) function.

G) **AFTER DEATH - ANATOMICAL GIFTS**: (It is now possible to transplant human organs and tissue in order to save and improve the lives of others. Organs, tissues and other body parts are also used for therapy, medical research and education. This section allows you to indicate your desire to make an anatomical gift and if so, to provide instructions for any limitations or special uses.)

Initial the statements which express your wishes:

1.   _____ I wish to make the following anatomical gift to take effect upon my death:

     A.   _____   any needed organs or body parts

B. _____ only the following organs or parts

_____

_____

for the purposes of transplantation, therapy, medical research or education, or

C. _____ my body for anatomical study, if needed.

D. _____ special limitations, if any:

_____

_____

_____

_____

If you wish to provide additional instructions, such as indicating your preference that your organs be given to a specific person or institution, or be used for a specific purpose, please do so in the space provided below.

_____

_____

_____

_____

2. _____ I do not wish to make an anatomical gift upon my death.

PART THREE: SIGNATURE AND WITNESSES

H) **COPIES**: The original or a copy of this document has been given to the following people (NOTE: If you have chosen to designate a health care representative, it is important that you provide him or her with a copy of your directive.)

Name #1:	_____	Name #2:	_____
Address:	_____	Address:	_____
City:	_____	City:	_____

State: _____   State: _____
Telephone: _____   Telephone: _____

I) **SIGNATURE**: By writing this advance directive, I inform those who may become entrusted with my health care of my wishes and intend to ease the burdens of decision making which this responsibility may impose. I have discussed the terms of this designation with my health care representative and he or she has willingly agreed to accept the responsibility for acting on my behalf in accordance with this directive. I understand the purpose and effect of this document and sign it knowingly, voluntarily and after careful deliberation.

Signed this _____ day of _____, 20_____
Signature   _____
Address   _____
City   _____
State   _____

J) **WITNESSES**: I declare that the person who signed this document, or asked another to sign this document on his or her behalf, did so in my presence, that he or she is personally known to me and that he or she appears to be of sound mind and free of duress or undue influence. I am 18 years of age or older, and am not designated by this or any other document as the person's health care representative nor as an alternate health care representative.

1.   Witness   _____
    Address   _____
    City   _____
    State   _____
    Signature   _____
    Date   _____

2.   Witness   _____
    Address   _____
    City   _____
    State   _____
    Signature   _____
    Date   _____

New Mexico State Forms

OPTIONAL ADVANCE HEALTH-CARE DIRECTIVE

Explanation

You have the right to give instructions about your own health care. You also have the right to name someone else to make health-care decisions for you. This form lets you do either or both of these things. It also lets you express your wishes regarding the designation of your primary physician.

THIS FORM IS OPTIONAL. Each paragraph and word of this form is also optional. If you use this form, you may cross out, complete or modify all or any part of it. You are free to use a different form. If you use this form, be sure to sign it and date it.

PART 1 of this form is a power of attorney for health care. PART 1 lets you name another individual as agent to make health-care decisions for you if you become incapable of making your own decisions or if you want someone else to make those decisions for you now even though you are still capable. You may also name an alternate agent to act for you if your first choice is not willing, able or reasonably available to make decisions for you. Unless related to you, your agent may not be an owner, operator or employee of a health-care institution at which you are receiving care.

Unless the form you sign limits the authority of your agent, your agent may make all health-care decisions for you. This form has a place for you to limit the authority of your agent. You need not limit the authority of your agent if you wish to rely on your agent for all health-care decisions that may have to be made. If you choose not to limit the authority of your agent, your agent will have the right to:

(a)   consent or refuse consent to any care, treatment, service or procedure to maintain, diagnose or otherwise affect a physical or mental condition;

(b)   select or discharge health-care providers and institutions;

(c)   approve or disapprove diagnostic tests, surgical procedures, programs of medication and orders not to resuscitate; and

(d)   direct the provision, withholding or withdrawal of artificial nutrition and hydration and all other forms of health care.

PART 2 of this form lets you give specific instructions about any aspect of your health care. Choices are provided for you to express your wishes regarding life-sustaining treatment, including the provision of artificial nutrition and hydration, as well as the provision of pain relief. In addition, you may express your wishes regarding whether you want to make an anatomical gift of some or all of your organs and tissue. Space is also provided for you to add to the choices you have made or for you to write out any additional wishes.

PART 3 of this form lets you designate a physician to have primary responsibility for your health care.

After completing this form, sign and date the form at the end. It is recommended but not required that you request two other individuals to sign as witnesses. Give a copy of the signed and completed form to your physician, to any other health-care providers you may have, to any health-care institution at which you are receiving care and to any health-care agents you have named. You should talk to the person you have named as agent to make sure that he or she understands your wishes and is willing to take the responsibility.

You have the right to revoke this advance health-care directive or replace this form at any time.

* * * * * * * * * * * * * * * * * * *

PART 1 POWER OF ATTORNEY FOR HEALTH CARE

(1) **DESIGNATION OF AGENT**: I designate the following individual as my agent to make health-care decisions for me:

_____

(name of individual you choose as agent)

_____

(address)   (city)   (state)   (zip code)

_____

(home phone)   (work phone)

If I revoke my agent's authority or if my agent is not willing, able or reasonably available to make a health-care decision for me, I designate as my first alternate agent:

_____

(name of individual you choose as agent)

_____

(address)   (city)   (state)   (zip code)

_____

(home phone)   (work phone)

If I revoke the authority of my agent and first alternate agent or if neither is willing, able or reasonably available to make a health-care decision for me, I designate as my second alternate agent:

_____

(name of individual you choose as agent)

_____

(address)   (city)   (state)   (zip code)

_____

(home phone)   (work phone)

(2) **AGENT'S AUTHORITY**: My agent is authorized to obtain and review medical records, reports and information about me and to make all health-care decisions for me, including decisions to provide, withhold or withdraw artificial nutrition, hydration and all other forms of health care to keep me alive, except as I state here:

_____

_____

(Add additional sheets if needed.)

(3)   **WHEN AGENT'S AUTHORITY BECOMES EFFECTIVE**: My agent's authority becomes effective when my primary physician and one other qualified health-care professional determine that I am unable to make my own health-care decisions. If I initial this box [ ], my agent's authority to make health-care decisions for me takes effect immediately.

(4)   **AGENT'S OBLIGATION**: My agent shall make health-care decisions for me in accordance with this power of attorney for health care, any instructions I give in Part 2 of this form and my other wishes to the extent known to my agent. To the extent my wishes are unknown, my agent shall make health-care decisions for me in accordance with what my agent determines to be in my best interest. In determining my best interest, my agent shall consider my personal values to the extent known to my agent.

(5)   **NOMINATION OF GUARDIAN**: If a guardian of my person needs to be appointed for me by a court, I nominate the agent designated in this form. If that agent is not willing, able or reasonably available to act as guardian, I nominate the alternate agents whom I have named, in the order designated.

PART 2 INSTRUCTIONS FOR HEALTH CARE

If you are satisfied to allow your agent to determine what is best for you in making end-of-life decisions, you need not fill out this part of the form. If you do fill out this part of the form, you may cross out any wording you do not want.

(6)   **END-OF-LIFE DECISIONS**: If I am unable to make or communicate decisions regarding my health care, and IF (i) I have an incurable or irreversible condition that will result in my death within a relatively short time, OR (ii) I become unconscious and, to a reasonable degree of medical certainty, I will not regain consciousness, OR (iii) the likely risks and burdens of treatment would outweigh the expected benefits, THEN I direct that my health-care providers and others involved in my care provide, withhold or withdraw treatment in accordance with the choice I have initialed below in one of the following three boxes:

[ ]   I CHOOSE NOT To Prolong Life
        I do not want my life to be prolonged.

[ ]   I CHOOSE To Prolong Life

254 | MAKE YOUR OWN LIVING WILL

I want my life to be prolonged as long as possible within the
limits of generally accepted health-care standards.

[ ]   I CHOOSE To Let My Agent Decide
My agent under my power of attorney for health care may make
life-sustaining treatment decisions for me.

(7)   **ARTIFICIAL NUTRITION AND HYDRATION**: If I have chosen above NOT to
prolong life, I also specify by marking my initials below:

[ ]   I DO NOT want artificial nutrition

OR

[ ]   I DO want artificial nutrition.

[ ]   I DO NOT want artificial hydration unless required for my comfort

OR

[ ]   I DO want artificial hydration.

(8)   **RELIEF FROM PAIN**: Regardless of the choices I have made in this form and except
as I state in the following space, I direct that the best medical care possible to keep me
clean, comfortable and free of pain or discomfort be provided at all times so that my
dignity is maintained, even if this care hastens my death:

_____

_____

_____

(9)   **ANATOMICAL GIFT DESIGNATION**: Upon my death I specify as marked below
whether I choose to make an anatomical gift of all or some of my organs or tissue:

[ ]   I CHOOSE to make an anatomical gift of all of my organs or tissue to be
determined by medical suitability at the time of death, and artificial support may
be maintained long enough for organs to be removed.

[ ]   I CHOOSE to make a partial anatomical gift of some of my organs and tissue as
specified below, and artificial support may be maintained long enough for organs
to be removed.

_____

_____

_____

[ ]   I REFUSE to make an anatomical gift of any of my organs or tissue.

[ ]   I CHOOSE to let my agent decide.

(10)   **OTHER WISHES:** (If you wish to write your own instructions, or if you wish to add to the instructions you have given above, you may do so here.) I direct that:

_____

_____

_____

(Add additional sheets if needed.)

PART 3 PRIMARY PHYSICIAN

(11)   I designate the following physician as my primary physician:

_____

(name of physician)

_____

(address)   (city)   (state)   (zip code)

_____

(phone)

If the physician I have designated above is not willing, able or reasonably available to act as my primary physician, I designate the following physician as my primary physician:

_____

(name of physician)

_____

(address)   (city)   (state)   (zip code)

_____

(phone)

(12)   **EFFECT OF COPY**: A copy of this form has the same effect as the original.

(13)   **REVOCATION**: I understand that I may revoke this OPTIONAL ADVANCE HEALTH-CARE DIRECTIVE at any time, and that if I revoke it, I should promptly notify my supervising health-care provider and any health-care institution where I am

receiving care and any others to whom I have given copies of this power of attorney. I understand that I may revoke the designation of an agent either by a signed writing or by personally informing the supervising health-care provider.

(14)   SIGNATURES: Sign and date the form here:

_____   _____
(date)   (sign your name)

_____   _____
(address)   (print your name)

_____
(city)

_____
(state)

_____
(your social security number) (Optional)

SIGNATURES OF WITNESSES:

First witness   Second witness

_____   _____
(print your name)   (print your name)

_____   _____
(address)   (address)

_____   _____
(city)   (city)

_____   _____
(state)   (state)

_____   _____
(signature of witness)   (signature of witness)

_____   _____
(date)   (date)

North Carolina State Forms

DECLARATION OF A DESIRE FOR A NATURAL DEATH

I, _____, being of sound mind, desire that, as specified below, my life not be prolonged by extraordinary means or by artificial nutrition or hydration if my condition is determined to be terminal and incurable or if I am diagnosed as being in a persistent vegetative state. I am aware and understand that this writing authorizes a physician to withhold or discontinue extraordinary means or artificial nutrition or hydration, in accordance with my specifications set forth below:

(Initial any of the following, as desired):

_____ If my condition is determined to be terminal and incurable, I authorize the following:

_____ My physician may withhold or discontinue extraordinary means only.

_____ In addition to withholding or discontinuing extraordinary means if such means are necessary, my physician may withhold or discontinue either artificial nutrition or hydration, or both.

_____ If my physician determines that I am in a persistent vegetative state, I authorize the following:

_____ My physician may withhold or discontinue extraordinary means only.

_____ In addition to withholding or discontinuing extraordinary means if such means are necessary, my physician may withhold or discontinue either artificial nutrition or hydration, or both.

This the _____ day of _____, 20___.

Signature _____

I hereby state that the declarant, _____, being of sound mind signed the above declaration in my presence and that I am not related to the declarant by blood or marriage and that I do not know or have a reasonable expectation that I would be entitled to any portion of the estate of the declarant under any existing will or codicil of the declarant or as an heir under the Intestate Succession Act if the declarant died on this date without a will. I also state that I am not the declarant's attending physician or an employee of the declarant's attending physician, or an employee of a health facility in which the declarant is a patient or an employee of a nursing home or any group-care home where the declarant resides. I further state that I do not now have any claim against the declarant.

Witness _____

Witness _____

The clerk or the assistant clerk, or a notary public may, upon proper proof, certify the declaration as follows:

Certificate

I, _____, Clerk (Assistant Clerk) of Superior Court or Notary Public (circle one as appropriate) for _____ County hereby certify that _____, the declarant, appeared before me and swore to me and to the witnesses in my presence that this instrument is his Declaration Of A Desire For A Natural Death, and that he had willingly and voluntarily made and executed it as his free act and deed for the purposes expressed in it.

I further certify that _____ and _____, witnesses, appeared before me and swore that they witnessed _____, declarant, sign the attached declaration, believing him to be of sound mind; and also swore that at the time they witnessed the declaration (i) they were not related within the third degree to the declarant or to the declarant's spouse, and (ii) they did not know or have a reasonable expectation that they would be entitled to any portion of the estate of the declarant upon the declarant's death under any will of the declarant or codicil thereto then existing or under the Intestate Succession Act as it provides at that time, and (iii) they were not a physician attending the declarant or an employee of an attending physician or an employee of a health facility in which the declarant was a patient or an employee of a nursing home or any group-care home in which the declarant resided, and (iv) they did not have a claim against the declarant. I further certify that I am satisfied as to the genuineness and due execution of the declaration.

This the _____ day of _____, 20___.

_____

Clerk (Assistant Clerk) of Superior Court or Notary Public

(circle one as appropriate) for the County of _____

North Dakota State Forms

HEALTH CARE DIRECTIVE

I_____ , understand this document allows me to do ONE OR ALL of the following:

PART I: Name another person (called the health care agent) to make health care

decisions for me if I am unable to make and communicate health care decisions for myself. My health care agent must make health care decisions for me based on the instructions I provide in this document (Part II), if any, the wishes I have made known to him or her, or my agent must act in my best interest if I have not made my health care wishes known.

AND/OR

PART II: Give health care instructions to guide others making health care decisions for me. If I have named a health care agent, these instructions are to be used by the agent. These instructions may also be used by my health care providers, others assisting with my health care and my family, in the event I cannot make and communicate decisions for myself.

AND/OR

PART III: Allows me to make an organ and tissue donation upon my death by signing a document of anatomical gift.

PART I: APPOINTMENT OF HEALTH CARE AGENT

THIS IS WHO I WANT TO MAKE HEALTH CARE DECISIONS FOR ME IF I AM UNABLE TO MAKE AND COMMUNICATE HEALTH CARE DECISIONS FOR MYSELF (I know I can change my agent or alternate agent at any time and I know I do not have to appoint an agent or an alternate agent)

NOTE: If you appoint an agent, you should discuss this health care directive with your agent and give your agent a copy. If you do not wish to appoint an agent, you may leave Part I blank and go to Part II and/or Part III. None of the following may be designated as your agent: your treating health care provider, a nonrelative employee of your treating health care provider, an operator of a long-term care facility, or a nonrelative employee of a long-term care facility.

When I am unable to make and communicate health care decisions for myself, I trust and appoint_____ to make health care decisions for me. This person is called my health care agent.

Relationship of my health care agent to me: _____

Telephone number of my health care agent: _____

Address of my health care agent:

_____

_____

_____

_____

(OPTIONAL) APPOINTMENT OF ALTERNATE HEALTH CARE AGENT: If my health care agent is not reasonably available, I trust and appoint _____ to be my health care agent instead.

Relationship of my alternate health care agent to me: _____

Telephone number of my alternate health care agent: _____
Address of my alternate health care agent:

_____

_____

_____

_____

THIS IS WHAT I WANT MY HEALTH CARE AGENT TO BE ABLE TO DO IF I AM UNABLE TO MAKE AND COMMUNICATE HEALTH CARE DECISIONS FOR MYSELF (I know I can change these choices)

My health care agent is automatically given the powers listed below in (A) through (D).

My health care agent must follow my health care instructions in this document or any other instructions I have given to my agent. If I have not given health care instructions, then my agent must act in my best interest.

Whenever I am unable to make and communicate health care decisions for myself, my health care agent has the power to:

(A)   Make any health care decision for me. This includes the power to give, refuse, or withdraw consent to any care, treatment, service, or procedures. This includes deciding whether to stop or not start health care that is keeping me or might keep me alive and deciding about mental health treatment.

(B)   Choose my health care providers.

(C)   Choose where I live and receive care and support when those choices relate to my health care needs.

(D)   Review my medical records and have the same rights that I would have to give my medical records to other people.

If I DO NOT want my health care agent to have a power listed above in (A) through (D) OR if I want to LIMIT any power in (A) through (D), I MUST say that here: _____

_____

_____

_____

My health care agent is NOT automatically given the powers listed below in (1) and (2). If I WANT my agent to have any of the powers in (1) and (2), I must INITIAL the line in front of the power; then my agent WILL HAVE that power.

_____   (1) To decide whether to donate any parts of my body, including organs, tissues, and eyes, when I die.

_____   (2) To decide what will happen with my body when I die (burial, cremation).

If I want to say anything more about my health care agent's powers or limits on the powers, I can say it here:

_____

_____

_____

PART II: HEALTH CARE INSTRUCTIONS

NOTE: Complete this Part II if you wish to give health care instructions. If you appointed an agent in Part I, completing this Part II is optional but would be very helpful to your agent. However, if you chose not to appoint an agent in Part I, you MUST complete, at a minimum, Part II (B) if you wish to make a valid health care directive. These are instructions for my health care when I am unable to make and communicate health care decisions for myself. These instructions must be followed (so long as they address my needs).

(A) THESE ARE MY BELIEFS AND VALUES ABOUT MY HEALTH CARE

(I know I can change these choices or leave any of them blank)

I want you to know these things about me to help you make decisions about my health care:

My goals for my health care:

_____

_____

_____

My fears about my health care:

_____

_____

_____

My spiritual or religious beliefs and traditions:

_____

_____

_____

My beliefs about when life would be no longer worth living:

_____

_____

_____

My thoughts about how my medical condition might affect my family:

_____

_____

_____

(B) THIS IS WHAT I WANT AND DO NOT WANT FOR MY HEALTH CARE

(I know I can change these choices or leave any of them blank)

Many medical treatments may be used to try to improve my medical condition or to prolong my life. Examples include artificial breathing by a machine connected to a tube in the lungs, artificial feeding or fluids through tubes, attempts to start a stopped heart, surgeries, dialysis, antibiotics, and blood transfusions. Most medical treatments can be tried for a while and then stopped if they do not help.

I have these views about my health care in these situations:

(Note: You can discuss general feelings, specific treatments, or leave any of them blank).

If I had a reasonable chance of recovery and were temporarily unable to make and communicate health care decisions for myself, I would want:

_____

_____

_____

If I were dying and unable to make and communicate health care decisions for myself, I would want:

_____

_____

_____

If I were permanently unconscious and unable to make and communicate health care decisions for myself, I would want:

_____

_____

_____

If I were completely dependent on others for my care and unable to make and communicate health care decisions for myself, I would want:

_____

_____

_____

In all circumstances, my doctors will try to keep me comfortable and reduce my pain. This is how I feel about pain relief if it would affect my alertness or if it could shorten my life:

_____

_____

_____

There are other things that I want or do not want for my health care, if possible:

Who I would like to be my doctor:

_____

_____

_____

Where I would like to live to receive health care:

_____

_____

_____

Where I would like to die and other wishes I have about dying:

_____

_____

_____

My wishes about what happens to my body when I die (cremation, burial):

_____

_____

_____

Any other things:

_____

_____

_____

PART III: MAKING AN ANATOMICAL GIFT

I would like to be an organ donor at the time of my death. I have told my family my decision and ask my family to honor my wishes. I wish to donate the following

(initial one Statement):

[_____] Any needed organs and tissue.

[_____] Only the following organs and tissue: _____

_____

_____

_____

PART IV: MAKING THE DOCUMENT LEGAL

PRIOR DESIGNATIONS REVOKED

I revoke any prior health care directive.

DATE AND SIGNATURE OF PRINCIPAL

(YOU MUST DATE AND SIGN THIS HEALTH CARE DIRECTIVE)

I sign my name to this Health Care Directive Form on _____ at (date)_____

_____

(city)

_____

(state)

_____

(you sign here)

(THIS HEALTH CARE DIRECTIVE WILL NOT BE VALID UNLESS IT IS NOTARIZED OR SIGNED BY TWO QUALIFIED WITNESSES WHO ARE PRESENT WHEN YOU SIGN OR ACKNOWLEDGE YOUR SIGNATURE. IF YOU HAVE ATTACHED ANY

ADDITIONAL PAGES TO THIS FORM, YOU MUST DATE AND SIGN EACH OF THE ADDITIONAL PAGES AT THE SAME TIME YOU DATE AND SIGN THIS HEALTH CARE DIRECTIVE.)

NOTARY PUBLIC OR STATEMENT OF WITNESSES

This document must be (1) notarized or (2) witnessed by two qualified adult witnesses. The person notarizing this document may be an employee of a health care or long-term care provider providing your care. At least one witness to the execution of the document must not be a health care or long-term care provider providing you with direct care or an employee of the health care or long-term care provider providing you with direct care. None of the following may be used as a notary or witness:

1.   A person you designate as your agent or alternate agent;

2.   Your spouse;

3.   A person related to you by blood, marriage, or adoption;

4.   A person entitled to inherit any part of your estate upon your death; or

5.   A person who has, at the time of executing this document, any claim against your estate.

Option 1: Notary Public

In my presence on _____ (date), _____ (name of declarant) acknowledged the declarant's signature on this document or acknowledged that the declarant directed the person signing this document to sign on the declarant's behalf.

_____
(Signature of Notary Public)
My commission expires _____ , 20__.

Option 2: Two Witnesses

Witness One:

(1)   In my presence on _____ (date), _____ (name of declarant) acknowledged the declarant's signature on this document or acknowledged that the declarant directed the person signing this document to sign on the declarant's behalf.

(2)   I am at least eighteen years of age.

(3)   If I am a health care provider or an employee of a health care provider giving direct care to the declarant, I must initial this box: [ ].

I certify that the information in (1) through (3) is true and correct.

_____

(Signature of Witness One)

_____

(Address)

Witness Two:

(1)   In my presence on _____ (date), _____ (name of declarant) acknowledged the declarant's signature on this document or acknowledged that the declarant directed the person signing this document to sign on the declarant's behalf.

(2)   I am at least eighteen years of age.

(3)   If I am a health care provider or an employee of a health care provider giving direct care to the declarant, I must initial this box: [ ].

I certify that the information in (1) through (3) is true and correct.

_____

(Signature of Witness Two)

_____

(Address)

ACCEPTANCE OF APPOINTMENT OF POWER OF ATTORNEY

I accept this appointment and agree to serve as agent for health care decisions. I understand I have a duty to act consistently with the desires of the principal as expressed in this appointment. I understand that this document gives me authority over health care decisions for the principal only if the principal becomes incapacitated. I understand that I must act in good faith in exercising my authority under this power of attorney. I understand that the principal may revoke this power of attorney at any time in any manner.

If I choose to withdraw during the time the principal is competent, I must notify the principal of my decision. If I choose to withdraw when the principal is not able to make health care decisions, I must notify the principal's physician.

_____

(Signature of agent/date)

_____

(Signature of alternate agent/date)

PRINCIPAL'S STATEMENT

I have read a written explanation of the nature and effect of an appointment of a health care agent that is attached to my health care directive.

Dated this _____ day of _____ , 20 _____. _____

(Signature of Principal)

Ohio State Forms

STATE OF OHIO

LIVING WILL DECLARATION

of

_____

(Print Full Name)

_____

(Birth Date)

I state that this is my Ohio Living Will Declaration. I am of sound mind and not under or subject to duress, fraud or undue influence. I am a competent adult who understands and accepts the consequences of this action. I voluntarily declare my wish that my dying not be artificially prolonged. If I am unable to give directions regarding the use of lifesustaining treatment when I am in a terminal condition or a permanently unconscious state, I intend that this Living Will Declaration be honored by my family and physicians as the final expression of my legal right to refuse health care.

DEFINITIONS

Several legal and medical terms are used in this document. For convenience they are explained below.

Anatomical gift means a donation of all or part of a human body to take effect upon or after death.

Artificially or technologically supplied nutrition or hydration means the providing of food and fluids through intravenous or tube "feedings."

Cardiopulmonary resuscitation or **CPR** means treatment to try to restart breathing or heartbeat. CPR may be done by breathing into the mouth, pushing on the chest, putting a tube through the mouth or nose into the throat, administering medication, giving electric shock to the chest, or by other means.

Declarant means the person signing this document.

Donor Registry Enrollment Form means a form that has been designed to allow individuals to specifically register their wishes regarding organ, tissue and eye donation with the Ohio Bureau of Motor Vehicles Donor Registry.

Do Not Resuscitate or **DNR Order** means a medical order given by my physician and written in my medical records that cardiopulmonary resuscitation or CPR is not to be administered to me.

Health care means any medical (including dental, nursing, psychological, and surgical) procedure, treatment, intervention or other measure used to maintain, diagnose or treat any physical or mental condition.

Health Care Power of Attorney means another document that allows me to name an adult person to act as my agent to make health care decisions for me if I become unable to do so.

Life-sustaining treatment means any health care, including artificially or technologically supplied nutrition and hydration, that will serve mainly to prolong the process of dying.

Living Will Declaration or **Living Will** means this document that lets me specify the health care I want to receive if I become terminally ill or permanently unconscious and cannot make my wishes known.

Permanently unconscious state means an irreversible condition in which I am permanently unaware of myself and my surroundings. My physician and one other physician must examine me and agree that the total loss of higher brain function has left me unable to feel pain or suffering.

Terminal condition or **terminal illness** means an irreversible, incurable and untreatable condition caused by disease, illness or injury. My physician and one other physician will have examined me and believe that I cannot recover and that death is likely to occur within a relatively short time if I do not receive life-sustaining treatment.

[Instructions and other information to assist in completing this document are set forth within brackets and in italic type.]

Health Care if I Am in a Terminal Condition.

If I am in a terminal condition and unable to make my own health care decisions, I direct that my physician shall:

1. Administer no life-sustaining treatment, including CPR and artificially or technologically supplied nutrition or hydration; and

2. Withdraw such treatment, including CPR, if such treatment has started; and

3. Issue a DNR Order; and

4. Permit me to die naturally and take no action to postpone my death, providing me with only that care necessary to make me comfortable and to relieve my pain.

Health Care if I Am in a Permanently Unconscious State.

If I am in a permanently unconscious state, I direct that my physician shall:

1. Administer no life-sustaining treatment, including CPR, except for the provision of artificially or technologically supplied nutrition or hydration unless, in the following paragraph, I have authorized its withholding or withdrawal; and

2. Withdraw such treatment, including CPR, if such treatment has started; and

3. Issue a DNR Order; and

4. Permit me to die naturally and take no action to postpone my death, providing me with only that care necessary to make me comfortable and to relieve my pain.

Special Instructions: By placing my initials at number 3 below, I want to specifically authorize my physician to withhold or to withdraw artificially or technologically supplied nutrition or hydration if:

1. I am in a permanently unconscious state; and

2. My physician and at least one other physician who has examined me have determined, to a reasonable degree of medical certainty, that artificially or technologically supplied nutrition and hydration will not provide comfort to me or relieve my pain; and

3. I have placed my initials on this line: _____

Notifications. [Note: You do not need to name anyone. If no one is named, the law requires your attending physician to make a reasonable effort to notify one of the following persons in the order named: your guardian, your spouse, your adult children who are available, your parents, or a majority of your adult siblings who are available.]

In the event my attending physician determines that life-sustaining treatment should be withheld or withdrawn, my physician shall make a reasonable effort to notify one of the persons named below, in the following order of priority:

[Note: If you do not name two contacts, you may wish to cross out the unused lines.]

First Contact: **Second Contact:**

Name: _____   Name: _____

Address: _____   Address: _____

_____   _____

_____   _____

Telephone: _____ Telephone: _____

ANATOMICAL GIFT

(optional)

INSTRUCTIONS: If you elect to make an anatomical gift, please complete and file the attached "Donor Registry Enrollment Form" with the Ohio Bureau of Motor Vehicles to ensure that your wishes will be honored.

_____ I wish to make an anatomical gift.

_____ I do not wish to make an anatomical gift.

Upon my death, the following are my directions regarding donation of all or part of my body:

In the hope that I, _____ (name of donor), may help others upon my death, I hereby give the following body parts:

_____

_____

(indicate specific parts or all body parts)

for any purpose authorized by law: transplantation, therapy, research or education. [Cross out any purpose that is unacceptable to you.]

This is a legal document under the Uniform Anatomical Gift Act or similar laws.

If I do not indicate a desire to donate all or part of my body by filling in the lines above, no presumption is created about my desire to make or refuse to make an anatomical gift.

DONOR REGISTRY ENROLLMENT FORM

I have completed the Donor Registry Enrollment

Form: _____Yes _____No

NOTE: If you modify or revoke your decision regarding anatomical gifts, please remember to make those changes in your Living Will, Health Care Power of Attorney, and Donor Registry Enrollment Form.

No Expiration Date. This Living Will Declaration will have no expiration date.

However, I may revoke it at any time.

Copies the Same as Original. Any person may rely on a copy of this document.

Out of State Application. I intend that this document be honored in any jurisdiction to the extent allowed by law.

Health Care Power of Attorney. I have completed a Health Care Power of Attorney:

_____ Yes _____ No

SIGNATURE

[See below for witness or notary requirements.]

I understand the purpose and effect of this document and sign my name to this
Living Will Declaration on _____, 20 _____, at
_____, Ohio.

_____

DECLARANT

[You are responsible for telling members of your family, the agent named in your Health Care Power of Attorney (if you have one), and your physician about this document. You also may wish to tell your religious advisor and your lawyer that you have signed a Living Will Declaration. You may wish to give a copy to each person notified.]

[You may choose to file a copy of this Living Will Declaration with your county recorder for safekeeping.]

WITNESSES OR NOTARY ACKNOWLEDGMENT

[Choose one.]

[This Living Will Declaration will not be valid unless it either is signed by two eligible witnesses who are present when you sign or are present when you acknowledge your signature, or it is acknowledged before a Notary Public.]

[The following persons cannot serve as a witness to this Living Will Declaration: the agent or any successor agent named in your Health Care Power of Attorney; your spouse; your children; anyone else related to you by blood, marriage or adoption; your attending physician; or, if you are in a nursing home, the administrator of the nursing home.]

WITNESSES

I attest that the Declarant signed or acknowledged this Living Will Declaration in my presence, and that the Declarant appears to be of sound mind and not under or subject to duress, fraud or undue influence. I further attest that I am not an agent designated in the Declarant's Health Care Power of Attorney, I am not the attending physician of the Declarant, I am not the administrator of a nursing home in which the Declarant is receiving care, and I am an adult not related to the Declarant by blood, marriage or adoption.

_____   Residing at   _____

Signature   _____

                                                                                 _____

_____

Print Name

_____   Residing at   _____

Signature   _____

                                                                                 _____

_____

Print Name

Dated: _____ , 20____.

OR

NOTARY ACKNOWLEDGMENT

State of Ohio

County of _____ ss.

On _____ , 20_____, before me, the undersigned Notary Public, personally appeared _____ , known to me or satisfactorily proven to be the person whose name is subscribed to the above Living Will Declaration as the Declarant, and who has acknowledged that (s)he executed the same for the purposes expressed therein. I attest that the Declarant appears to be of sound mind and not under or subject to duress, fraud or undue influence._____

Notary Public
My Commission Expires: _____

Oklahoma State Forms

ADVANCE DIRECTIVE FOR HEALTH CARE

If I am incapable of making an informed decision regarding my health care, I direct my health care providers to follow my instructions below.

I. Living Will

If my attending physician and another physician determine that I am no longer able to make decisions regarding my medical treatment, I direct my attending physician and other health care providers, pursuant to the Oklahoma Advance Directive Act, to follow my instructions as set forth below:

(1)   If I have a terminal condition, that is, an incurable and irreversible condition that even with the administration of life-sustaining treatment will, in the opinion of the attending physician and another physician, result in death within six (6) months:

_____ I direct that my life not be extended by life-sustaining treatment, except that if I am unable to take food and water by mouth, I wish to receive artificially administered nutrition and hydration.

Initial only   _____ I direct that my life not be extended by life-sustaining
one option   treatment, including artificially administered nutrition and hydration.

_____ I direct that I be given life-sustaining treatment and, if I am unable to take food and water by mouth, I wish to receive artificially administered nutrition and hydration.

_____   See my more specific instructions in paragraph (4) below. (Initial if applicable)

(2)   If I am persistently unconscious, that is, I have an irreversible condition, as determined by the attending physician and another physician, in which thought and awareness of

self and environment are absent:

_____ I direct that my life not be extended by life-sustaining treatment, except that if I am unable to take food and water by mouth, I wish to receive artificially administered nutrition and hydration.

Initial only
one option
_____ I direct that my life not be extended by life-sustaining treatment, including artificially administered nutrition and hydration.

_____ I direct that I be given life-sustaining treatment and, if I am unable to take food and water by mouth, I wish to receive artificially administered nutrition and hydration.

_____ See my more specific instructions in paragraph (4) below. (Initial if applicable)

(3)   If I have an end-stage condition, that is, a condition caused by injury, disease, or illness, which results in severe and permanent deterioration indicated by incompetency and complete physical dependency for which treatment of the irreversible condition would be medically ineffective:

_____ I direct that my life not be extended by life-sustaining treatment, except that if I am unable to take food and water by mouth, I wish to receive artificially administered nutrition and hydration.

Initial only
one option
_____ I direct that my life not be extended by life-sustaining treatment, including artificially administered nutrition and hydration.

_____ I direct that I be given life-sustaining treatment and, if I am unable to take food and water by mouth, I wish to receive artificially administered nutrition and hydration.

_____   See my more specific instructions in paragraph (4) below.
(Initial if applicable)

(4)   OTHER.

Here you may:

(a)   describe other conditions in which you would want life-sustaining treatment or artificially administered nutrition and hydration provided, withheld, or withdrawn,

(b)   give more specific instructions about your wishes concerning life-sustaining treatment or artificially administered nutrition and hydration if you have a terminal condition, are persistently unconscious, or have an end-stage condition, or

(c)   do both of these:

_____

_____

_____

_____

_____
Initial

II. My Appointment of My Health Care Proxy

If my attending physician and another physician determine that I am no longer able to make decisions regarding my medical treatment, I direct my attending physician and other health care providers pursuant to the Oklahoma Advance Directive Act to follow the instructions of _____, whom I appoint as my health care proxy. If my health care proxy is unable or unwilling to serve, I appoint _____ as my alternate health care proxy with the same authority. My health care proxy is authorized to make whatever medical treatment decisions I could make if I were able, except that decisions regarding life-sustaining treatment and artificially administered nutrition and hydration can be made by my health care proxy or alternate health care proxy only as I have indicated in the foregoing sections.

If I fail to designate a health care proxy in this section, I am deliberately declining to designate a health care proxy.

III. Anatomical Gifts

Pursuant to the provisions of the Uniform Anatomical Gift Act, I direct that at the time of my death my entire body or designated body organs or body parts be donated for purposes of:

(Initial all that apply)

_____ transplantation

_____ therapy

_____ advancement of medical science, research, or education

_____ advancement of dental science, research, or education

Death means either irreversible cessation of circulatory and respiratory functions or irreversible cessation of all functions of the entire brain, including the brain stem. If I initial the "yes" line below, I specifically donate:

My entire body

or

The following body organs or parts:

_____	lungs	_____	liver
_____	pancreas	_____	heart
_____	kidneys	_____	brain
_____	skin	_____	bones/marrow
_____	blood/fluids	_____	tissue
_____	arteries	_____	eyes/cornea/lens

IV. General Provisions

a. I understand that I must be eighteen (18) years of age or older to execute this form.

b. I understand that my witnesses must be eighteen (18) years of age or older and shall not be related to me and shall not inherit from me.

c. I understand that if I have been diagnosed as pregnant and that diagnosis is known to my attending physician, I will be provided with life-sustaining treatment and artificially administered hydration and nutrition unless I have, in my own words, specifically authorized that during a course of pregnancy, life-sustaining treatment and/or artificially administered hydration and/or nutrition shall be withheld or withdrawn.

d. In the absence of my ability to give directions regarding the use of life-sustaining procedures, it is my intention that this advance directive shall be honored by my family and physicians as the final expression of my legal right to choose or refuse medical or surgical treatment including, but not limited to, the administration of life-sustaining procedures, and I accept the consequences of such choice or refusal.

e. This advance directive shall be in effect until it is revoked.

f. I understand that I may revoke this advance directive at any time.

g. I understand and agree that if I have any prior directives, and if I sign this advance directive, my prior directives are revoked.

h. I understand the full importance of this advance directive and I am emotionally and mentally competent to make this advance directive.

i. I understand that my physician(s) shall make all decisions based upon his or her best judgment applying with ordinary care and diligence the knowledge and skill that is possessed and used by members of the physician's profession in good standing engaged in the same field of practice at that time, measured by national standards.

Signed this _____ day of _____, 20 _____.

_____
(Signature)

_____
City of

_____
County, Oklahoma

_____

Date of birth

_____

(Optional for identification purposes)

This advance directive was signed in my presence.

_____

Witness

_____, Oklahoma Residence

_____

Witness

_____, Oklahoma Residence

Oregon State Forms

ADVANCE DIRECTIVE

YOU DO NOT HAVE TO FILL OUT AND SIGN THIS FORM

PART A: IMPORTANT INFORMATION ABOUT THIS ADVANCE DIRECTIVE

This is an important legal document. It can control critical decisions about your health care. Before signing, consider these important facts:

Facts About Part B (Appointing a Health Care Representative)

You have the right to name a person to direct your health care when you cannot do so. This person is called your "health care representative." You can do this by using Part B of this form. Your representative must accept on Part E of this form.

You can write in this document any restrictions you want on how your representative will make decisions for you. Your representative must follow your desires as stated in this document or otherwise made known. If your desires are unknown, your representative must try to act in your best interest. Your representative can resign at any time.

Facts About Part C (Giving Health Care Instructions)

You also have the right to give instructions for health care providers to follow if you become unable to direct your care. You can do this by using Part C of this form.

Facts About Completing This Form

This form is valid only if you sign it voluntarily and when you are of sound mind. If you do not want an advance directive, you do not have to sign this form.

Unless you have limited the duration of this advance directive, it will not expire. If you have set an expiration date, and you become unable to direct your health care before that date, this advance directive will not expire until you are able to make those decisions again.

You may revoke this document at any time. To do so, notify your representative and your health care provider of the revocation.

Despite this document, you have the right to decide your own health care as long as you are able to do so.

If there is anything in this document that you do not understand, ask a lawyer to explain it to you.

You may sign PART B, PART C, or both parts. You may cross out words that don't express your wishes or add words that better express your wishes. Witnesses must sign PART D.

Print your NAME, BIRTHDATE AND ADDRESS here:

Name:- _____
Birthdate:- _____
Address:- _____
_____
_____
_____

Unless revoked or suspended, this advance directive will continue for:

INITIAL ONE:

_____ My entire life
_____ Other period (__ Years)

PART B: APPOINTMENT OF HEALTH CARE REPRESENTATIVE

I appoint _____ as my health care representative. My representative's address is _____ and telephone number is _____.

I appoint _____ as my alternate health care representative. My alternate's address is _____ and telephone number is _____.

I authorize my representative (or alternate) to direct my health care when I can't do so.

NOTE: You may not appoint your doctor, an employee of your doctor, or an owner, operator or employee of your health care facility, unless that person is related to you by blood, marriage or adoption or that person was appointed before your admission into the health care facility.

1.   **Limits**

Special Conditions or Instructions:

_____

_____

_____

INITIAL IF THIS APPLIES:

_____ I have executed a Health Care Instruction or Directive to Physicians. My representative is to honor it.

2.   **Life Support**

"Life support" refers to any medical means for maintaining life, including procedures, devices and medications. If you refuse life support, you will still get routine measures to keep you clean and comfortable.

INITIAL IF THIS APPLIES:

_____ My representative MAY decide about life support for me. (If you don't initial this space, then your representative MAY NOT decide about life support.)

3.   **Tube Feeding**

One sort of life support is food and water supplied artificially by medical device, known as tube feeding.

INITIAL IF THIS APPLIES:

_____ My representative MAY decide about tube feeding for me. (If you don't initial this space, then your representative MAY NOT decide about tube feeding.)

_____

(Date)

SIGN HERE TO APPOINT A HEALTH CARE REPRESENTATIVE

_____

(Signature of person making appointment)

PART C: HEALTH CARE INSTRUCTIONS

NOTE: In filling out these instructions, keep the following in mind:

- The term "as my physician recommends" means that you want your physician to try life support if your physician believes it could be helpful and then discontinue it if it is not helping your health condition or symptoms.

- "Life support" and "tube feeding" are defined in Part B above.

- If you refuse tube feeding, you should understand that malnutrition, dehydration and death will probably result.

- You will get care for your comfort and cleanliness, no matter what choices you make.

- You may either give specific instructions by filling out Items 1 to 4 below, or you may use the general instruction provided by Item 5.

Here are my desires about my health care if my doctor and another knowledgeable doctor confirm that I am in a medical condition described below:

1.   **Close to Death**

If I am close to death and life support would only postpone the moment of my death:

A.   INITIAL ONE:

_____ I want to receive tube feeding.
_____ I want tube feeding only as my physician recommends.
_____ I DO NOT WANT tube feeding.

B.   INITIAL ONE:

_____ I want any other life support that may apply.
_____ I want life support only as my physician recommends.
_____ I want NO life support.

2. **Permanently Unconscious**

If I am unconscious and it is very unlikely that I will ever become conscious again:

A.   INITIAL ONE:

_____   I want to receive tube feeding.
_____   I want tube feeding only as my physician recommends.
_____   I DO NOT WANT tube feeding.

B.   INITIAL ONE:

_____   I want any other life support that may apply.
_____   I want life support only as my physician recommends.
_____   I want NO life support.

3. **Advanced Progressive Illness**

If I have a progressive illness that will be fatal and is in an advanced stage, and I am consistently and permanently unable to communicate by any means, swallow food and water safely, care for myself and recognize my family and other people, and it is very unlikely that my condition will substantially improve:

A.   INITIAL ONE:

_____   I want to receive tube feeding.
_____   I want tube feeding only as my physician recommends.
_____   I DO NOT WANT tube feeding.

B.   INITIAL ONE:
_____   I want any other life support that may apply.
_____   I want life support only as my physician recommends.
_____   I want NO life support.

4. **Extraordinary Suffering**

If life support would not help my medical condition and would make me suffer permanent and severe pain:

A.   INITIAL ONE:

_____   I want to receive tube feeding.
_____   I want tube feeding only as my physician recommends.
_____   I DO NOT WANT tube feeding.

B.   INITIAL ONE:

_____   I want any other life support that may apply.
_____   I want life support only as my physician recommends.
_____   I want NO life support.

5.   **General Instruction**

INITIAL IF THIS APPLIES:

_____   I do not want my life to be prolonged by life support. I also do not want tube feeding as life support. I want my doctors to allow me to die naturally if my doctor and another knowledgeable doctor confirm I am in any of the medical conditions listed in Items 1 to 4 above.

6.   **Additional Conditions or Instructions**

_____

_____

_____

(Insert description of what you want done.)

7.   **Other Documents**

A "health care power of attorney" is any document you may have signed to appoint a representative to make health care decisions for you.

INITIAL ONE:

_____   I have previously signed a health care power of attorney. I want it to remain in effect unless I appointed a health care representative after signing the health care power of attorney.

_____ I have a health care power of attorney, and I REVOKE IT.

_____ I DO NOT have a health care power of attorney.

_____

(Date)

SIGN HERE TO GIVE INSTRUCTIONS

_____

(Signature)

PART D: DECLARATION OF WITNESSES

We declare that the person signing this advance directive:

(a)   Is personally known to us or has provided proof of identity;

(b)   Signed or acknowledged that person's signature on this advance directive in our presence;

(c)   Appears to be of sound mind and not under duress, fraud or undue influence;

(d)   Has not appointed either of us as health care representative or alternative representative; and

(e)   Is not a patient for whom either of us is attending physician.

Witnessed By:

_____ _____

(Signature of   (Printed Name

Witness/Date) of Witness)

_____ _____
(Signature of   (Printed Name
Witness/Date) of Witness)

NOTE: One witness must not be a relative (by blood, marriage or adoption) of the person signing this advance directive. That witness must also not be entitled to any portion of the person's estate upon death. That witness must also not own, operate or be employed at a health care facility where the person is a patient or resident.

PART E: ACCEPTANCE BY HEALTH CARE REPRESENTATIVE

I accept this appointment and agree to serve as health care representative. I understand I must act consistently with the desires of the person I represent, as expressed in this advance directive or otherwise made known to me. If I do not know the desires of the person I represent, I have a duty to act in what I believe in good faith to be that person's best interest. I understand that this document allows me to decide about that person's health care only while that person cannot do so. I understand that the person who appointed me may revoke this appointment. If I learn that this document has been suspended or revoked, I will inform the person's current health care provider if known to me.

_____
(Signature of Health Care Representative/Date)

_____
(Printed name)

_____
(Signature of Alternate Health Care Representative/Date)

_____
(Printed name)

Pennsylvania State Forms

DURABLE HEALTH CARE POWER OF ATTORNEY AND HEALTH CARE TREATMENT INSTRUCTIONS

(LIVING WILL)

PART I

INTRODUCTORY REMARKS ON HEALTH CARE DECISION MAKING

You have the right to decide the type of health care you want.

Should you become unable to understand, make or communicate decisions about medical care, your wishes for medical treatment are most likely to be followed if you express those wishes in advance by:

(1)   naming a health care agent to decide treatment for you; and

(2)   giving health care treatment instructions to your health care agent or health care provider.

An advance health care directive is a written set of instructions expressing your wishes for medical treatment. It may contain a health care power of attorney, where you name a person called a "health care agent" to decide treatment for you, and a living will, where you tell your health care agent and health care providers your choices regarding the initiation, continuation, withholding or withdrawal of life-sustaining treatment and other specific directions.

You may limit your health care agent's involvement in deciding your medical treatment so that your health care agent will speak for you only when you are unable to speak for yourself or you may give your health care agent the power to speak for you immediately. This combined form gives your health care agent the power to speak for you only when you are unable to speak for yourself. A living will cannot be followed unless your attending physician determines that you lack the ability to understand, make or communicate health care decisions for yourself and you are either permanently unconscious or you have an end-stage medical condition, which is a condition that will result in death despite the introduction or continuation of medical treatment. You, and not your health care agent, remain responsible for the cost of your medical care.

If you do not write down your wishes about your health care in advance, and if later you become unable to understand, make or communicate these decisions, those wishes may not be honored because they may remain unknown to others.

A health care provider who refuses to honor your wishes about health care must tell you of its refusal and help to transfer you to a health care provider who will honor your wishes.

You should give a copy of your advance health care directive (a living will, health care power of attorney or a document containing both) to your health care agent, your physicians, family members and others whom you expect would likely attend to your needs if you become unable to understand, make or communicate decisions about medical care.

If your health care wishes change, tell your physician and write a new advance health care directive to replace your old one. It is important in selecting a health care agent that you choose a person you trust who is likely to be available in a medical situation where you cannot make decisions for yourself. You should inform that person that you have appointed him or her as your health care agent and discuss your beliefs and values with him or her so that your health care agent will understand your health care objectives.

You may wish to consult with knowledgeable, trusted individuals such as family members, your physician or clergy when considering an expression of your values and health care wishes. You are free to create your own advance health care directive to convey your wishes regarding medical treatment.

The following form is an example of an advance health care directive that combines a health care power of attorney with a living will.

NOTES ABOUT THE USE OF THIS FORM

If you decide to use this form or create your own advance health care directive, you should consult with your physician and your attorney to make sure that your wishes are clearly expressed and comply with the law.

If you decide to use this form but disagree with any of its statements, you may cross out those statements. You may add comments to this form or use your own form to help your physician or health care agent decide your medical care.

This form is designed to give your health care agent broad powers to make health care decisions for you whenever you cannot make them for yourself. It is also designed to express a desire to limit or authorize care if you have an end-stage medical condition or are permanently unconscious.

If you do not desire to give your health care agent broad powers, or you do not wish to limit your care if you have an end-stage medical condition or are permanently unconscious, you may wish to use a different form or create your own.

YOU SHOULD ALSO USE A DIFFERENT FORM IF YOU WISH TO EXPRESS YOUR PREFERENCES IN MORE DETAIL THAN THIS FORM ALLOWS OR IF YOU WISH FOR YOUR HEALTH CARE AGENT TO BE ABLE TO SPEAK FOR YOU IMMEDIATELY.

In these situations, it is particularly important that you consult with your attorney and physician to make sure that your wishes are clearly expressed.

This form allows you to tell your health care agent your goals if you have an end-stage medical condition or other extreme and irreversible medical condition, such as advanced Alzheimer's disease. Do you want medical care applied aggressively in these situations or would you consider such aggressive medical care burdensome and undesirable?

You may choose whether you want your health care agent to be bound by your instructions or whether you want your health care agent to be able to decide at the time what course of treatment the health care agent thinks most fully reflects your wishes and values.

If you are a woman and diagnosed as being pregnant at the time a health care decision would otherwise be made pursuant to this form, the laws of this Commonwealth prohibit implementation of that decision if it directs that life-sustaining treatment, including nutrition and hydration, be withheld or withdrawn from you, unless your attending physician and an obstetrician who have examined you certify in your medical record that the life-sustaining treatment:

(1)   will not maintain you in such a way as to permit the continuing development and live birth of the unborn child;

(2)   will be physically harmful to you; or

(3)   will cause pain to you that cannot be alleviated by medication.

A physician is not required to perform a pregnancy test on you unless the physician has reason to believe that you may be pregnant.

Pennsylvania law protects your health care agent and health care providers from any legal liability for following in good faith your wishes as expressed in the form or by your health care agent's direction. It does not otherwise change professional standards or excuse negligence in the way your wishes are carried out. If you have any questions about the law, consult an attorney for guidance.

This form and explanation is not intended to take the place of specific legal or medical advice for which you should rely upon your own attorney and physician.

PART II

DURABLE HEALTH CARE POWER OF ATTORNEY

I, _____, of _____ County, Pennsylvania, appoint the person named below to be my health care agent to make health and personal care decisions for me.

Effective immediately and continuously until my death or revocation by a writing signed by me or someone authorized to make health care treatment decisions for me, I authorize all health care providers or other covered entities to disclose to my health care agent, upon my agent's request, any information, oral or written, regarding my physical or mental health, including, but not limited to, medical and hospital records and what is otherwise private, privileged, protected or personal health information, such as health information as defined and described in the Health Insurance Portability and Accountability Act of 1996 (Public Law 104-191, 110 Stat. 1936), the regulations promulgated thereunder and any other State or local laws and rules. Information disclosed by a health care provider or other covered entity may be redisclosed and may no longer be subject to the privacy rules provided by 45 C.F.R. Pt. 164.

The remainder of this document will take effect when and only when I lack the ability to understand, make or communicate a choice regarding a health or personal care decision as verified by my attending physician. My health care agent may not delegate the authority to make decisions.

MY HEALTH CARE AGENT HAS ALL OF THE FOLLOWING POWERS SUBJECT TO THE HEALTH CARE TREATMENT INSTRUCTIONS THAT FOLLOW IN PART III (CROSS OUT ANY POWERS YOU DO NOT WANT TO GIVE YOUR HEALTH CARE AGENT):

1. To authorize, withhold or withdraw medical care and surgical procedures.

2. To authorize, withhold or withdraw nutrition (food) or hydration (water) medically supplied by tube through my nose, stomach, intestines, arteries or veins.

3. To authorize my admission to or discharge from a medical, nursing, residential or similar facility and to make agreements for my care and health insurance for my care, including hospice and/or palliative care.

4. To hire and fire medical, social service and other support personnel responsible for my care.

5. To take any legal action necessary to do what I have directed.

6. To request that a physician responsible for my care issue a do-not-resuscitate (DNR) order, including an out-of-hospital DNR order, and sign any required documents and consents.

APPOINTMENT OF HEALTH CARE AGENT

I appoint the following health care agent:

Health Care Agent:
    Name: _____
    Relationship: _____
    Address: _____
    _____
    _____

    Telephone Number: _____
                        (Home)

    Telephone Number: _____
                        (Work)

    E-mail: _____

IF YOU DO NOT NAME A HEALTH CARE AGENT, HEALTH CARE PROVIDERS WILL ASK YOUR FAMILY OR AN ADULT WHO KNOWS YOUR PREFERENCES AND VALUES FOR HELP IN DETERMINING YOUR WISHES FOR TREATMENT. NOTE THAT YOU MAY NOT APPOINT YOUR DOCTOR OR OTHER HEALTH CARE PROVIDER AS YOUR HEALTH CARE AGENT UNLESS RELATED TO YOU BY BLOOD, MARRIAGE OR ADOPTION.

If my health care agent is not readily available or if my health care agent is my spouse and an action for divorce is filed by either of us after the date of this document, I appoint the person or persons named below in the order named. (It is helpful, but not required, to name alternative health care agents.)

First Alternative Health Care Agent:

Name: _____

Relationship: _____

Address: _____

_____

Telephone Number: _____

(Home)

Telephone Number: _____

(Work)

E-mail: _____

Second Alternative Health Care Agent:

Name: _____

Relationship: _____

Address: _____

_____

Telephone Number: _____

(Home)

Telephone Number: _____

(Work)

GUIDANCE FOR HEALTH CARE AGENT

(OPTIONAL)

GOALS

If I have an end-stage medical condition or other extreme irreversible medical condition, my goals in making medical decisions are as follows (insert your personal priorities such as comfort, care, preservation of mental function, etc.):

_____

_____

_____

SEVERE BRAIN DAMAGE OR BRAIN DISEASE

If I should suffer from severe and irreversible brain damage or brain disease with no realistic hope of significant recovery, I would consider such a condition intolerable and the application of aggressive medical care to be burdensome.

I therefore request that my health care agent respond to any intervening (other and separate) life-threatening conditions in the same manner as directed for an end-stage medical condition or state of permanent unconsciousness as I have indicated below.

Initials _____ I agree

Initials _____ I disagree

PART III

HEALTH CARE TREATMENT INSTRUCTIONS IN THE EVENT OF END-STAGE MEDICAL CONDITION OR PERMANENT UNCONSCIOUSNESS

(LIVING WILL)

The following health care treatment instructions exercise my right to make my own health care decisions. These instructions are intended to provide clear and convincing evidence of my wishes to be followed when I lack the capacity to understand, make or communicate my treatment decisions:

IF I HAVE AN END-STAGE MEDICAL CONDITION (WHICH WILL RESULT IN MY DEATH, DESPITE THE INTRODUCTION OR CONTINUATION OF MEDICAL TREATMENT) OR AM PERMANENTLY UNCONSCIOUS SUCH AS AN IRREVERSIBLE COMA OR AN IRREVERSIBLE VEGETATIVE STATE AND THERE IS NO REALISTIC HOPE OF SIGNIFICANT RECOVERY, ALL OF THE FOLLOWING APPLY (CROSS OUT ANY TREATMENT INSTRUCTIONS WITH WHICH YOU DO NOT AGREE):

1.   I direct that I be given health care treatment to relieve pain or provide comfort even if such treatment might shorten my life, suppress my appetite or my breathing, or be habit forming.

2.   I direct that all life prolonging procedures be withheld or withdrawn.

3.   I specifically do not want any of the following as life prolonging procedures: (If you wish to receive any of these treatments, write "I do want" after the treatment)

Heart-lung resuscitation (CPR)   _____
Mechanical ventilator (breathing machine) _____
Dialysis (kidney machine)   _____
Surgery   _____
Chemotherapy   _____
Radiation treatment   _____
Antibiotics   _____

Please indicate whether you want nutrition (food) or hydration (water) medically supplied by a tube into your nose, stomach, intestine, arteries, or veins if you have an end-stage medical condition or are permanently unconscious and there is no realistic hope of significant recovery.

(Initial only one statement.)

TUBE FEEDINGS

_____   I want tube feedings to be given

OR

NO TUBE FEEDINGS

_____   I do not want tube feedings to be given.

HEALTH CARE AGENT'S USE OF INSTRUCTIONS

(INITIAL ONE OPTION ONLY).

_____   My health care agent must follow these instructions.

OR

_____   These instructions are only guidance. My health care agent shall
                   have final say and may override any of my instructions. (Indicate any
                   exceptions) _____

                   _____

                   _____

If I did not appoint a health care agent, these instructions shall be followed.

LEGAL PROTECTION

Pennsylvania law protects my health care agent and health care providers from any legal
liability for their good faith actions in following my wishes as expressed in this form or
in complying with my health care agent's direction. On behalf of myself, my executors
and heirs, I further hold my health care agent and my health care providers harmless and
indemnify them against any claim for their good faith actions in recognizing my health
care agent's authority or in following my treatment instructions.

ORGAN DONATION

(INITIAL ONE OPTION ONLY.)

_____   I consent to donate my organs and tissues at the time of my death
                   for the purpose of transplant, medical study or education. (Insert any
                   limitations you desire on donation of specific organs or tissues or uses
                   for donation of organs and tissues.)

                   _____

_____

_____

OR

_____   I do not consent to donate my organs or tissues at the
time of my death.

SIGNATURE

Having carefully read this document, I have signed it this.......day of............., 20..., revoking all
previous health care powers of attorney and health care treatment instructions.

_____

(SIGN FULL NAME HERE FOR HEALTH CARE POWER OF ATTORNEY AND

HEALTH CARE TREATMENT INSTRUCTIONS)

WITNESS:

    Name: _____

    Address: _____

    _____

    _____

WITNESS:

    Name: _____

    Address: _____

    _____

    _____

Two witnesses at least 18 years of age are required by Pennsylvania law and should witness your
signature in each other's presence. A person who signs this document on behalf of and at the
direction of a principal may not be a witness.

(It is preferable if the witnesses are not your heirs, nor your creditors, nor employed by any of
your health care providers.)

NOTARIZATION
(OPTIONAL)

(Notarization of document is not required by Pennsylvania law, but if the document is both witnessed and notarized, it is more likely to be honored by the laws of some other states.)

On this _____ day of _____, 20____, before me personally appeared the aforesaid declarant and principal, to me known to be the person described in and who executed the foregoing instrument and acknowledged that he/she executed the same as his/her free act and deed.

IN WITNESS WHEREOF, I have hereunto set my hand and affixed my official seal in the County of_____, State of_____ the day and year first above written.

_____   _____   Notary

    Public   My commission expires

Rhode Island State Forms

DECLARATION

I, _____, being of sound mind willfully and voluntarily make known my desire that my dying shall not be artificially prolonged under the circumstances set forth below, do hereby declare:

If I should have an incurable or irreversible condition that will cause my death and if I am unable to make decisions regarding my medical treatment, I direct my attending physician to withhold or withdraw procedures that merely prolong the dying process and are not necessary to my comfort, or to alleviate pain.

This authorization

      includes   [   ]
      does not include   [   ]

the withholding or withdrawal of artificial feeding (check only one box above).

Signed this _____ day of _____, 20___.
Signature   _____
Address   _____
               _____
               _____
               _____

The declarant is personally known to me and voluntarily signed this document in my presence.

Signature of witness   _____
Address   _____
                    _____
                    _____
                    _____

Signature of witness   _____

Address   _____

_____

_____

_____

STATUTORY FORM DURABLE POWER OF ATTORNEY FOR HEALTH CARE

WARNING TO PERSON EXECUTING THIS DOCUMENT

This is an important legal document which is authorized by the general laws of this state. Before executing this document, you should know these important facts:

You must be at least eighteen (18) years of age and a resident of the state for this document to be legally valid and binding.

This document gives the person you designate as your agent (the attorney in fact) the power to make health care decisions for you. Your agent must act consistently with your desires as stated in this document or otherwise made known.

Except as you otherwise specify in this document, this document gives your agent the power to consent to your doctor not giving treatment or stopping treatment necessary to keep you alive.

Notwithstanding this document, you have the right to make medical and other health care decisions for yourself so long as you can give informed consent with respect to the particular decision. In addition, no treatment may be given to you over your objection at the time, and health care necessary to keep you alive may not be stopped or withheld if you object at the time.

This document gives your agent authority to consent, to refuse to consent, or to withdraw consent to any care, treatment, service, or procedure to maintain, diagnose, or treat a physical or mental condition. This power is subject to any statement of your desires and any limitation that you include in this document. You may state in this document any types of treatment that you do not desire. In addition, a court can take away the power of your agent to make health care decisions for you if your agent:

    (1) Authorizes anything that is illegal,

304 | MAKE YOUR OWN LIVING WILL

(2) Acts contrary to your known desires, or

(3) Where your desires are not known, does anything that is clearly contrary to your best interests.

Unless you specify a specific period, this power will exist until you revoke it. Your agent's power and authority ceases upon your death except to inform your family or next of kin of your desire, if any, to be an organ and tissue owner.

You have the right to revoke the authority of your agent by notifying your agent or your treating doctor, hospital, or other health care provider orally or in writing of the revocation.

Your agent has the right to examine your medical records and to consent to their disclosure unless you limit this right in this document.

This document revokes any prior durable power of attorney for health care.

You should carefully read and follow the witnessing procedure described at the end of this form. This document will not be valid unless you comply with the witnessing procedure.

If there is anything in this document that you do not understand, you should ask a lawyer to explain it to you.

Your agent may need this document immediately in case of an emergency that requires a decision concerning your health care. Either keep this document where it is immediately available to your agent and alternate agents or give each of them an executed copy of this document. You may also want to give your doctor an executed copy of this document.

RHODE ISLAND DURABLE POWER OF ATTORNEY FOR HEALTHCARE

(1)   **DESIGNATION OF HEALTH CARE AGENT**

I, _____ (insert your name and address) do hereby designate and appoint:

_____

(insert name, address, and telephone number of one individual only as your agent to make health care decisions for you. None of the following may be designated as your agent: (1) your treating health

care provider, (2) a nonrelative employee of your treating health care provider, (3) an operator of a community care facility, or (4) a nonrelative employee of an operator of a community care facility.)

as my attorney in fact (agent) to make health care decisions for me as authorized in this document. For the purposes of this document, "health care decision" means consent, refusal of consent, or withdrawal of consent to any care, treatment, service, or procedure to maintain, diagnose, or treat an individual's physical or mental condition.

(2) **CREATION OF DURABLE POWER OF ATTORNEY FOR HEALTH CARE**

By this document I intend to create a durable power of attorney for health care.

(3) **GENERAL STATEMENT OF AUTHORITY GRANTED**

Subject to any limitations in this document, I hereby grant to my agent full power and authority to make health care decisions for me to the same extent that I could make such decisions for myself if I had the capacity to do so. In exercising this authority, my agent shall make health care decisions that are consistent with my desires as stated in this document or otherwise made known to my agent, including, but not limited to, my desires concerning obtaining or refusing or withdrawing life-prolonging care, treatment, services, and procedures and informing my family or next of kin of my desire, if any, to be an organ or tissue donor.

(If you want to limit the authority of your agent to make health care decisions for you, you can state the limitations in paragraph (4) ("Statement of Desires, Special Provisions, and Limitations") below. You can indicate your desires by including a statement of your desires in the same paragraph.)

(4) **STATEMENT OF DESIRES, SPECIAL PROVISIONS, AND LIMITATIONS**

(Your agent must make health care decisions that are consistent with your known desires. You can, but are not required to, state your desires in the space provided below. You should consider whether you want to include a statement of your desires concerning life-prolonging care, treatment, services, and procedures. You can also include a statement of your desires concerning other matters relating to your health care. You can also make your desires known to your agent by discussing your desires with your agent or by some other means. If there are any types of treatment that you do not want to be used, you should

state them in the space below. If you want to limit in any other way the authority given your agent by this document, you should state the limits in the space below. If you do not state any limits, your agent will have broad powers to make health care decisions for you, except to the extent that there are limits provided by law.)

In exercising the authority under this durable power of attorney for health care, my agent shall act consistently with my desires as stated below and is subject to the special provisions and limitations stated below:

(a)   Statement of desires concerning life-prolonging care, treatment, services, and procedures:

_____
_____
_____

(b)   Additional statement of desires, special provisions, and limitations regarding health care decisions:

_____
_____
_____

(c)   Statement of desire regarding organ and tissue donation:

_____
_____
_____

Initial if applicable:

[   ]   In the event of my death, I request that my agent inform my family/next of kin of my desire to be an organ and tissue donor, if possible.

_____
_____
_____

(You may attach additional pages if you need more space to complete your statement. If you attach additional pages, you must date and sign EACH of the additional pages at the same time you date and sign this document.)

(5) **INSPECTION AND DISCLOSURE OF INFORMATION RELATING TO MY PHYSICAL OR MENTAL HEALTH**

Subject to any limitations in this document, my agent has the power and authority to do all of the following:

(a) Request, review, and receive any information, verbal or written, regarding my physical or mental health, including, but not limited to, medical and hospital records.

(b) Execute on my behalf any releases or other documents that may be required in order to obtain this information.

(c) Consent to the disclosure of this information.

(If you want to limit the authority of your agent to receive and disclose information relating to your health, you must state the limitations in paragraph (4) ("Statement of desires, special provisions, and limitations") above.)

(6) **SIGNING DOCUMENTS, WAIVERS, AND RELEASES**

Where necessary to implement the health care decisions that my agent is authorized by this document to make, my agent has the power and authority to execute on my behalf all of the following:

(a) Documents titled or purporting to be a "Refusal to Permit Treatment" and "Leaving Hospital Against Medical Advice."

(b) Any necessary waiver or release from liability required by a hospital or physician.

(7) **DURATION**

(Unless you specify a shorter period in the space below, this power of attorney will exist until it is revoked.)

This durable power of attorney for health care expires on _____.

(Fill in this space ONLY if you want the authority of your agent to end on a specific date.)

(8)   **DESIGNATION OF ALTERNATE AGENTS**

(You are not required to designate any alternate agents but you may do so. Any alternate agent you designate will be able to make the same health care decisions as the agent you designated in paragraph (1), above, in the event that agent is unable or ineligible to act as your agent. If the agent you designated is your spouse, he or she becomes ineligible to act as your agent if your marriage is dissolved.)

If the person designated as my agent in paragraph (1) is not available or becomes ineligible to act as my agent to make a health care decision for me or loses the mental capacity to make health care decisions for me, or if I revoke that person's appointment or authority to act as my agent to make health care decisions for me, then I designate and appoint the following persons to serve as my agent to make health care decisions for me as authorized in this document, such persons to serve in the order listed below:

(A) First Alternate Agent:

(Insert name, address, and telephone number of first alternate agent.)

(B) Second Alternate Agent:

(Insert name, address, and telephone number of second alternate agent.)

(9)   **PRIOR DESIGNATIONS REVOKED**

I revoke any prior durable power of attorney for health care.

DATE AND SIGNATURE OF PRINCIPAL

(YOU MUST DATE AND SIGN THIS POWER OF ATTORNEY)

I sign my name to this Statutory Form Durable Power of Attorney for Health Care on

_____

(Date)

At _____

(Address) (City) (State)

_____

(You sign here)

(THIS POWER OF ATTORNEY WILL NOT BE VALID UNLESS IT IS SIGNED BY ONE NOTARY PUBLIC OR TWO (2) QUALIFIED WITNESSES WHO ARE PRESENT WHEN YOU SIGN OR ACKNOWLEDGE YOUR SIGNATURE. IF YOU HAVE ATTACHED ANY ADDITIONAL PAGES TO THIS FORM, YOU MUST DATE AND SIGN EACH OF THE ADDITIONAL PAGES AT THE SAME TIME YOU DATE AND SIGN THIS POWER OF ATTORNEY.)

STATEMENT OF WITNESSES

(This document must be witnessed by two (2) qualified adult witnesses or one (1) notary public. None of the following may be used as a witness:

(1)   A person you designate as your agent or alternate agent,

(2)   A health care provider,

(3)   An employee of a health care provider,

(4)   The operator of a community care facility,

(5)   An employee of an operator of a community care facility.

I declare under penalty of perjury that the person who signed or acknowledged this document is personally known to me to be the principal, that the principal signed or acknowledged this durable power of attorney in my presence, that the principal appears to be of sound mind and under no duress, fraud, or undue influence, that I am not the person appointed as attorney in fact by this document, and that I am not a health care provider, an employee of a health care provider, the operator of a community care facility, nor an employee of an operator of a community care facility.

Option 1 – Two (2) Qualified Witnesses

Signature of witness   _____

Name of witness   _____

Address   _____

_____

_____

_____

Date   _____

Signature of witness   _____

Name of witness   _____

Address   _____

_____

_____

_____

Date   _____

Option 2 – One Notary Public

Signature   _____, Notary Public

Print Name   _____

Date   _____

My commission expires on: _____

(AT LEAST ONE OF THE ABOVE WITNESSES OR THE NOTARY PUBLIC MUST ALSO SIGN THE FOLLOWING DECLARATION.)

I further declare under penalty of perjury that I am not related to the principal by blood, marriage, or adoption, and, to the best of my knowledge, I am not entitled to any part of the estate of the principal upon the death of the principal under a will now existing or by operation of law.

Signature   _____

Print Name   _____

South Carolina State Forms

STATE OF SOUTH CAROLINA   **COUNTY OF** _____

DECLARATION OF A DESIRE FOR A NATURAL DEATH

I, _____, Declarant, being at least eighteen years of age and a resident of and domiciled in the City of _____, County of _____, State of South Carolina, make this Declaration this ___ day of _____, 20___.

I wilfully and voluntarily make known my desire that no life-sustaining procedures be used to prolong my dying if my condition is terminal or if I am in a state of permanent unconsciousness, and I declare:

If at any time I have a condition certified to be a terminal condition by two physicians who have personally examined me, one of whom is my attending physician, and the physicians have determined that my death could occur within a reasonably short period of time without the use of life-sustaining procedures or if the physicians certify that I am in a state of permanent unconsciousness and where the application of life-sustaining procedures would serve only to prolong the dying process, I direct that the procedures be withheld or withdrawn, and that I be permitted to die naturally with only the administration of medication or the performance of any medical procedure necessary to provide me with comfort care.

INSTRUCTIONS CONCERNING ARTIFICIAL NUTRITION AND HYDRATION

INITIAL ONE OF THE FOLLOWING STATEMENTS

If my condition is terminal and could result in death within a reasonably short time,

_____ I direct that nutrition and hydration BE PROVIDED through any medically indicated means, including medically or surgically implanted tubes.

_____ I direct that nutrition and hydration NOT BE PROVIDED through any medically indicated means, including medically or surgically implanted tubes.
INITIAL ONE OF THE FOLLOWING STATEMENTS

If I am in a persistent vegetative state or other condition of permanent unconsciousness,

_____ I direct that nutrition and hydration BE PROVIDED through any medically indicated means, including medically or surgically implanted tubes.

_____ I direct that nutrition and hydration NOT BE PROVIDED through any medically indicated means, including medically or surgically implanted tubes.

In the absence of my ability to give directions regarding the use of life-sustaining procedures, it is my intention that this Declaration be honored by my family and physicians and any health facility in which I may be a patient as the final expression of my legal right to refuse medical or surgical treatment, and I accept the consequences from the refusal.

I am aware that this Declaration authorizes a physician to withhold or withdraw life-sustaining procedures. I am emotionally and mentally competent to make this Declaration.

APPOINTMENT OF AN AGENT

(OPTIONAL)

1. You may give another person authority to revoke this declaration on your behalf. If you wish to do so, please enter that person's name in the space below.

Name of Agent with Power to Revoke: _____
Address: _____
_____
_____
Telephone Number: _____

2. You may give another person authority to enforce this declaration on your behalf. If you

wish to do so, please enter that person's name in the space below.

Name of Agent with Power to enforcec: _____

Address: _____

_____

_____

Telephone Number: _____

REVOCATION PROCEDURES

THIS DECLARATION MAY BE REVOKED BY ANY ONE OF THE FOLLOWING METHODS. HOWEVER, A REVOCATION IS NOT EFFECTIVE UNTIL IT IS COMMUNICATED TO THE ATTENDING PHYSICIAN.

(1) BY BEING DEFACED, TORN, OBLITERATED, OR OTHERWISE DESTROYED, IN EXPRESSION OF YOUR INTENT TO REVOKE, BY YOU OR BY SOME PERSON IN YOUR PRESENCE AND BY YOUR DIRECTION. REVOCATION BY DESTRUCTION OF ONE OR MORE OF MULTIPLE ORIGINAL DECLARATIONS REVOKES ALL OF THE ORIGINAL DECLARATIONS;

(2) BY A WRITTEN REVOCATION SIGNED AND DATED BY YOU EXPRESSING YOUR INTENT TO REVOKE;

(3) BY YOUR ORAL EXPRESSION OF YOUR INTENT TO REVOKE THE DECLARATION. AN ORAL REVOCATION COMMUNICATED TO THE ATTENDING PHYSICIAN BY A PERSON OTHER THAN YOU IS EFFECTIVE ONLY IF:

(a) THE PERSON WAS PRESENT WHEN THE ORAL REVOCATION WAS MADE;

(b) THE REVOCATION WAS COMMUNICATED TO THE PHYSICIAN WITHIN A REASONABLE TIME;

(c) YOUR PHYSICAL OR MENTAL CONDITION MAKES IT IMPOSSIBLE FOR THE PHYSICIAN TO CONFIRM THROUGH SUBSEQUENT CONVERSATION WITH YOU THAT THE REVOCATION HAS OCCURRED.

TO BE EFFECTIVE AS A REVOCATION, THE ORAL EXPRESSION CLEARLY MUST INDICATE YOUR DESIRE THAT THE DECLARATION NOT BE GIVEN

EFFECT OR THAT LIFE-SUSTAINING PROCEDURES BE ADMINISTERED;

(4)   IF YOU, IN THE SPACE ABOVE, HAVE AUTHORIZED AN AGENT TO REVOKE THE   DECLARATION, THE AGENT MAY REVOKE ORALLY OR BY A WRITTEN, SIGNED, AND DATED INSTRUMENT. AN AGENT MAY REVOKE ONLY IF YOU ARE INCOMPETENT TO DO SO. AN AGENT MAY REVOKE THE DECLARATION PERMANENTLY OR TEMPORARILY.

(5)   BY YOUR EXECUTING ANOTHER DECLARATION AT A LATER TIME.

_____

Signature of Declarant

STATE OF _____   COUNTY OF _____

AFFIDAVIT

We, _____ and _____, the undersigned witnesses to the foregoing Declaration, dated the ____ day of _____, 20____, at least one of us being first duly sworn, declare to the undersigned authority, on the basis of our best information and belief, that the Declaration was on that date signed by the declarant as and for his DECLARATION OF A DESIRE FOR A NATURAL DEATH in our presence and we, at his request and in his presence, and in the presence of each other, subscribe our names as witnesses on that date. The declarant is personally known to us, and we believe him to be of sound mind. Each of us affirms that he is qualified as a witness to this Declaration under the provisions of the South Carolina Death With Dignity Act in that he is not related to the declarant by blood, marriage, or adoption, either as a spouse, lineal ancestor, descendant of the parents of the declarant, or spouse of any of them; nor directly financially responsible for the declarant's medical care; nor entitled to any portion of the declarant's estate upon his decease, whether under any will or as an heir by intestate succession; nor the beneficiary of a life insurance policy of the declarant; nor the declarant's attending physician; nor an employee of the attending physician; nor a person who has a claim against the declarant's decedent's estate as of this time. No more than one of us is an employee of a health facility in which the declarant is a patient. If the declarant is a resident in a hospital or nursing care facility at the date of execution of this Declaration, at least one of us is an ombudsman designated by the State Ombudsman, Office of the Governor.

_____

Witness

_____
Witness

Subscribed before me by _____, the declarant, and subscribed and sworn to before me by _____, the witnesses, this ___ day of _____, 20___.

_____
Signature

Notary Public for _____

My commission expires: _____

SEAL

South Dakota State Forms

LIVING WILL DECLARATION

This is an important legal document. A living will directs the medical treatment you are to receive in the event you are in a terminal condition and are unable to participate in your own medical decisions. This living will may state what kind of treatment you want or do not want to receive.

Prepare this living will carefully. If you use this form, read it completely. You may want to seek professional help to make sure the form does what you intend and is completed without mistakes.

This living will remains valid and in effect until and unless you revoke it. Review this living will periodically to make sure it continues to reflect your wishes. You may amend or revoke this living will at any time by notifying your physician and other health care providers. You should give copies of this living will to your family, your physician, and your health care facility. This form is entirely optional. If you choose to use this form, please note that the form provides signature lines for you, the two witnesses whom you have selected, and a notary public.

TO MY FAMILY, HEALTH CARE PROVIDER, AND ALL THOSE CONCERNED WITH MY CARE:

I, _____ direct you to follow my wishes for care if I am in a terminal condition, my death is imminent, and I am unable to communicate my decisions about my medical care.

With respect to any life-sustaining treatment, I direct the following:

(Initial only one of the following options. If you do not agree with either of the following options, space is provided below for you to write your own instructions.)

_____ If my death is imminent or I am permanently unconscious, I choose not to prolong my life. If life sustaining treatment has been started, stop it, but keep me comfortable and control my pain.

_____ Even if my death is imminent or I am permanently unconscious, I choose to prolong my life.

_____   I choose neither of the above options, and here are my instructions should I become terminally ill and my death is imminent or I am permanently unconscious:

_____

_____

_____

_____

Artificial Nutrition and Hydration: food and water provided by means of a tube inserted into the stomach or intestine or needle into a vein.

With respect to artificial nutrition and hydration, I direct the following:

(Initial only one)

_____   If my death is imminent or I am permanently unconscious, I do not want artificial nutrition and hydration. If it has been started, stop it.

_____   Even if my death is imminent or I am permanently unconscious, I want artificial nutrition and hydration.

Date: _____

(your signature)

_____

(your address)   (type or print your signature)

The declarant voluntarily signed this document in my presence.

Witness _____

Address _____

Witness _____

Address _____

On this the _____ day of _____, 20___, the declarant, _____, and witnesses _____, and _____ personally appeared before the undersigned officer and signed the foregoing instrument in my presence.

Dated this _____ day of day of _____, 20___.

_____ Notary Public

My commission expires: _____.

Tennessee State Forms

LIVING WILL

I, _____, willfully and voluntarily make known my desire that my dying shall not be artificially prolonged under the circumstances set forth below, and do hereby declare:

If at any time I should have a terminal condition and my attending physician has determined there is no reasonable medical expectation of recovery and which, as a medical probability, will result in my death, regardless of the use or discontinuance of medical treatment implemented for the purpose of sustaining life, or the life process, I direct that medical care be withheld or withdrawn, and that I be permitted to die naturally with only the administration of medications or the performance of any medical procedure deemed necessary to provide me with comfortable care or to alleviate pain.

ARTIFICIALLY PROVIDED NOURISHMENT AND FLUIDS

By checking the appropriate line below, I specifically:

[ ]   Authorize the withholding or withdrawal of artificially provided

food, water or other nourishment or fluids.

[ ]   DO NOT authorize the withholding or withdrawal of
artificially provided food, water or other nourishment or fluids.

ORGAN DONOR CERTIFICATION

Notwithstanding my previous declaration relative to the withholding or withdrawal of life-prolonging procedures, if as indicated below I have expressed my desire to donate my organs and/or tissues for transplantation, or any of them as specifically designated herein, I do direct my attending physician, if I have been determined dead according to Tennessee Code Annotated, § 68-3-501(b), to maintain me on artificial support systems only for the period of time required to maintain the viability of and to remove such organs and/or tissues. By checking the appropriate line below, I specifically:

320 | MAKE YOUR OWN LIVING WILL

[ ]   Desire to donate my organs and/or tissues for transplantation.

[ ]   Desire to donate my _____ (Insert specific organs and/or tissues for.

[ ]   DO NOT desire to donate my organs or tissues for transplantation.

In the absence of my ability to give directions regarding my medical care, it is my intention that this declaration shall be honored by my family and physician as the final expression of my legal right to refuse medical care and accept the consequences of such refusal.

The definitions of terms used herein shall be as set forth in the Tennessee Right to Natural Death Act, Tennessee Code Annotated, § 32-11-103.

I understand the full import of this declaration, and I am emotionally and mentally competent to make this declaration.In acknowledgment whereof, I do hereinafter affix my signature on

this the _____ day of_____, 20___.

_____

Declarant

We, the subscribing witnesses hereto, are personally acquainted with and subscribe our names hereto at the request of the declarant, an adult, whom we believe to be of sound mind, fully aware of the action taken herein and its possible consequence.

We, the undersigned witnesses, further declare that we are not related to the declarant by blood or marriage; that we are not entitled to any portion of the estate of the declarant upon the declarant's decease under any will or codicil thereto presently existing or by operation of law then existing; that we are not the attending physician, an employee of the attending physician or a health facility in which the declarant is a patient; and that we are not persons who, at the present time, have a claim against any portion of the estate of the declarant upon the declarant's death.

Witness: _____
Witness: _____

STATE OF TENNESSEE   **COUNTY OF** _____

Subscribed, sworn to and acknowledged before me by _____, the declarant, and subscribed and sworn to before me by _____ and _____, witnesses, this day of _____, 20___.

_____

Notary Public

My Commission Expires:

Texas State Forms

DIRECTIVE TO PHYSICIANS AND FAMILY OR SURROGATES

<u>Instructions for completing this document</u>:

This is an important legal document known as an Advance Directive. It is designed to help you communicate your wishes about medical treatment at some time in the future when you are unable to make your wishes known because of illness or injury. These wishes are usually based on personal values. In particular, you may want to consider what burdens or hardships of treatment you would be willing to accept for a particular amount of benefit obtained if you were seriously ill.

You are encouraged to discuss your values and wishes with your family or chosen spokesperson, as well as your physician. Your physician, other health care provider, or medical institution may provide you with various resources to assist you in completing your advance directive. Brief definitions are listed below and may aid you in your discussions and advance planning. Initial the treatment choices that best reflect your personal preferences. Provide a copy of your directive to your physician, usual hospital, and family or spokesperson. Consider a periodic review of this document. By periodic review, you can best assure that the directive reflects your preferences.

In addition to this advance directive, Texas law provides for two other types of directives that can be important during a serious illness. These are the Medical Power of Attorney and the Out-of-Hospital Do-Not-Resuscitate Order. You may wish to discuss these with your physician, family, hospital representative, or other advisers. You may also wish to complete a directive related to the donation of organs and tissues.

DIRECTIVE

I, _____, recognize that the best health care is based upon a partnership of trust and communication with my physician. My physician and I will make health care decisions together as long as I am of sound mind and able to make my wishes known. If there comes a time that I am unable to make medical decisions about myself because of illness or injury, I direct that the following treatment preferences be honored:

If, in the judgment of my physician, I am suffering with a terminal condition from which I am expected to die within six months, even with available life-sustaining treatment provided in accordance with prevailing standards of medical care:

_____   I request that all treatments other than those needed to keep me comfortable be discontinued or withheld and my physician allow me to die as gently as possible; OR

_____   I request that I be kept alive in this terminal condition using available life-sustaining treatment. (THIS SELECTION DOES NOT APPLY TO HOSPICE CARE.)

If, in the judgment of my physician, I am suffering with an irreversible condition so that I cannot care for myself or make decisions for myself and am expected to die without life-sustaining treatment provided in accordance with prevailing standards of care:

_____   I request that all treatments other than those needed to keep me comfortable be discontinued or withheld and my physician allow me to die as gently as possible; OR

_____   I request that I be kept alive in this irreversible condition using available life-sustaining treatment. *(THIS SELECTION DOES NOT APPLY TO HOSPICE CARE.)*

Additional requests: *(After discussion with your physician, you may wish to consider listing particular treatments in this space that you do or do not want in specific circumstances, such as artificial nutrition and fluids, intravenous antibiotics, etc. Be sure to state whether you do or do not want the particular treatment.)*

_____

After signing this directive, if my representative or I elect hospice care, I understand and agree that only those treatments needed to keep me comfortable would be provided and I would not be given available life-sustaining treatments.

If I do not have a Medical Power of Attorney, and I am unable to make my wishes known, I designate the following person(s) to make treatment decisions with my physician compatible with my personal values:

1. _____

2. _____

(If a Medical Power of Attorney has been executed, then an agent already has been named and you should not list additional names in this document.)

If the above persons are not available, or if I have not designated a spokesperson, I understand that a spokesperson will be chosen for me following standards specified in the laws of Texas. If, in the judgment of my physician, my death is imminent within minutes to hours, even with the use of all available medical treatment provided within the prevailing standard of care, I acknowledge that all treatments may be withheld or removed except those needed to maintain my comfort. I understand that under Texas law this directive has no effect if I have been diagnosed as pregnant. This directive will remain in effect until I revoke it. No other person may do so.

Signed _____ Date_____ City, County, State of Residence _____

Two competent adult witnesses must sign below, acknowledging the signature of the declarant. The witness designated as Witness 1 may not be a person designated to make a treatment decision for the patient and may not be related to the patient by blood or marriage. This witness may not be entitled to any part of the estate and may not have a claim against the estate of the patient. This witness may not be the attending physician or an employee of the attending physician. If this witness is an employee of a health care facility in which the patient is being cared for, this witness may not be involved in providing direct patient care to the patient. This witness may not be an officer, director, partner, or business office employee of a health care facility in which the patient is being cared for or of any parent organization of the health care facility.

Witness 1 _____

Witness 2 _____

Definitions:

"Artificial nutrition and hydration" means the provision of nutrients or fluids by a tube inserted in a vein, under the skin in the subcutaneous tissues, or in the stomach (gastrointestinal tract).

"Irreversible condition" means a condition, injury, or illness:

    (1)   that may be treated, but is never cured or eliminated;

    (2)   that leaves a person unable to care for or make decisions for the person's own self; and

    (3)   that, without life-sustaining treatment provided in accordance with the prevailing standard of medical care, is fatal.

Explanation: Many serious illnesses such as cancer, failure of major organs (kidney, heart, liver, or lung), and serious brain disease such as Alzheimer's dementia may be considered irreversible early on. There is no cure, but the patient may be kept alive for prolonged periods of time if the patient receives life-sustaining treatments. Late in the course of the same illness, the disease may be considered terminal when, even with treatment, the patient is expected to die. You may wish to consider which burdens of treatment you would be willing to accept in an effort to achieve a particular outcome. This is a very personal decision that you may wish to discuss with your physician, family, or other important persons in your life.

"Life-sustaining treatment" means treatment that, based on reasonable medical judgment, sustains the life of a patient and without which the patient will die. The term includes both life-sustaining medications and artificial life support such as mechanical breathing machines, kidney dialysis treatment, and artificial hydration and nutrition. The term does not include the administration of pain management medication, the performance of a medical procedure necessary to provide comfort care, or any other medical care provided to alleviate a patient's pain.

"Terminal condition" means an incurable condition caused by injury, disease, or illness that according to reasonable medical judgment will produce death within six months, even with available life-sustaining treatment provided in accordance with the prevailing standard of medical care.

Explanation: Many serious illnesses may be considered irreversible early in the course of the illness, but they may not be considered terminal until the disease is fairly advanced. In thinking about terminal illness and its treatment, you again may wish to consider the relative benefits and burdens of treatment and discuss your wishes with your physician, family, or other important persons in your life.

Utah State Forms

DIRECTIVE TO PHYSICIANS AND PROVIDERS OF MEDICAL SERVICES

(Pursuant to Section 75-2-1104, UCA)

This directive is made this _____ day of _____, 20___.

1. I, _____, being of sound mind, willfully and voluntarily make known my desire that my life not be artificially prolonged by life-sustaining procedures except as I may otherwise provide in this directive.

2. I declare that if at any time I should have an injury, disease, or illness, which is certified in writing to be a terminal condition or persistent vegetative state by two physicians who have personally examined me, and in the opinion of those physicians the application of life-sustaining procedures would serve only to unnaturally prolong the moment of my death and to unnaturally postpone or prolong the dying process, I direct that these procedures be withheld or withdrawn and my death be permitted to occur naturally.

3. I expressly intend this directive to be a final expression of my legal right to refuse medical or surgical treatment and to accept the consequences from this refusal which shall remain in effect notwithstanding my future inability to give current medical directions to treating physicians and other providers of medical services.

4. I understand that the term "life-sustaining procedure" includes artificial nutrition and hydration and any other procedures that I specify below to be considered life-sustaining but does not include the administration of medication or the performance of any medical procedure which is intended to provide comfort care or to alleviate pain:_____

    _____

    _____

    _____

5. I reserve the right to give current medical directions to physicians and other providers of medical services so long as I am able, even though these directions may conflict with the above written directive that life-sustaining procedures be withheld or withdrawn.

6. I understand the full import of this directive and declare that I am emotionally and mentally competent to make this directive.

_____

Declarant's signature

_____

City, County, and State of Residence

We witnesses certify that each of us is 18 years of age or older and each personally witnessed the declarant sign or direct the signing of this directive; that we are acquainted with the declarant and believe him to be of sound mind; that the declarant's desires are as expressed above; that neither of us is a person who signed the above directive on behalf of the declarant; that we are not related to the declarant by blood or marriage nor are we entitled to any portion of declarant's estate according to the laws of intestate succession of this state or under any will or codicil of declarant; that we are not directly financially responsible for declarant's medical care; and that we are not agents of any health care facility in which the declarant may be a patient at the time of signing this directive.

_____   _____

Signature of Witness   Signature of Witness

_____   _____

Address of Witness   Address of Witness

SPECIAL POWER OF ATTORNEY

I, _____, of _____, this _____ day of _____, 20____, being of sound mind, willfully and voluntarily appoint _____ of _____ as my agent and attorney-in-fact, without substitution, with lawful authority to execute a directive on my behalf under Section 75-2-1105, governing the care and treatment to be administered to or withheld from me at any time after I incur an injury, disease, or illness which renders me unable to give current directions to attending physicians and other providers of medical services.

I have carefully selected my above-named agent with confidence in the belief that this person's familiarity with my desires, beliefs, and attitudes will result in directions to attending physicians and providers of medical services which would probably be the same as I would give if able to do so.

This power of attorney shall be and remain in effect from the time my attending physician certifies that I have incurred a physical or mental condition rendering me unable to give current directions to attending physicians and other providers of medical services as to my care and treatment.

_____
Signature of Principal

State of _____)
                       ): ss.
County of _____)

On the _____ day of _____, 20____, personally appeared before me _____, who duly acknowledged to me that he has read and fully understands the foregoing power of attorney, executed the same of his own volition and for the purposes set forth, and that he was acting under no constraint or undue influence whatsoever.

_____
Notary Public

My commission expires:

Residing at: _____

_____

Vermont State Forms

STATE OF VERMONT

INFORMATION CONCERNING THE DURABLE POWER OF ATTORNEY FOR HEALTH CARE

THIS IS AN IMPORTANT LEGAL DOCUMENT. BEFORE SIGNING THIS DOCUMENT, YOU SHOULD KNOW THESE IMPORTANT FACTS:

Except to the extent you state otherwise, this document gives the person your name as your agent the authority to make any and all health care decisions for you when you are no longer capable of making them yourself. "Health care" means any treatment, service or procedure to maintain, diagnose or treat your physical or mental condition. Your agent therefore can have the power to make a broad range of health care decisions for you. Your agent may consent, refuse to consent, or withdraw consent to medical treatment and may make decisions about withdrawing or withholding life-sustaining treatment.

You may state in this document any treatment you do not desire or treatment you want to be sure you receive. Your agent's authority will begin when your doctor certifies that you lack the capacity to make health care decisions. You may attach additional pages if you need more space to complete your statement.

Your agent will be obligated to follow your instructions when making decisions on your behalf. Unless you state otherwise, your agent will have the same authority to make decisions about your health care as you would have had.

It is important that you discuss this document with your physician or other health care providers before you sign it to make sure that you understand the nature and range of decisions which may be made on your behalf. If you do not have a physician, you should talk with someone else who is knowledgeable about these issues and can answer your questions. You do not need a lawyer's assistance to complete this document, but if there is anything in this document that you do not understand, you should ask a lawyer to explain it to you.

The person you appoint as agent should be someone you know and trust and must be at least 18 years old. If you appoint your health or residential care provider (e.g. your physician, or an employee of a home health agency, hospital, nursing home, or residential care home, other than a relative), that person will have to choose between acting as your agent or as your health or residential care provider; the law does not permit a person to do both at the same time.

You should inform the person you appoint that you want him or her to be your health care agent. You should discuss this document with your agent and your physician and give each a signed copy. You should indicate on the document itself the people and institutions who will have signed copies. Your agent will not be liable for health care decisions made in good faith on your behalf.

Even after you have signed this document, you have the right to make health care decisions for yourself as long as you are able to do so, and treatment cannot be given to you or stopped over your objection. You have the right to revoke the authority granted to your agent by informing him or her or your health care provider orally or in writing.

This document may not be changed or modified. If you want to make changes in the document you must make an entirely new one.

You may wish to designate an alternate agent in the event that your agent is unwilling, unable or ineligible to act as your agent. Any alternate agent you designate will have the same authority to make health care decisions for you.

THIS POWER OF ATTORNEY WILL NOT BE VALID UNLESS IT IS SIGNED IN THE PRESENCE OF TWO (2) OR MORE QUALIFIED WITNESSES WHO MUST BOTH BE PRESENT WHEN YOU SIGN OR ACKNOWLEDGE YOUR SIGNATURE. THE FOLLOWING PERSONS MAY NOT ACT AS WITNESSES:

- the person you have designated as your agent;
- your health or residential care provider or one of their employees;

- your spouse;

- your lawful heirs or beneficiaries named in your will or a deed;

- creditors or persons who have a claim against you.

(Recodified 2003, No. 162 (Adj. Sess.), § 15.)

DURABLE POWER OF ATTORNEY FOR HEALTH CARE

I, _____, hereby appoint _____ of
_____ as my agent to make any and all health care decisions for me,
except to the extent I state otherwise in this document. This durable power of attorney for
health care shall take effect in the event I become unable to make my own health care decisions.

(a)   **STATEMENT OF DESIRES, SPECIAL PROVISIONS, AND LIMITATIONS
REGARDING HEALTH CARE DECISIONS**

Here you may include any specific desires or limitations you deem appropriate, such
as when or what life-sustaining measures should be withheld; directions whether to
continue or discontinue artificial nutrition and hydration; or instructions to refuse
any specific types of treatment that are inconsistent with your religious beliefs or
unacceptable to you for any other reason.

_____

_____

_____

(attach additional pages as necessary)

(b)   **THE SUBJECT OF LIFE-SUSTAINING TREATMENT IS OF PARTICULAR
IMPORTANCE**

For your convenience in dealing with that subject, some general statements concerning
the withholding or removal of life-sustaining treatment are set forth below.

**IF YOU AGREE WITH ONE OF THESE STATEMENTS, YOU MAY
INCLUDE THE STATEMENT IN THE BLANK SPACE ABOVE:**

If I suffer a condition from which there is no reasonable prospect of regaining my
ability to think and act for myself, I want only care directed to my comfort and dignity,
and authorize my agent to decline all treatment (including artificial nutrition and
hydration) the primary purpose of which is to prolong my life. If I suffer a condition
from which there is no reasonable prospect of regaining the ability to think and act
for myself, I want care directed to my comfort and dignity and also want artificial
nutrition and hydration if needed, but authorize my agent to decline all other treatment

the primary purpose of which is to prolong my life. I want my life sustained by any reasonable medical measures, regardless of my condition. In the event the person I appoint above is unable, unwilling or unavailable to act as my health care agent, I hereby appoint _____ of _____ _ as alternate agent. I hereby acknowledge that I have been provided with a disclosure statement explaining the effect of this document. I have read and understand the information contained in the disclosure statement. The original of this document will be kept at _____ and the following persons and institutions will have signed copies:

_____

_____

_____

In witness whereof, I have hereunto signed my name this _____ day of _____, 20 _____.

_____
Signature

I declare that the principal appears to be of sound mind and free from duress at the time the durable power of attorney for health care is signed and that the principal has affirmed that he or she is aware of the nature of the document and is signing it freely and voluntarily.

Witness: _____
Address: _____
Witness: _____
Address: _____

Statement of ombudsman, hospital representative or other authorized person (to be signed only if the principal is in or is being admitted to a hospital, nursing home or residential care home): I declare that I have personally explained the nature and effect of this durable power of attorney to the principal and that the principal understands the same.

Date: _____
Address: _____
Name: _____

Virginia State Forms

ADVANCE MEDICAL DIRECTIVE

I, _____, willfully and voluntarily make known my wishes in the event that I am incapable of making an informed decision, as follows:

I understand that my advance directive may include the selection of an agent as well as set forth my choices regarding health care. The term "health care"

means the furnishing of services to any individual for the purpose of preventing, alleviating, curing, or healing human illness, injury or physical disability, including but not limited to, medications; surgery; blood transfusions; chemotherapy; radiation therapy; admission to a hospital, assisted living facility, or other health care facility; psychiatric or other mental health treatment; and life-prolonging procedures and palliative care.

The phrase "incapable of making an informed decision" means unable to understand the nature, extent and probable consequences of a proposed health care decision or unable to make a rational evaluation of the risks and benefits of a proposed health care decision as compared with the risks and benefits of alternatives to that decision, or unable to communicate such understanding in any way.

The determination that I am incapable of making an informed decision shall be made by my attending physician and a second physician or licensed clinical psychologist after a personal examination of me and shall be certified in writing. The second physician or licensed clinical psychologist shall not be otherwise currently involved in my treatment, unless such independent physician or licensed clinical psychologist is not reasonably available. Such certification shall be required before health care is provided, continued, withheld or withdrawn, before any named agent shall be granted authority to make health care decisions on my behalf, and before, or as soon as reasonably practicable after, health care is provided, continued, withheld or withdrawn *and every 180 days thereafter while the need for health care continues.*

If, at any time, I am determined to be incapable of making an informed decision, I shall be notified, to the extent I am capable of receiving such notice, that such determination has been made before health care is provided, continued, withheld, or withdrawn. Such notice shall also be provided, as soon as practical, to my named agent or person authorized by § 54.1-2986 to make health care decisions on my behalf. If I am later determined to be capable of making an informed decision by a physician, in writing, upon personal examination, any further health care decisions will require my informed consent.

(SELECT ANY OR ALL OF THE OPTIONS BELOW.)

OPTION I: APPOINTMENT OF AGENT

(CROSS THROUGH OPTIONS I AND II BELOW IF YOU DO NOT WANT TO APPOINT AN AGENT TO MAKE HEALTH CARE DECISIONS FOR YOU.)

I hereby appoint _____ (primary agent), of _____ (address and telephone number), as my agent to make health care decisions on my behalf as authorized in this document. If _____ (primary agent) is not reasonably available or is unable or unwilling to act as my agent, then I appoint _____ (successor agent), of _____ (address and telephone number), to serve in that capacity.

I hereby grant to my agent, named above, full power and authority to make health care decisions on my behalf as described below whenever I have been determined to be incapable of making an informed decision. My agent's authority hereunder is effective as long as I am incapable of making an informed decision.

In exercising the power to make health care decisions on my behalf, my agent shall follow my desires and preferences as stated in this document or as otherwise known to my agent. My agent shall be guided by my medical diagnosis and prognosis and any information provided by my physicians as to the intrusiveness, pain, risks, and side effects associated with treatment or non-treatment. My agent shall not make any decision regarding my health care which he knows, or upon reasonable inquiry ought to know, is contrary to my religious beliefs or my basic values, whether expressed orally or in writing. If my agent cannot determine what health care choice I would have made on my own behalf, then my agent shall make a choice for me based upon what he believes to be in my best interests.

OPTION II: POWERS OF MY AGENT

(CROSS THROUGH ANY LANGUAGE YOU DO NOT WANT AND ADD ANY LANGUAGE YOU DO WANT.)

The powers of my agent shall include the following:

A.   To consent to or refuse or withdraw consent to any type of health care, treatment, surgical procedure, diagnostic procedure, medication and the use of mechanical or other procedures that affect any bodily function, including, but not limited to, artificial respiration, artificially administered nutrition and hydration, and cardiopulmonary resuscitation. This authorization specifically includes the power to consent to the administration of dosages of pain-relieving medication in excess of recommended dosages in an amount sufficient to relieve pain, even if such medication carries the risk of addiction or of inadvertently hastening my death;

B.   To request, receive, and review any information, verbal or written, regarding my physical or mental health, including but not limited to, medical and hospital records, and to consent to the disclosure of this information;

C.   To employ and discharge my health care providers;

D.   To authorize my admission to or discharge (including transfer to another facility) from any hospital, hospice, nursing home, assisted living facility or other medical care facility. If I have authorized admission to a health care facility for treatment of mental illness, that authority is stated elsewhere in this advance directive;

E.   To authorize my admission to a health care facility for the treatment of mental illness for no more than 10 calendar days provided I do not protest the admission and a physician on the staff of or designated by the proposed admitting facility examines me and states in writing that I have a mental illness and I am incapable of making an informed decision about my admission, and that I need treatment in the facility; and to authorize my discharge (including transfer to another facility) from the facility;

F.   To authorize my admission to a health care facility for the treatment of mental illness for no more than 10 calendar days, even over my protest, if a physician on the staff of or designated by the proposed admitting facility examines me and states in writing that I have a mental illness and I am incapable of making an informed decision about my admission, and that I need treatment in the facility; and to authorize my discharge (including transfer to another facility) from the facility. [My physician or licensed clinical psychologist hereby attests that I am capable of making an informed decision and that I understand the consequences of this provision of my advance directive: _____ _____ ;

G.   To authorize the specific types of health care identified in this advance directive [specify cross-reference to other sections of directive] even over my protest. [My physician or licensed clinical psychologist hereby attests that I am capable of making an informed decision and that I understand the consequences of this provision of my advance directive: _____];

H.   To continue to serve as my agent even in the event that I protest the agent's authority after I have been determined to be incapable of making an informed decision;

I.   To authorize my participation in any health care study approved by an institutional review board or research review committee according to applicable federal or state law that offers the prospect of direct therapeutic benefit to me;

J.   To authorize my participation in any health care study approved by an institutional review board or research review committee pursuant to applicable federal or state law that aims to increase scientific understanding of any condition that I may have or otherwise to promote human well-being, even though it offers no prospect of direct benefit to me;

K.   To make decisions regarding visitation during any time that I am admitted to any health care facility, consistent with the following directions:

_____

_____

_____

_____; and

L.   To take any lawful actions that may be necessary to carry out these decisions, including the granting of releases of liability to medical providers.

Further, my agent shall not be liable for the costs of health care pursuant to his authorization, based solely on that authorization.

OPTION III: HEALTH CARE INSTRUCTIONS

(CROSS THROUGH PARAGRAPHS A AND/OR B IF YOU DO NOT WANT TO GIVE ADDITIONAL SPECIFIC INSTRUCTIONS ABOUT YOUR HEALTH CARE.)

A.   I specifically direct that I receive the following health care if it is medically appropriate under the circumstances as determined by my attending physician:

_____.

B.   I specifically direct that the following health care not be provided to me under the following circumstances (you may specify that certain health care not be provided under any circumstances):

_____

_____

_____

_____

OPTION IV: END OF LIFE INSTRUCTIONS

(CROSS THROUGH THIS OPTION IF YOU DO NOT WANT TO GIVE INSTRUCTIONS ABOUT YOUR HEALTH CARE IF YOU HAVE A TERMINAL CONDITION.)

If at any time my attending physician should determine that I have a terminal condition where the application of life-prolonging procedures - including artificial respiration, cardiopulmonary resuscitation, artificially administered nutrition, and artificially administered hydration - would serve only to artificially prolong the dying process, I direct that such procedures be withheld or withdrawn, and that I be permitted to die naturally with only the administration of medication or the performance of any medical procedure deemed necessary to provide me with comfort care or to alleviate pain.

OPTION: OTHER DIRECTIONS ABOUT LIFE-PROLONGING PROCEDURES

(If you wish to provide your own directions, or if you wish to add to the directions you have given above, you may do so here. If you wish to give specific instructions regarding certain life-prolonging procedures, such as artificial respiration, cardiopulmonary resuscitation, artificially administered nutrition, and artificially administered hydration, this is where you should write them.) I direct that:

_____

_____

_____

My other instructions regarding my care if I have a terminal condition are as follows:

_____

_____

_____

In the absence of my ability to give directions regarding the use of such life-prolonging procedures, it is my intention that this advance directive shall be honored by my family and physician as the final expression of my legal right to refuse health care and acceptance of the consequences of such refusal.

OPTION V: APPOINTMENT OF AN AGENT TO MAKE AN ANATOMICAL GIFT OR ORGAN, TISSUE OR EYE DONATION

(CROSS THROUGH IF YOU DO NOT WANT TO APPOINT AN AGENT TO MAKE AN ANATOMICAL GIFT OR ANY ORGAN, TISSUE OR EYE DONATION FOR YOU.)

Upon my death, I direct that an anatomical gift of all of my body or certain organ, tissue or eye donations may be made pursuant to Article 2 (§ 32.1-289.2 et seq.) of Chapter 8 of Title 32.1 and in accordance with my directions, if any. I hereby appoint _____ as my agent, of _____ (address and telephone number), to make any such an atomical gift or organ, tissue or eye donation following my death. I further direct that: _____ (declarant's directions concerning anatomical gift or organ, tissue or eye donation).

This advance directive shall not terminate in the event of my disability.

AFFIRMATION AND RIGHT TO REVOKE: By signing below, I indicate that I am emotionally and mentally capable of making this advance directive and that I understand the purpose and effect of this document. I understand I may revoke all or any part of this document at any time (i) with a signed, dated writing; (ii) by physical cancellation or destruction of this advance directive by myself or by directing someone else to destroy it in my presence; or (iii) by my oral expression of intent to revoke.

_____ _____

(Date)   (Signature of Declarant)

The declarant signed the foregoing advance directive in my presence.

(Witness) _____
(Witness) _____

Washington State Forms

HEALTH CARE DIRECTIVE

Directive made this _____ day of _____, 20___ (month, year).

I _____, having the capacity to make health care decisions, willfully, and voluntarily make known my desire that my dying shall not be artificially prolonged under the circumstances set forth below, and do hereby declare that:

(a)   If at any time I should be diagnosed in writing to be in a terminal condition by the attending physician, or in a permanent unconscious condition by two physicians, and where the application of life-sustaining treatment would serve only to artificially prolong the process of my dying, I direct that such treatment be withheld or withdrawn, and that I be permitted to die naturally. I understand by using this form that a terminal condition means an incurable and irreversible condition caused by injury, disease, or illness, that would within reasonable medical judgment cause death within a reasonable period of time in accordance with accepted medical standards, and where the application of life-sustaining treatment would serve only to prolong the process of dying. I further understand in using this form that a permanent unconscious condition means an incurable and irreversible condition in which I am medically assessed within reasonable medical judgment as having no reasonable probability of recovery from an irreversible coma or a persistent vegetative state.

(b)   In the absence of my ability to give directions regarding the use of such life-sustaining treatment, it is my intention that this directive shall be honored by my family and physician(s) as the final expression of my legal right to refuse medical or surgical treatment and I accept the consequences of such refusal. If another person is appointed to make these decisions for me, whether through a durable power of attorney or otherwise, I request that the person be guided by this directive and any other clear expressions of my desires.

(c)   If I am diagnosed to be in a terminal condition or in a permanent unconscious condition (check one):

_____   I DO want to have artificially provided nutrition and hydration.

_____   I DO NOT want to have artificially provided nutrition and hydration.

(d)   If I have been diagnosed as pregnant and that diagnosis is known to my physician, this directive shall have no force or effect during the course of my pregnancy.

(e)   I understand the full import of this directive and I am emotionally and mentally capable to make the health care decisions contained in this directive.

(f)   I understand that before I sign this directive, I can add to or delete from or otherwise change the wording of this directive and that I may add to or delete from this directive at any time and that any changes shall be consistent with Washington state law or federal constitutional law to be legally valid.

(g)   It is my wish that every part of this directive be fully implemented. If for any reason any part is held invalid it is my wish that the remainder of my directive be implemented.

Signed:-   _____

City, County, and State of Residence:- _____

The declarer has been personally known to me and I believe him or her to be capable of making health care decisions.

Witness:-   _____

Witness:-   _____

West Virginia State Forms

STATE OF WEST VIRGINIA
LIVING WILL

Living will made this _____ day of _____
(month, year).

I,_____, being of sound mind,
willfully and voluntarily declare that I want my wishes to be respected if I am very sick and
not able to communicate my wishes for myself. In the absence of my ability to give directions
regarding the use of life-prolonging medical intervention, it is my desire that my dying shall not
be prolonged under the following circumstances:

If I am very sick and not able to communicate my wishes for myself and I am certified by one
physician, who has personally examined me, to have a terminal condition or to be in a persistent
vegetative state (I am unconscious and am neither aware of my environment nor able to interact
with others), I direct that life-prolonging medical intervention that would serve solely to prolong
the dying process or maintain me in a persistent vegetative state be withheld or withdrawn. I
want to be allowed to die naturally and only be given medications or other medical procedures
necessary to keep me comfortable. I want to receive as much medication as is necessary to
alleviate my pain.

I give the following SPECIAL DIRECTIVES OR LIMITATIONS: (Comments about tube
feedings, breathing machines, cardiopulmonary resuscitation, dialysis and mental health
treatment may be placed here. My failure to provide special directives or limitations does not
mean that I want or refuse certain treatments.) _____
_____
_____
_____

It is my intention that this living will be honored as the final expression of my legal right to
refuse medical or surgical treatment and accept the consequences resulting from such refusal.

I understand the full import of this living will.

Signed:-   _____
Address:-   _____

_____

_____

I did not sign the principal's signature above for or at the direction of the principal. I am at least eighteen years of age and am not related to the principal by blood or marriage, entitled to any portion of the estate of the principal to the best of my knowledge under any will of principal or codicil thereto, or directly financially responsible for principal's medical care. I am not the principal's attending physician or the principal's medical power of attorney representative or successor medical power of attorney representative under a medical power of attorney.

_____ _____ Witness
DATE

_____ _____ Witness
DATE

_____

STATE OF

_____

COUNTY OF

I, _____, a Notary Public of said County, do certify that _____ _____, as principal, and _____ and _____, as witnesses, whose names are signed to the writing above bearing date on the _____ day of _____, 20____, have this day acknowledged the same before me.

Given under my hand this _____ day of _____, 20__.

My commission expires:_____

_____

Notary Public

STATE OF WEST VIRGINIA

MEDICAL POWER OF ATTORNEY

Dated: _____ , 20_____

I,_____, hereby
(Insert your name and address) appoint as my representative to act on my behalf to give, withhold or withdraw informed consent to health care decisions in the event that I am not able to do so myself.

The person I choose as my representative is: _____
_____ *(Insert the name, address, area code and telephone number of the person you wish to designate as your representative)*

The person I choose as my successor representative is: If my representative is unable, unwilling or disqualified to serve, then I appoint:

_____*(Insert the name, address, area code and telephone number of the person you wish to designate as your successor representative)*

This appointment shall extend to, but not be limited to, health care decisions relating to medical treatment, surgical treatment, nursing care, medication, hospitalization, care and treatment in a nursing home or other facility, and home health care. The representative appointed by this document is specifically authorized to be granted access to my medical records and other health information and to act on my behalf to consent to, refuse or withdraw any and all medical treatment or diagnostic procedures, or autopsy if my representative determines that I, if able to do so, would consent to, refuse or withdraw such treatment or procedures. Such authority shall include, but not be limited to, decisions regarding the withholding or withdrawal of life-prolonging interventions.

I appoint this representative because I believe this person understands my wishes and values and will act to carry into effect the health care decisions that I would make if I were able to do so and because I also believe that this person will act in my best interest when my wishes are unknown. It is my intent that my family, my physician and all legal authorities be bound by the decisions that are made by the representative appointed by this document and it is my intent that these decisions should not be the subject of review by any health care provider or administrative or judicial agency.

It is my intent that this document be legally binding and effective and that this document be taken as a formal statement of my desire concerning the method by which any health care decisions should be made on my behalf during any period when I am unable to make such decisions.

In exercising the authority under this medical power of attorney, my representative shall act consistently with my special directives or limitations as stated below.

I am giving the following SPECIAL DIRECTIVES OR LIMITATIONS ON THIS POWER: (Comments about tube feedings, breathing machines, cardiopulmonary resuscitation, dialysis, funeral arrangements, autopsy and organ donation may be placed here. My failure to provide special directives or limitations does not mean that I want or refuse certain treatments.)

_____

_____

_____

THIS MEDICAL POWER OF ATTORNEY SHALL BECOME EFFECTIVE ONLY UPON MY INCAPACITY TO GIVE, WITHHOLD OR WITHDRAW INFORMED CONSENT TO MY OWN MEDICAL CARE.

_____

Signature of the Principal

I did not sign the principal's signature above. I am at least eighteen years of age and am not related to the principal by blood or marriage. I am not entitled to any portion of the estate of the principal or to the best of my knowledge under any will of the principal or codicil thereto, or legally responsible for the costs of the principal's medical or other care. I am not the principal's attending physician, nor am I the representative or successor representative of the principal.

_____   _____ Witness
                DATE

_____   _____ Witness
                DATE

_____
STATE OF

_____
COUNTY OF

I, _____, a Notary Public of said County, do certify that _____

_____, as principal, and _____ and

_____, as witnesses, whose names are signed to the writing above bearing date on the _____ day of _____, 20_____,have this day acknowledged the same before me.

Given under my hand this _____ day of _____, 20__.

My commission expires:_____

_____

Notary Public

STATE OF WEST VIRGINIA

COMBINED MEDICAL POWER OF ATTORNEY

AND LIVING WILL

Dated: _____, 20_____.

I, _____, hereby *(Insert your name and address)* appoint as my representative to act on my behalf to give, withhold or withdraw informed consent to health care decisions in the event that I am not able to do so myself.

The person I choose as my representative is:

_____

(Insert the name, address, area code and telephone number of the person you wish to designate as your representative).

If my representative is unable, unwilling or disqualified to serve, then I appoint as my successor representative:

_____

(Insert the name, address, area code and telephone number of the person you wish to designate as your successor representative).

This appointment shall extend to, but not be limited to, health care decisions relating to medical treatment, surgical treatment, nursing care, medication, hospitalization, care and treatment in a nursing home or other facility, and home

health care. The representative appointed by this document is specifically authorized to be granted access to my medical records and other health information and to act on my behalf to consent to, refuse or withdraw any and all medical treatment or diagnostic procedures, or autopsy if my representative determines that I, if able to do so, would consent to, refuse or withdraw such treatment or procedures. Such authority shall include, but not be limited to, decisions regarding the withholding or withdrawal of life-prolonging interventions.

I appoint this representative because I believe this person understands my wishes and values and will act to carry into effect the health care decisions that I would make if I were able to do so, and because I also believe that this person will act in my best interest when my wishes are unknown. It is my intent that my family, my physician and all legal authorities be bound by the decisions that are made by the representative appointed by this document, and it is my intent that these decisions should not be the subject of review by any health care provider or administrative or judicial agency.

It is my intent that this document be legally binding and effective and that this document be taken as a formal statement of my desire concerning the method by which any health care decisions should be made on my behalf during any period when I am unable to make such decisions.

In exercising the authority under this medical power of attorney, my representative shall act consistently with my special directives or limitations as stated below.

I am giving the following SPECIAL DIRECTIVES OR LIMITATIONS ON THIS POWER: (Comments about tube feedings, breathing machines, cardiopulmonary resuscitation, dialysis, mental health treatment, funeral arrangements, autopsy, and organ donation may be placed here. My failure to provide special directives or limitations does not mean that I want or refuse certain treatments).

1.   If I am very sick and not able to communicate my wishes for myself and I am certified by one physician who has personally examined me, to have a terminal condition or to be in a persistent vegetative state (I am unconscious and am neither aware of my environment nor able to interact with others,) I direct that life-prolonging medical intervention that would serve solely to prolong the dying process or maintain me in a

persistent vegetative state be withheld or withdrawn. I want to be allowed to die naturally and only be given medications or other medical procedures necessary to keep me comfortable. I want to receive as much medication as is necessary to alleviate my pain.

2.   Other directives: _____

            _____

            _____

            _____

            _____

THIS MEDICAL POWER OF ATTORNEY SHALL BECOME EFFECTIVE ONLY UPON MY INCAPACITY TO GIVE, WITHHOLD OR WITHDRAW INFORMED CONSENT TO MY OWN MEDICAL CARE.

_____

Signature of the Principal

I did not sign the principal's signature above. I am at least eighteen years of age and am not related to the principal by blood or marriage. I am not entitled to any portion of the estate of the principal or to the best of my knowledge under any will of the principal or codicil thereto, or legally responsible for the costs of the principal's medical or other care. I am not the principal's attending physician, nor am I the representative or successor representative of the principal.

_____   _____ Witness
           DATE

_____   _____ Witness
           DATE

_____

STATE OF

_____

COUNTY OF

I, _____, a Notary Public of said County, do certify that _____
_____, as principal, and _____ and
_____, as witnesses, whose names are signed to the writing above bearing

date on the _____ day of _____, 20____,have this day acknowledged the same before me.

Given under my hand this _____ day of _____, 20__.

My commission expires:_____

_____

Notary Public

Wisconsin State Forms

DECLARATION TO PHYSICIANS

(WISCONSIN LIVING WILL)

I, _____, being of sound mind, voluntarily state my desire that my dying not be prolonged under the circumstances specified in this document. Under those circumstances, I direct that I be permitted to die naturally. If I am unable to give directions regarding the use of life☐ sustaining procedures or feeding tubes, I intend that my family and physician honor this document as the final expression of my legal right to refuse medical or surgical treatment.

1.   If I have a TERMINAL CONDITION, as determined by 2 physicians who have personally examined me, I do not want my dying to be artificially prolonged and I do not want life☐ sustaining procedures to be used. In addition, the following are my directions regarding the use of feeding tubes:

_____ YES, I want feeding tubes used if I have a terminal condition.

_____ NO, I do not want feeding tubes used if I have a terminal condition.

If you have not checked either box, feeding tubes will be used.

2.   If I am in a PERSISTENT VEGETATIVE STATE, as determined by 2 physicians who have personally examined me, the following are my directions regarding the use of life☐ sustaining procedures:

_____ YES, I want life☐ sustaining procedures used if I am in a persistent vegetative state.

_____ NO, I do not want life☐ sustaining procedures used if I am in a persistent vegetative state.

If you have not checked either box, life☐ sustaining procedures will be used.

3.   If I am in a PERSISTENT VEGETATIVE STATE, as determined by 2 physicians who have personally examined me, the following are my directions regarding the use of feeding tubes:

     _____   YES, I want feeding tubes used if I am in a persistent vegetative state.

     _____   NO, I do not want feeding tubes used if I am in a persistent vegetative state.

If you have not checked either box, feeding tubes will be used.

If you are interested in more information about the significant terms used in this document, see section 154.01 of the Wisconsin Statutes or the information accompanying this document.

ATTENTION: You and the 2 witnesses must sign the document at the same time.

Signed: _____

Date: _____

Address: _____

    _____

    _____

    _____

Date of birth: _____

I believe that the person signing this document is of sound mind. I am an adult and am not related to the person signing this document by blood, marriage or adoption. I am not entitled to and do not have a claim on any portion of the person's estate and am not otherwise restricted by law from being a witness.

Witness signature: _____

Date signed: _____

Print name: _____

Witness signature: _____

Date signed: _____

Print name: _____

DIRECTIVES TO ATTENDING PHYSICIAN

1. This document authorizes the withholding or withdrawal of life☐ sustaining procedures or of feeding tubes when 2 physicians, one of whom is the attending physician, have personally examined and certified in writing that the patient has a terminal condition or is in a persistent vegetative state.

2. The choices in this document were made by a competent adult. Under the law, the patient's stated desires must be followed unless you believe that withholding or withdrawing life☐ sustaining procedures or feeding tubes would cause the patient pain or reduced comfort and that the pain or discomfort cannot be alleviated through pain relief measures. If the patient's stated desires are that life☐ sustaining procedures or feeding tubes be used, this directive must be followed.

3. If you feel that you cannot comply with this document, you must make a good faith attempt to transfer the patient to another physician who will comply. Refusal or failure to make a good faith attempt to do so constitutes unprofessional conduct.

4. If you know that the patient is pregnant, this document has no effect during her pregnancy.

The person making this living will may use the following space to record the names of those individuals and health care providers to whom he or she has given copies of this document:

_____

_____

_____

_____

NOTICE TO PERSON MAKING THIS DOCUMENT

YOU HAVE THE RIGHT TO MAKE DECISIONS ABOUT YOUR HEALTH CARE. NO HEALTH CARE MAY BE GIVEN TO YOU OVER YOUR OBJECTION, AND NECESSARY

HEALTH CARE MAY NOT BE STOPPED OR WITHHELD IF YOU OBJECT.

BECAUSE YOUR HEALTH CARE PROVIDERS IN SOME CASES MAY NOT HAVE HAD THE OPPORTUNITY TO ESTABLISH A LONG TERM RELATIONSHIP WITH YOU, THEY ARE OFTEN UNFAMILIAR WITH YOUR BELIEFS AND VALUES AND THE DETAILS OF YOUR FAMILY RELATIONSHIPS. THIS POSES A PROBLEM IF YOU BECOME PHYSICALLY OR MENTALLY UNABLE TO MAKE DECISIONS ABOUT YOUR HEALTH CARE.

IN ORDER TO AVOID THIS PROBLEM, YOU MAY SIGN THIS LEGAL DOCUMENT TO SPECIFY THE PERSON WHOM YOU WANT TO MAKE HEALTH CARE DECISIONS FOR YOU IF YOU ARE UNABLE TO MAKE THOSE DECISIONS PERSONALLY. THAT PERSON IS KNOWN AS YOUR HEALTH CARE AGENT. YOU SHOULD TAKE SOME TIME TO DISCUSS YOUR THOUGHTS AND BELIEFS ABOUT MEDICAL TREATMENT WITH THE PERSON OR PERSONS WHOM YOU HAVE SPECIFIED. YOU MAY STATE IN THIS DOCUMENT ANY TYPES OF HEALTH CARE THAT YOU DO OR DO NOT DESIRE, AND YOU MAY LIMIT THE AUTHORITY OF YOUR HEALTH CARE AGENT. IF YOUR HEALTH CARE AGENT IS UNAWARE OF YOUR DESIRES WITH RESPECT TO A PARTICULAR HEALTH CARE DECISION, HE OR SHE IS REQUIRED TO DETERMINE WHAT WOULD BE IN YOUR BEST INTERESTS IN MAKING THE DECISION.

THIS IS AN IMPORTANT LEGAL DOCUMENT. IT GIVES YOUR AGENT BROAD POWERS TO MAKE HEALTH CARE DECISIONS FOR YOU. IT REVOKES ANY PRIOR POWER OF ATTORNEY FOR HEALTH CARE THAT YOU MAY HAVE MADE. IF YOU WISH TO CHANGE YOUR POWER OF ATTORNEY FOR HEALTH CARE, YOU MAY REVOKE THIS DOCUMENT AT ANY TIME BY DESTROYING IT, BY DIRECTING ANOTHER PERSON TO DESTROY IT IN YOUR PRESENCE, BY SIGNING A WRITTEN AND DATED STATEMENT OR BY STATING THAT IT IS REVOKED IN THE PRESENCE OF TWO WITNESSES. IF YOU REVOKE, YOU SHOULD NOTIFY YOUR AGENT, YOUR HEALTH CARE PROVIDERS AND ANY OTHER PERSON TO WHOM YOU HAVE GIVEN A COPY. IF YOUR AGENT IS YOUR SPOUSE OR DOMESTIC PARTNER AND YOUR MARRIAGE IS ANNULLED OR YOU

ARE DIVORCED OR THE DOMESTIC PARTNERSHIP IS TERMINATED AFTER SIGNING THIS DOCUMENT, THE DOCUMENT IS INVALID.

YOU MAY ALSO USE THIS DOCUMENT TO MAKE OR REFUSE TO MAKE AN ANATOMICAL GIFT UPON YOUR DEATH. IF YOU USE THIS DOCUMENT TO MAKE OR REFUSE TO MAKE AN ANATOMICAL GIFT, THIS DOCUMENT REVOKES ANY PRIOR RECORD OF GIFT THAT YOU MAY HAVE MADE. YOU MAY REVOKE OR CHANGE ANY ANATOMICAL GIFT THAT YOU MAKE BY THIS DOCUMENT BY CROSSING OUT THE ANATOMICAL GIFTS PROVISION IN THIS DOCUMENT.

DO NOT SIGN THIS DOCUMENT UNLESS YOU CLEARLY UNDERSTAND IT.

IT IS SUGGESTED THAT YOU KEEP THE ORIGINAL OF THIS DOCUMENT ON FILE WITH YOUR PHYSICIAN.

POWER OF ATTORNEY FOR HEALTH CARE

Document made this _____ day of_____ (month), 20___ (year).

CREATION OF POWER OF ATTORNEY FOR HEALTH CARE

I, _____ (print name,
address and date of birth), being of sound mind, intend by this document to create a power
of attorney for health care. My executing this power of attorney for health care is voluntary.
Despite the creation of this power of attorney for health care, I expect to be fully informed
about and allowed to participate in any health care decision for me, to the extent that I am
able. For the purposes of this document, "health care decision" means an informed decision
to accept, maintain, discontinue or refuse any care, treatment, service or procedure to maintain,
diagnose or treat my physical or mental condition.

In addition, I may, by this document, specify my wishes with respect to making an anatomical
gift upon my death.

DESIGNATION OF HEALTH CARE AGENT

If I am no longer able to make health care decisions for myself, due to my incapacity, I hereby
designate _____ (print name, address and
telephone number) to be my health care agent for the purpose of making health care decisions
on my behalf. If he or she is ever unable or unwilling to do so, I hereby designate _____
_____ (print name, address and telephone number) to be my alternate
health care agent for the purpose of making health care decisions on my behalf. Neither my
health care agent nor my alternate health care agent whom I have designated is my health care
provider, an employee of my health care provider, an employee of a health care facility in which
I am a patient or a spouse of any of those persons, unless he or she is also my relative. For
purposes of this document, "incapacity" exists if 2 physicians or a physician and a psychologist
who have personally examined me sign a statement that specifically expresses their opinion that
I have a condition that means that I am unable to receive and evaluate information effectively
or to communicate decisions to such an extent that I lack the capacity to manage my health care

decisions. A copy of that statement must be attached to this document.

GENERAL STATEMENT OF AUTHORITY GRANTED

Unless I have specified otherwise in this document, if I ever have incapacity I instruct my health care provider to obtain the health care decision of my health care agent, if I need treatment, for all of my health care and treatment. I have discussed my desires thoroughly with my health care agent and believe that he or she understands my philosophy regarding the health care decisions I would make if I were able. I desire that my wishes be carried out through the authority given to my health care agent under this document.

If I am unable, due to my incapacity, to make a health care decision, my health care agent is instructed to make the health care decision for me, but my health care agent should try to discuss with me any specific proposed health care if I am able to communicate in any manner, including by blinking my eyes. If this communication cannot be made, my health care agent shall base his or her decision on any health care choices that I have expressed prior to the time of the decision. If I have not expressed a health care choice about the health care in question and communication cannot be made, my health care agent shall base his or her health care decision on what he or she believes to be in my best interest.

LIMITATIONS ON MENTAL HEALTH TREATMENT

My health care agent may not admit or commit me on an inpatient basis to an institution for mental diseases, an intermediate care facility for persons with mental retardation, a state treatment facility or a treatment facility. My health care agent may not consent to experimental mental health research or psychosurgery, electroconvulsive treatment or drastic mental health treatment procedures for me.

ADMISSION TO NURSING HOMES OR COMMUNITY□ BASED RESIDENTIAL FACILITIES

My health care agent may admit me to a nursing home or community☐ based residential facility for short☐ term stays for recuperative care or respite care.

If I have checked "Yes" to the following, my health care agent may admit me for a purpose other than recuperative care or respite care, but if I have checked "No" to the following, my health care agent may not so admit me:

1.   A nursing home — Yes _____ No _____

2.   A community☐ based residential facility —   Yes _____   No _____

If I have not checked either "Yes" or "No" immediately above, my health care agent may admit me only for short☐ term stays for recuperative care or respite care.

PROVISION OF A FEEDING TUBE

If I have checked "Yes" to the following, my health care agent may have a feeding tube withheld or withdrawn from me, unless my physician has advised that, in his or her professional judgment, this will cause me pain or will reduce my comfort. If I have checked "No" to the following, my health care agent may not have a feeding tube withheld or withdrawn from me.

My health care agent may not have orally ingested nutrition or hydration withheld or withdrawn from me unless provision of the nutrition or hydration is medically contraindicated.

Withhold or withdraw a feeding tube —   Yes _____   No _____

If I have not checked either "Yes" or "No" immediately above, my health care agent may not have a feeding tube withdrawn from me.

HEALTH CARE DECISIONS FOR PREGNANT WOMEN

If I have checked "Yes" to the following, my health care agent may make health care decisions for me even if my agent knows I am pregnant. If I have checked "No" to the following, my health care agent may not make health care decisions for me if my health care agent knows I am pregnant.

Health care decision if I am pregnant —   Yes _____   No _____

If I have not checked either "Yes" or "No" immediately above, my health care agent may not make health care decisions for me if my health care agent knows I am pregnant.

STATEMENT OF DESIRES, SPECIAL PROVISIONS OR LIMITATIONS

In exercising authority under this document, my health care agent shall act consistently with my following stated desires, if any, and is subject to any special provisions or limitations that I specify. The following are specific desires, provisions or limitations that I wish to state (add more items if needed):

1) ☐ _____

2) ☐ _____

3) ☐ _____

INSPECTION AND DISCLOSURE OF INFORMATION RELATING TO MY HYSICAL OR MENTAL HEALTH

Subject to any limitations in this document, my health care gent has the authority to do all of the following:

(a)   Request, review and receive any information, oral or written, regarding my physical or mental health, including medical and hospital records.

(b)   Execute on my behalf any documents that may be required in order to obtain this information.

(c)   Consent to the disclosure of this information.

(The principal and the witnesses all must sign the document at the same time.)

SIGNATURE OF PRINCIPAL

(person creating the power of attorney for health care)

Signature: _____   Date: _____

(The signing of this document by the principal revokes all previous powers of attorney for health care documents.)

STATEMENT OF WITNESSES

I know the principal personally and I believe him or her to be of sound mind and at least 18 years of age. I believe that his or her execution of this power of attorney for health care is voluntary.

I am at least 18 years of age, am not related to the principal by blood, marriage, or adoption, am not the domestic partner under ch. 770 of the principal, and am not directly financially responsible for the principal's health care. I am not a health care provider who is serving the principal at this time, an employee of the health care provider, other than a chaplain or a social worker, or an employee, other than a chaplain or a social worker, of an inpatient health care facility in which the declarant is a patient. I am not the principal's health care agent. To the best of my knowledge, I am not entitled to and do not have a claim on the principal's estate.

Witness No. 1:

        Print Name:- _____
        Date:- _____
        Address:- _____
                _____
                _____
                _____

        Signature:- _____

Witness No. 2:

        Print Name:- _____

Date:-   _____

Address:-   _____

_____

_____

_____

Signature:-   _____

STATEMENT OF HEALTH CARE AGENT AND ALTERNATE HEALTH CARE AGENT

I understand that _____ (name of principal) has designated me to be his or her health care agent or alternate health care agent if he or she is ever found to have incapacity and unable to make health care decisions himself or herself. .... (name of principal) has discussed his or her desires regarding health care decisions with me.

Agent's signature: _____

Address: _____

_____

_____

Alternate's signature: _____

Address: _____

_____

_____

Failure to execute a power of attorney for health care document under chapter 155 of the Wisconsin Statutes creates no presumption about the intent of any individual with regard to his or her health care decisions.

This power of attorney for health care is executed as provided in chapter 155 of the Wisconsin Statutes.

ANATOMICAL GIFTS

(optional)

Upon my death:

_____   I wish to donate only the following organs or parts:

_____

_____

_____

(specify the organs or parts).

_____   I wish to donate any needed organ or part.
_____   I wish to donate my body for anatomical study if needed.
_____   I refuse to make an anatomical gift. (If this revokes a prior commitment that I have made to make an anatomical gift to a designated donee, I will attempt to notify the donee to which or to whom I agreed to donate.)

Failing to check any of the lines immediately above creates no presumption about my desire to make or refuse to make an anatomical gift.

Signature: _____   Date: _____

Wyoming State Forms

WYOMING LIVING WILL

NOTICE

This document has significant medical, legal and possible ethical implications and effects. Before you sign this document, you should become completely familiar with these implications and effects. The operation, effects and implications of this document may be discussed with a physician, a lawyer and a clergyman of your choice.

The following declaration must dated and signed by the person making the declaration, or by another person in the declarant's presence and by the declarant's expressed direction, and in the presence of two (2) or more adult witnesses. The witnesses shall not be:

(i)   The person who signed the declaration on behalf of and at the direction of the person making the declaration;

(ii)   Related to the declarant by blood or marriage;

(iii)   Entitled to any portion of the estate of the declarant according to laws of intestate succession of this state or under any will of the declarant or codicil thereto; or

(iv)   Directly financially responsible for declarant's medical care.

DECLARATION

Declaration made this _____ day of _____(month, year). I, _____, being of sound mind, willfully and voluntarily make known my desire that my dying shall not be artificially prolonged under the circumstances set forth below, do hereby declare:

If at any time I should have an incurable injury, disease or other illness certified to be a terminal condition by two (2) physicians who have personally examined me, one (1) of whom shall be my attending physician, and the physicians have determined that my death will occur whether or not life-sustaining procedures are utilized and where the application of life-sustaining procedures would serve only to artificially prolong the dying process, I direct that such procedures be withheld or withdrawn, and that I be permitted to die naturally with only the administration of medication or the performance of any medical procedure deemed necessary to provide me with comfort care.

If, in spite of this declaration, I am comatose or otherwise unable to make treatment decisions for myself, I HEREBY designate _____ to make treatment decisions for me.

In the absence of my ability to give directions regarding the use of life-sustaining procedures, it is my intention that this declaration shall be honored by my family and physician(s) and agent as the final expression of my legal right to refuse medical or surgical treatment and accept the consequences from this refusal. I understand the full import of this declaration and I am emotionally and mentally competent to make this declaration.

Signed _____

City, County and State of Residence _____

The declarant has been personally known to me and I believe him or her to be of sound mind. I did not sign the declarant's signature above for or at the direction of the declarant. I am not related to the declarant by blood or marriage, entitled to any portion of the estate of the declarant according to the laws of intestate succession or under any will of the declarant or codicil thereto, or directly financially responsible for declarant's medical care.

Witness: _____
Printed Name: _____
Date: _____

Witness: _____
Printed Name: _____
Date: _____

APPENDIX B:

STANDARD LIVING WILL FOR USE IN MASSACHUSETTS AND MICHIGAN

CD-ROM & Downloadable Forms

Blank copies of all of the forms contained in this book are available on the CD-ROM which accompanies this book. Alternatively all forms can be downloaded from the enodare website.

Web: http://www.enodare.com/downloadarea/

Unlock Code: XYZ10412

enodare

Appendix B

APPENDIX B

Standard Living Will

(for use in Massachusetts and Michigan)

LIVING WILL DECLARATION

I, _____, (hereinafter referred to as the Declarant), aged eighteen years and upwards and a resident at _____ make this Declaration this _____ day of _____ , 20___ .

1. **DECLARATION**

1.1   I, being of sound and disposing mind, memory and understanding, do hereby wilfully and voluntarily make known and declare this to be my Living Will, making known my desire that my life shall not be artificially prolonged under the circumstances (if any) set forth below, and do hereby declare:-

    (a)   In the absence of my ability to give directions regarding the use of life-sustaining procedures, it is my intention that this Declaration be honored by my family and physicians and any health facility in which I may be a patient as the final expression of my legal right to refuse or accept medical or surgical treatment, and I accept the consequences from such refusal.

    (b)   I understand the full import of this Declaration and am aware that this Declaration may authorize a physician to withhold or withdraw life-sustaining procedures.

    (c)   I am emotionally and mentally competent to make this Declaration.

2.   TREATMENT OPTIONS

(initial only those options which apply)
<u>Terminal Condition</u>

_____ If, at any time, I have a medical condition certified to be a terminal condition by two physicians who have personally examined me, and the physicians have determined that my death could occur within a reasonably short period of time without the use of life-sustaining procedures then I direct that, save as may be set out herein, such life-sustaining procedures (SHALL)/(SHALL NOT) be applied to prolong my life within the limits of generally accepted health care standards.

Specifically, if I am suffering from a terminal condition:

_____ I [want]/[do not want] artificial nutrition or hydration.

_____ I [want]/[do not want] to receive cardiac resuscitation or a cardiac pacemaker.

_____ I [want]/[do not want] to receive blood or blood products.

_____ I [want]/[do not want] to receive mechanical respiration.

_____ I [want]/[do not want] to receive kidney dialysis.

_____ I [want]/[do not want] to receive antibiotics.

_____ I [want]/[do not want] to receive any form of surgery or invasive diagnostic tests.

_____ I [want]/[do not want] to receive an organ.

<u>Permanent Unconsciousness</u>

_____ If, at any time, I have a medical condition certified to be a terminal condition by two physicians who have personally examined me, and the physicians have certified that I am in a state of permanent unconsciousness and the application of life-sustaining procedures would serve only to prolong the dying process then I direct that, save as may be set out herein, such life-sustaining procedures (SHALL)/(SHALL NOT)be withheld or withdrawn and that I be permitted to die naturally with, unless otherwise set out below, only the administration of medication or the performance of any medical procedure necessary to provide me with comfort care.

Specifically, if I am in a persistent vegetative state or other condition of permanent unconsciousness:

_____ I [want]/[do not want] artificial nutrition or hydration.

_____ I [want]/[do not want] to receive cardiac resuscitation or a cardiac pacemaker.

_____ I [want]/[do not want] to receive blood or blood products.

_____ I [want]/[do not want] to receive mechanical respiration.

_____ I [want]/[do not want] to receive kidney dialysis.

_____ I [want]/[do not want] to receive antibiotics.

_____ I [want]/[do not want] to receive any form of surgery or invasive diagnostic tests.

_____ I [want]/[do not want] to receive an organ.

Maximum Treatment

_____ I want to receive the maximum treatment in all possible circumstances to prolong my life.

3.   **RELIEF FROM PAIN**

(initial one choice only)

_____   I want to receive treatment for the alleviation of pain or discomfort.

_____   I do not want to receive treatment for the alleviation of pain or discomfort.

4.   **PREGNANCY** (Optional)

(If applicable, initial your choice below. If no choice is initialled, this clause shall cease to apply)

4.1   Should I become unconscious and I am pregnant, I direct that this document shall, unless applicable laws prescribe otherwise:
(initial one choice below)

_____ continue to have full effect
_____ cease to have full effect

5.   **REVOCATION PROCEDURES**

5.1   This Declaration may be revoked by any one of the following methods:

(a)   by being defaced, torn, obliterated, or otherwise destroyed, in expression of my intent to revoke by me or by some person in my presence and acting on my direction. For the avoidance of doubt, revocation by destruction of one or more of multiple original Declarations revokes all of the original Declarations;

(b)   by a written revocation signed and dated by me; and

(c)   by my oral expression of my intent to revoke this Declaration. An oral revocation communicated to the attending physician by a person other than me is effective only if:

(i)   such person was present when the oral revocation was made;

(ii)   the revocation was communicated to the physician within a reasonable time;

(iii)   my physical or mental condition makes it impossible for the physician to confirm through subsequent conversation with me whether or not the revocation has in fact occurred. To be effective as a revocation, the oral expression must clearly indicate my desire that the Declaration not be given effect or that life-sustaining procedures be administered; and

(iv)   by executing another Declaration at a later time.

5.2   Any revocation of this Declaration shall not be effective until such time as notice of same is communicated to the attending physician.

6.   **EFFECT OF COPY**

6.1   A copy of this declaration has the same effect as the original.

I understand the full import of this declaration and I am emotionally and mentally competent to make this declaration.

IN WITNESS WHEREOF, I have hereunto subscribed my name and affixed my seal at _____, _____, this _____ day of _____, 20_____, in the presence of the subscribing witnesses whom I have requested to become attesting witnesses hereto.

_____

Signature of Declarant

Name of Witness: _____
Signature of Witness: _____
Address: _____
                                        _____
                                        _____
                                        _____

Name of Witness: _____
Signature of Witness: _____
Address: _____
                                        _____
                                        _____
                                        _____

APPENDIX C:
SAMPLE COMPLETED LIVING WILL FORMS FOR ALASKA

CD-ROM & Downloadable Forms

Blank copies of all of the forms contained in this book are available on the CD-ROM which accompanies this book. Alternatively all forms can be downloaded from the enodare website.

Web: http://www.enodare.com/downloadarea/

Unlock Code: XYZ10412

enodare

Appendix C

APPENDIX C

Sample completed living will forms for Alaska

Sample Completed Alaska State Forms

ADVANCE HEALTH CARE DIRECTIVE

Explanation

You have the right to give instructions about your own health care to the extent allowed by law. You also have the right to name someone else to make health care decisions for you to the extent allowed by law.

This form lets you do either or both of these things. It also lets you express your wishes regarding the designation of your health care provider. If you use this form, you may complete or modify all or any part of it. You are free to use a different form if the form complies with the requirements of A.S. 13.52.

Part 1 of this form is a durable power of attorney for health care. A durable power of attorney for health care means the designation of an agent to make health care decisions for you. Part 1 lets you name another individual as an agent to make health care decisions for you if you do not have the capacity to make your own decisions or if you want someone else to make those decisions for you now even though you still have the capacity to make those decisions. You may name an alternate agent to act for you if your first choice is not willing, able, or reasonably available to make decisions for you. Unless related to you, your agent may not be an owner, operator, or employee of a health care institution where you are receiving care.

Unless the form you sign limits the authority of your agent, your agent may make all health care decisions for you that you could legally make for yourself. This form has a place for you to limit the authority of your agent. You do not have to limit the authority of your agent if you wish to rely on your agent for all health care decisions that may have to be made. If you choose not to limit the authority of your agent, your agent will have the right, to the extent allowed by law, to

(a) consent or refuse consent to any care, treatment, service, or procedure to maintain, diagnose, or otherwise affect a physical or mental condition, including the administration or discontinuation of psychotropic medication;

(b) select or discharge health care providers and institutions;

(c) approve or disapprove proposed diagnostic tests, surgical procedures, and programs of medication;

(d) direct the provision, withholding, or withdrawal of artificial nutrition and hydration and all other forms of health care; and

(e) make an anatomical gift following your death.

Part 2 of this form lets you give specific instructions for any aspect of your health care to the extent allowed by law, except you may not authorize mercy killing, assisted suicide, or euthanasia. Choices are provided for you to express your wishes regarding the provision, withholding, or withdrawal of treatment to keep you alive, including the provision of artificial nutrition and hydration, as well as the provision of pain relief medication. Space is provided for you to add to the choices you have made or for you to write out any additional wishes.

Part 3 of this form lets you express an intention to make an anatomical gift following your death.

Part 4 of this form lets you make decisions in advance about certain types of mental health treatment.

Part 5 of this form lets you designate a physician to have primary responsibility for your health care.

After completing this form, sign and date the form at the end and have the form witnessed by one of the two alternative methods listed below. Give a copy of the signed and completed form to your physician, to any other health care providers you may have, to any health care institution at which you are receiving care, and to any health care agents you have named. You should talk to the person you have named as your agent to make sure that the person understands your wishes and is willing to take the responsibility.

You have the right to revoke this advance health care directive or replace this form at any time, except that you may not revoke this declaration when you are determined not to be competent by a court, by two physicians, at least one of whom shall be a psychiatrist, or by both a physician and a professional mental health clinician. In this advance health care directive, "competent" means that you have the capacity

(1)   to assimilate relevant facts and to appreciate and understand your situation with regard to those facts; and

(2)   to participate in treatment decisions by means of a rational thought process.

ADVANCE HEALTH CARE DIRECTIVE

PART 1
DURABLE POWER OF ATTORNEY FOR HEALTH CARE DECISIONS

(1)   **DESIGNATION OF AGENT**

I designate the following individual as my agent to make health care decisions for me:

John Doe

(name of individual you choose as agent)

3451003 East 99th St   Fairbanks   _Alaska_   _99508_

(address)   (city)   (state)   (zip code)

_(971) 12376891_   _(971) 231328878_

(home telephone)   (work telephone)

OPTIONAL: If I revoke my agent's authority or if my agent is not willing, able, or reasonably available to make a health care decision for me, I designate as my first alternate agent

Paul Doe

(name of individual you choose as first alternate agent)

1234099 41st Avenue   Anchorage   _Alaska_   _99501_

(address)   (city)   (state)   (zip code)

_(972) 123417891_   _(972) 123417891_

(home telephone)   (work telephone)

OPTIONAL: If I revoke the authority of my agent and first alternate agent or if neither is willing, able, or reasonably available to make a health care decision for me, I designate as my second alternate agent

Susan Doe

(name of individual you choose as first alternate agent)

5656561 E39 st   Juneau   _Alaska_   _99801_

(address)   (city)   (state)   (zip code)

_(907) 123417891_   _(907) 123417891_

(home telephone)   (work telephone)

(2)   AGENT'S AUTHORITY

My agent is authorized and directed to follow my individual instructions and my other wishes to the extent known to the agent in making all health care decisions for me. If these are not known, my agent is authorized to make these decisions in accordance with my best interest, including decisions to provide, withhold, or withdraw artificial hydration and nutrition and other forms of health care to keep me alive, except as I state here:

I do not wish to be kept alive by artificial devices

Under this authority, "best interest" means that the benefits to you resulting from a treatment outweigh the burdens to you resulting from that treatment after assessing

(A)   the effect of the treatment on your physical, emotional, and cognitive functions;

(B)   the degree of physical pain or discomfort caused to you by the treatment or the withholding or withdrawal of the treatment;

(C)   the degree to which your medical condition, the treatment, or the withholding or withdrawal of treatment, results in a severe and continuing impairment;

(D)   the effect of the treatment on your life expectancy;

(E)   your prognosis for recovery, with and without the treatment;

(F)   the risks, side effects, and benefits of the treatment or the withholding of treatment; and

(G)   your religious beliefs and basic values, to the extent that these may assist in determining benefits and burdens.

(3)   **WHEN AGENT'S AUTHORITY BECOMES EFFECTIVE**

Except in the case of mental illness, my agent's authority becomes effective when my primary physician determines that I am unable to make my own health care decisions unless I mark the following box. In the case of mental illness, unless I mark the following box, my agent's authority becomes effective when a court determines I am unable to make my own decisions, or, in an emergency, if my primary physician or another health care provider determines I am unable to make my own decisions. _____ If I mark this box, my agent's authority to make health care decisions for me takes effect immediately.

(4)   **AGENT'S OBLIGATION**

My agent shall make health care decisions for me in accordance with this durable power of attorney for health care, any instructions I give in Part 2 of this form, and my other wishes to the extent known to my agent. To the extent my wishes are unknown, my agent shall make health care decisions for me in accordance with what my agent determines to be in my best interest. In determining my best interest, my agent shall consider my personal values to the extent known to my agent.

(5)   **NOMINATION OF GUARDIAN**

If a guardian of my person needs to be appointed for me by a court, I nominate the agent designated in this form. If that agent is not willing, able, or reasonably available to act as guardian, I nominate the alternate agents whom I have named under (1) above, in the order designated.

PART 2
INSTRUCTIONS FOR HEALTH CARE

If you are satisfied to allow your agent to determine what is best for you in making health care decisions, you do not need to fill out this part of the form. If you do fill out this part of the form, you may strike any wording you do not want. There is a state protocol that governs the use of do not resuscitate orders by physicians and other health care providers. You may obtain a copy of the protocol from the Alaska Department of Health and Social Services. A "do not resuscitate order" means a directive from a licensed physician that emergency cardiopulmonary resuscitation should not be administered to you.

(6) END-OF-LIFE DECISIONS

Except to the extent prohibited by law, I direct that my health care providers and others involved in my care provide, withhold, or withdraw treatment in accordance with the choice I have marked below:

(Check only one box.)

(A) _X_ Choice To Prolong Life

I want my life to be prolonged as long as possible within the limits of generally accepted health care standards; OR

(B) ___ Choice Not To Prolong Life

I want comfort care only and I do not want my life to be prolonged with medical treatment if, in the judgment of my physician, I have

(check all choices that represent your wishes)

_X_ (i) a condition of permanent unconsciousness: a condition that, to a high degree of medical certainty, will last permanently without improvement; in which, to a high degree of medical certainty, thought, sensation, purposeful action, social interaction, and awareness of myself and the environment are absent; and for which, to a high degree of medical certainty, initiating or continuing life-sustaining procedures for me, in light of my medical outcome, will provide only minimal medical benefit for me; or

___ (ii) a terminal condition: an incurable or irreversible illness or injury that without the administration of life-sustaining procedures will result in my death in a short period of time, for which there is no reasonable prospect of cure or recovery, that imposes severe pain or otherwise imposes an inhumane burden on me, and for which, in light of my medical condition, initiating or continuing life-sustaining procedures will provide only minimal medical benefit.

Additional instructions: _____

_____

(C) <u>Artificial Nutrition and Hydration</u>

If I am unable to safely take nutrition, fluids, or nutrition and fluids (check your choices or write your instructions),

__X__ I wish to receive artificial nutrition and hydration indefinitely;

____ I wish to receive artificial nutrition and hydration indefinitely, unless it clearly increases my suffering and is no longer in my best interest;

____ I wish to receive artificial nutrition and hydration on a limited trial basis to see if I can improve;

____ In accordance with my choices in (6)(B) above, I do not wish to receive artificial nutrition and hydration.

Other instructions:_____

_____

(D) <u>Relief from Pain</u>

__X__ I direct that adequate treatment be provided at all times for the sole purpose of the alleviation of pain or discomfort; or I give these instructions: _____

_____

(E) <u>Should I become unconscious and I am pregnant</u>, I direct that: N/A _____

(7) OTHER WISHES

(If you do not agree with any of the optional choices above and wish to write your own, or if you wish to add to the instructions you have given above, you may do so here.) I direct that _____

_____

_____

Conditions or limitations: *I impose no conditions or limitations on my directions above*
(Add additional sheets if needed.)

PART 3
(OPTIONAL)
ANATOMICAL GIFT AT DEATH

If you are satisfied to allow your agent to determine whether to make an anatomical gift at your death, you do not need to fill out this part of the form.

(8)   Upon my death: (mark applicable box)

(A) ___ I give any needed organs, tissues, or other body parts, OR

(B) _X_ I give the following organs, tissues, or other body parts only:
Heart, Lungss and Eyes

(C) _X_ My gift is for the following purposes (mark any of the following you want):

        _X_ (i) transplant;

        ___ (ii) therapy;

        ___ (iii) research;

        ___ (iv) education.

(D) ___ I refuse to make an anatomical gift.

PART 4 - MENTAL HEALTH TREATMENT

This part of the declaration allows you to make decisions in advance about mental health treatment. The instructions that you include in this declaration will be followed only if a court, two physicians that include a psychiatrist, or a physician and a professional mental health clinician believe that you are not competent and cannot make treatment decisions. Otherwise, you will be considered to be competent and to have the capacity to give or withhold consent for the treatments.

If you are satisfied to allow your agent to determine what is best for you in making these mental health decisions, you do not need to fill out this part of the form. If you do fill out this part of the form, you may strike any wording you do not want.

(9)   **PSYCHOTROPIC MEDICATIONS**

If I do not have the capacity to give or withhold informed consent for mental health treatment, my wishes regarding psychotropic medications are as follows:

_X_ I consent to the administration of the following medications: _Haloperidol, Chlorpromazine, Loxapine_

_____ I do not consent to the administration of the following medications: _____

Conditions or limitations:. _____*No conditions or Limitations are to be applied*_____

_____

(10) ELECTROCONVULSIVE TREATMENT

If I do not have the capacity to give or withhold informed consent for mental health treatment, my wishes regarding electroconvulsive treatment are as follows:

_X_ I consent to the administration of electroconvulsive treatment.

_____ I do not consent to the administration of electroconvulsive treatment.

Conditions or limitations:._*No conditions or Limitations are to be applied*_____

_____

(11) _____ ADMISSION TO AND RETENTION IN FACILITY

If I do not have the capacity to give or withhold informed consent for mental health treatment, my wishes regarding admission to and retention in a mental health facility for mental health treatment are as follows:

_X_ I consent to being admitted to a mental health facility for mental health treatment for up to _12_ days. (The number of days not to exceed 17.)

_____ I do not consent to being admitted to a mental health facility for mental health treatment.

Conditions or limitations:. _____*No conditions or Limitations are to be applied*_____

OTHER WISHES OR INSTRUCTIONS

_____

_____

_____

Conditions

_____

_____

PART 5
PRIMARY PHYSICIAN
(OPTIONAL)

(12) I designate the following physician as my primary physician:

Dr Paul Doe
(name of physician)

9950823 C street	_Anchorage_	_Alaska_	_99508_
(address)	(city)	(state)	(zip code)

_(907) 1234567_
(telephone)

OPTIONAL: If the physician I have designated above is not willing, able, or reasonably available to act as my primary physician, I designate the following physician as my primary physician:

Dr Susan Bloggs
(name of physician)

97865464 Sherry street	_Anchorage_	_Alaska_	_99508_
(address)	(city)	(state)	(zip code)

_(907) 5678903_
(telephone)

(13)   **EFFECT OF COPY**

A copy of this form has the same effect as the original.

(14)   **SIGNATURES**

Sign and date the form here:

John Doe   _11/21/2010_   (date)
(sign your name)
John Doe
(print your name)

3451003 East 99th St	_Fairbanks_	_Alaska_	_99508_
(address)	(city)	(state)	(zip code)

(15)   **WITNESSES**

This advance care health directive will not be valid for making health care decisions unless it is

(A)   signed by two qualified adult witnesses who are personally known to you and who are present when you sign or acknowledge your signature; the witnesses may not be a health care provider employed at the health care institution or health care facility where you are receiving health care, an employee of the health care provider who is providing health care to you, an employee of the health care institution or health care facility where you are receiving health care, or the person appointed as your agent by this document; at least one of the two witnesses may not be related to you by blood, marriage, or adoption or entitled to a portion of your estate upon your death under your will or codicil; or

(B)   acknowledged before a notary public in the state.

ALTERNATIVE NO. 1

Witness Who is Not Related to or a Devisee of the Principal

I swear under penalty of perjury under AS 11.56.200 that the principal is personally known to me, that the principal signed or acknowledged this durable power of attorney for health care in my presence, that the principal appears to be of sound mind and under no duress, fraud, or undue influence, and that I am not

(1)   a health care provider employed at the health care institution or health care facility where the principal is receiving health care;

(2)   an employee of the health care provider providing health care to the principal;

(3)   an employee of the health care institution or health care facility where the principal is receiving health care;

(4)   the person appointed as agent by this document;

(5)   related to the principal by blood, marriage, or adoption; or

(6)   entitled to a portion of the principal's estate upon the principal's death under a will or codicil.

Peter Smith _____ _11/21/2010_ _____(date)

(signature of witness)

Peter Smith _____

(printed name of witness)

9010 H Street East 31st St   _Anchorage_ _____ _Alaska_ _____ _99508_ _____

(address)   (city)   (state)   (zip code)

Witness Who May be Related to or a Devisee of the Principal

I swear under penalty of perjury under AS 11.56.200 that the principal is personally known to me, that the principal signed or acknowledged this durable power of attorney for health care in my presence, that the principal appears to be of sound mind and under no duress, fraud, or undue influence, and that I am not

(1)   a health care provider employed at the health care institution or health care facility where the principal is receiving health care;

(2)   an employee of the health care provider who is providing health care to the principal;

(3)   an employee of the health care institution or health care facility where the principal is receiving health care; or

(4)   the person appointed as agent by this document.

_____

(date)   (signature of witness)

_____

(printed name of witness)

_____

(address)   (city)   (state)   (zip code)

ALTERNATIVE NO. 2

State of Alaska

_____ Judicial District

On this _____ day of _____, in the year _____, before me, _____
_____ (insert name of notary public) appeared _____
_____ , personally known to me (or proved to me on the basis of satisfactory evidence) to be the person whose name is subscribed to this instrument, and acknowledged that the person executed it.

Notary Seal

_____ (signature of notary public)

APPENDIX D:
SELF PROVING AFFIDAVITS

CD-ROM & Downloadable Forms

Blank copies of all of the forms contained in this book are available on the CD-ROM which accompanies this book. Alternatively all forms can be downloaded from the enodare website.

Web: http://www.enodare.com/downloadarea/

Unlock Code: XYZ10412

enodare

APPENDIX D

Self Proving Affidavits

SELF PROVING AFFIDAVIT – TYPE 1

FOR USE IN THE FOLLOWING STATES		
Alabama	Indiana	North Dakota
Alaska	Maine	Oregan
Arizona	Mississippi	South Carolina
Arkansas	Montana	South Dakota
Colorado	Nebraska	Tennessee
Hawaii	Nevada	Utah
Idaho	New Mexico	Washington
Illinois	New York	West Virginia

SELF-PROVING AFFIDAVIT

State of _____   County of _____

We,_____, _____
_____, and _____
_____, the declarant and the witnesses
respectively, whose names are signed to the attached instrument in those capacities, personally
appearing before the undersigned authority and first being duly sworn, do hereby declare to the

undersigned authority under penalty of perjury that the declarant declared, signed, and executed the instrument as his/her [living will]; he/she signed it willingly or willingly directed another to sign for him/her; he/she executed it as his/her free and voluntary act for the purposes therein expressed; and each of the witnesses, at the request of the declarant, in his or her hearing and presence, and in the presence of each other, signed the will as witness and that to the best of his or her knowledge the Declarant was at that time eighteen (18) years of age or older, of sound mind and under no constraint or undue influence.

_____ [Signature of Declarant]
_____ [Printed or typed name of Declarant]
_____ [Address of Declarant, Line 1]
_____ [Address of Declarant, Line 2]

_____ [Signature of Witness #1]
_____ [Printed or typed name of Witness #1]
_____ [Address of Witness #1, Line 1]
_____ [Address of Witness #1, Line 2]

_____ [Signature of Witness #2]
_____ [Printed or typed name of Witness #2]
_____ [Address of Witness #2, Line 1]
_____ [Address of Witness #2, Line 2]

Subscribed, sworn, and acknowledged before me, _____
_____, a notary public, by _____
_____, the Declarant, and by _____
_, and _____, the witnesses, this
_____ day of _____, 20_____.

[**NOTARIAL SEAL**]

_____
Notary Public's Signature

My Commission Expires: _____

SELF PROVING AFFIDAVIT – TYPE 2

FOR USE IN THE FOLLOWING STATES		
Delaware	Kentucky	Oklahoma
Florida	Massachusetts	Pennsylvania
Georgia	Missouri	Rhode Island
Iowa	New Jersey	Virginia
Kansas	North Carolina	Wyoming

SELF-PROVING AFFIDAVIT

State of _____   **County of** _____

I, the undersigned, an officer authorized to administer oaths, certify that_____
_____, the Declarant, and _____, and _____
_____, the witnesses, whose names are signed to the attached or foregoing
instrument and whose signatures appear below, having appeared together before me and
having been first duly sworn, each then declare to me that the attached or foregoing instrument
is the [living will] of the Declarant; the Declarant willingly and voluntarily declared, signed
and executed the will or willingly directed another to sign in the presence of the witnesses;
the witnesses signed the will upon request by the Declarant, in the presence and hearing of
the Declarant, and in the presence of each other; to the best knowledge of each witness the
Declarant was, at the time of the signing, eighteen (18) years of age or older, of sound mind,
and under no constraint or undue influence; and each witness was and is competent, and of the
proper age to witness a will.

_____ [Signature of Declarant]
_____ [Printed or typed name of Declarant]
_____ [Address of Declarant, Line 1]
_____ [Address of Declarant, Line 2]

_____ [Signature of Witness #1]
_____ [Printed or typed name of Witness #1]
_____ [Address of Witness #1, Line 1]
_____ [Address of Witness #1, Line 2]

_____ [Signature of Witness #2]
_____ [Printed or typed name of Witness #2]
_____ [Address of Witness #2, Line 1]
_____ [Address of Witness #2, Line 2]

Subscribed, sworn, and acknowledged before me, _____
_____, a notary public, by _____
_____, the Declarant, and by _____
_, and _____, the witnesses, this
_____ day of _____, 20_____.

SIGNED:

_____

_____

Official Capacity of Officer

APPENDIX E:
NOTICE OF REVOCATION OF A LIVING WILL

CD-ROM & Downloadable Forms

Blank copies of all of the forms contained in this book are available on the CD-ROM which accompanies this book. Alternatively all forms can be downloaded from the enodare website.

Web: http://www.enodare.com/downloadarea/

Unlock Code: XYZ10412

enodare

Appendix E

APPENDIX E

Notice of Revocation of a Living Will

&

Notice of Revocation of a Healthcare Power of Attorney

NOTICE OF REVOCATION OF LIVING WILL

I, _____ of _____ _____

_____aged eighteen years and upwards herby

REVOKE, countermand and make null and void the [Living Will] dated _____.

Executed this _____ day of _____, 20 ____, at _____

_____

THE GRANTOR

Name of Witness: _____

Signature of Witness: _____

Address: _____

                           _____

_____

_____

NOTICE OF REVOCATION OF POWER OF ATTORNEY

I, _____ of _____
_____aged eighteen
years and upwards hereby REVOKE, countermand and make null and void the Power of
Attorney dated _____ (the "Power of Attorney") and granted in favor of _____
_____ (the "Agent", which expression shall include any successor
agent appointed under the Power of Attorney) and all rights, powers and authority thereby given
to the aforesaid Agent hereby lapse and cease.

Executed this _____ day of _____, 20 _____,
at _____.

_____

THE GRANTOR

NOTARY AFFIDAVIT

STATE OF _____ **COUNTY OF** _____

On this day, before me, the undersigned authority, in and for and residing in the above County and State, personally appeared _____, who is personally known to me to be the same person whose name is subscribed to the forgoing document, and, being duly sworn, he/she verified that the information contained in the foregoing document is true and correct on personal knowledge and acknowledged that said document was signed as a free and voluntary act.

Subscribed and sworn this _____ day of _____, 20 _____.

_____

NAME AND SIGNATURE

My commission expires on: _____

APPENDIX F:
ADDEMDUM TO A LIVING WILL

Appendix F

CD-ROM & Downloadable Forms

Blank copies of all of the forms contained in this book are available on the CD-ROM which accompanies this book. Alternatively all forms can be downloaded from the enodare website.

Web: http://www.enodare.com/downloadarea/

Unlock Code: XYZ10412

enodare

APPENDIX F

Addendum to a Living Will

How to use this Form

This form can be used to add to or amend the terms of a state living will, power of attorney or advance directive. Simply complete the form below and attach it to your original living will, power of attorney or advance directive. Remember to initial only the options that you desire.

ADDENDUM TO LIVING WILL DECLARATION

I, _____, (hereinafter referred to as the Declarant), aged eighteen years and upwards and a resident at _____ make this Addendum this _____ day of _____ , 20___ .

This is an Addendum to my [Living Will] dated _____ day of _____, 20___ (my "Living Will").

The purpose of this Addendum is to amend and clarify the terms of my Living Will.
Except as expressly provided herein, these amendments shall not in any other way alter, modify, amend or in any way affect any of the terms, conditions or obligations contained in my Living Will, which shall continue in full force and effect as amended hereby.

1.   **TREATMENT OPTIONS**

(Initial only those options which apply)

Terminal Condition

_____ If, at any time, I have a medical condition certified to be a terminal condition by two physicians who have personally examined me, and the physicians have determined that my death could occur within a reasonably short period of time without the use of life-sustaining procedures then I direct that, save as may be set out herein, such life-sustaining procedures SHALL NOT be applied to prolong my life within the limits of generally accepted health care standards.

Specifically, I do not want the following forms of treatment if I am suffering from a terminal condition:

_____ I do not want artificial nutrition or hydration.

_____ I do not want to receive cardiac resuscitation or a cardiac pacemaker.

_____ I do not want to receive blood or blood products.

_____ I do not want to receive mechanical respiration.

_____ I do not want to receive kidney dialysis.

_____ I do not want to receive antibiotics.

_____ I do not want to receive any form of surgery or invasive diagnostic tests.

_____ I do not want to receive an organ.

Permanent Unconsciousness

_____ If, at any time, I have a medical condition certified to be a terminal condition by two physicians who have personally examined me, and the physicians have certified that I am in a state of permanent unconsciousness and the application of life-sustaining procedures would serve only to prolong the dying process then I direct that, save as may be set out herein, such life-sustaining procedures SHALL NOT be withheld or withdrawn and that I be permitted to die naturally with, unless otherwise set out below, only the administration of medication or the performance of any medical procedure necessary to provide me with comfort care.

Specifically, I do not want the following forms of treatment if I am in a persistent vegetative state or other condition of permanent unconsciousness:

_____ I do not want artificial nutrition or hydration.

_____ I do not want to receive cardiac resuscitation or a cardiac pacemaker.

_____ I do not want to receive blood or blood products.

_____ I do not want to receive mechanical respiration.

_____ I do not want to receive kidney dialysis.

_____ I do not want to receive antibiotics.

_____ I do not want to receive any form of surgery or invasive diagnostic tests.

_____ I do not want to receive an organ.

<u>Maximum Treatment</u>

_____ I want to receive the maximum treatment in all possible circumstances to prolong my life.

<u>My instructions in mw own words</u>

_____

_____

_____

_____(add more lines or pages if needed)

2.   **RELIEF FROM PAIN**

(initial one choice only)

_____ I want to receive treatment for the alleviation of pain or discomfort.

_____ I do not want to receive treatment for the alleviation of pain or discomfort.

3. **PREGNANCY** (Optional)

(If applicable, initial your choice below. If no choice is initialled, this clause shall cease to apply)

3.1 Should I become unconscious and I am pregnant, I direct that this document shall, unless applicable laws prescribe otherwise:

(initial one choice below)

_____ continue to have full effect

_____ cease to have full effect

4. **EFFECT OF COPY**

4.1 A copy of this declaration has the same effect as the original.
I understand the full import of this declaration and I am emotionally and mentally competent to make this declaration.

IN WITNESS WHEREOF, I have hereunto subscribed my name and affixed my seal at _____, _____, this _____ day of _____, 20_____, in the presence of the subscribing witnesses whom I have requested to become attesting witnesses hereto.

_____

Signature of Declarant

Name of Witness: _____
Signature of Witness: _____
Address: _____
                        _____

Name of Witness: _____

Signature of Witness: _____

Address: _____

_____

_____

INDEX

Will Writer - Estate Planning Software

Everything You Need to Create Your Estate Plan

Product Description

Enodare's Estate Planning Software helps you create wills, living trusts, living wills, powers of attorney and more from the comfort of your own home and without the staggering legal fees!

Through the use of a simple question and answer process, we'll guide you step-by-step through the process of preparing your chosen document. It only takes a few minutes of your time and comprehensive help and information is available at every stage of the process.

The documents are valid in all states (and tailored to the laws of your home state) except Louisiana.

Product Features:

Last Wills

Make gifts to your family, friends and charities, make funeral arrangements, appoint executors, appoint guardians to care for your minor children, make property management arrangements for young beneficiaries, release people from debts, and much more.

Living Trusts

Make gifts to your family and friends, make property management arrangements for young beneficiaries, transfer assets tax efficiently with AB Trusts, and much more.

Living Wills

Instruct doctors as to your choices regarding the receipt or non-receipt of medical treatments designed to prolong your life.

✓ Healthcare Power of Attorney

Appoint someone you trust to make medical decisions for you if you become mentally incapacitated.

Ensure Your Family's Protected

✓ Power of Attorney for Finance and Property

Appoint someone you trust to manage your financial affairs if you become mentally incapacitated, or if you are unable to do so for any reason.

✓ And More.........

As well as including a built in estate planning manual, Enodare's Will Writer software also includes documents such as Self-Proving Affidavits, Deeds of Assignment, Certifications of Trust, Estate Planning Worksheet, Revocation forms and more.

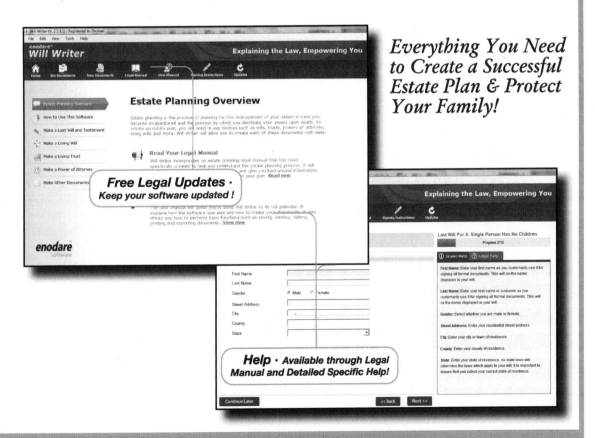

Everything You Need to Create a Successful Estate Plan & Protect Your Family!

409

Other Great Books from Enodare's
Estate Planning Series

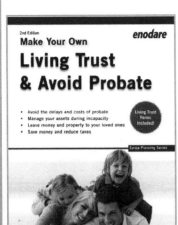
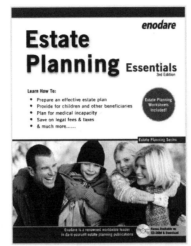

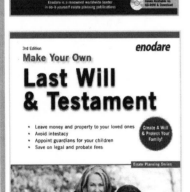
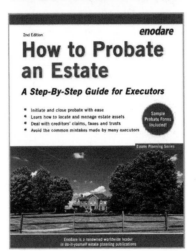

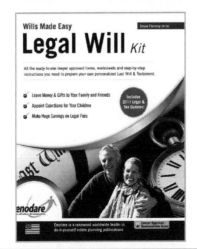

www.enodare.com

Entrepreneur's Guide to Starting a Business

Entrepreneur's Guide to Starting a Business takes the fear of the unknown out of starting your new business and provides a treasure chest of information that will help you be successful from the very start. First-time entrepreneurs face a daunting challenge in identifying all of the issues that must be addressed and mastered when starting a new business. If any item slips through the cracks, or is handled improperly, it could bring a new company crashing to the ground. Entrepreneur's Guide to Starting a Business helps you meet that challenge by walking you through all of the important aspects of successfully launching your own business.

When you finish reading this book, not alone will you know the step-by-step process needed to turn your business idea and vision into a successful reality, but you'll also have a wealth of practical knowledge about corporate structures, business & marketing plans, e-commerce, hiring staff & external advisors, finding commercial property, sales & marketing, legal & financial matters, tax and much more.

Features:

- Comprehensive overview of all major aspects of starting a new business

- Covers every stage of the process, from writing your business plan to marketing and selling your new product

- Plain English descriptions of complex subject matters

- Real-world case study showing you how things play out in an actual new business environment

NEW TITLE

Personal Budget Kit

Budgeting Made Easy

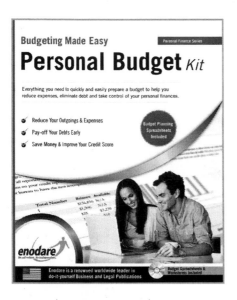

In this kit, we'll guide you step-by-step through the process of creating and living with a personal budget. We'll show you how analyze how you receive and spend your money and to set goals, both short and long-term.

You'll learn how to gain control of your personal cash flow. You'll discover when you need to make adjustments to your budget and how to do it wisely. Most of all, this kit will show you that budgeting isn't simply about adding limitations to your living but rather the foundation for living better by maximizing the resources you have.

This Personal Budget Kit provides you with step-by-step instructions, detailed information and all the budget worksheets and spreadsheets necessary to identify and understand your spending habits, reduce your expenses, set goals, prepare personal budgets, monitor your progress and take control over your finances.

- Reduce your spending painlessly and effortlessly

- Pay off your debts early

- Improve your credit rating

- Save & invest money

- Set & achieve financial goals

- Eliminate financial worries

Budget Planning Spreadsheets Included

enodare

NEW TITLE